RAT BASTARDS

RAT BASTARDS

THE LIFE AND TIMES OF SOUTH BOSTON'S
MOST HONORABLE IRISH MOBSTER

JOHN "RED" SHEA
WITH AN INTRODUCTION BY MARK WAHLBERG

wm

WILLIAM MORROW
An Imprint of HarperCollins*Publishers*

HarperCollins books may be purchased for educational, business, or sales promotional use. For information please write: Special Markets Department, HarperCollins Publishers, 10 East 53rd Street, New York, NY 10022.

FIRST EDITION

Designed by Kris Tobiassen

Printed on acid-free paper

Library of Congress Cataloging-in-Publication Data has been applied for.

ISBN-13: 978-0-06-083716-7
ISBN-10: 0-06-083716-0

06 07 08 09 10 JTC/RRD 10 9 8 7 6 5 4 3 2 1

This book is dedicated to all the stand-up guys out there.
Every day you can get up, look in the mirror,
and respect the man you see.

It takes a strong person to reach inside himself and say, "I'm here because of me."

—JAMES "WHITEY" BULGER

CONTENTS

ACKNOWLEDGMENTS

I want to thank everyone involved in this project. A special thank-you to the wonderful and giving people listed below.

To my editor, Maureen O'Brien, for her support and caring way throughout this process. I appreciate her keen eye for discovering diamonds in the rough like me. I want to thank her for her courage and loyalty in developing this project when others might have looked past it because of my lack of notoriety. Thanks to everyone at HarperCollins for all their help, but mostly for the opportunity to tell my story.

To Brian Lipson, my agent, for always being there for me, offering his guidance and unwavering support for this project. His straightforward manner and no-nonsense style is a perfect match for a guy like me. No bullshit from Brian. He tells it like it is.

I want to thank Steve Levinson for all his efforts in helping this project get off the ground. Thanks, Lev, for all your support.

Also, David Vigliano, my literary agent, whose tireless efforts on my behalf helped me realize something I didn't believe could become a reality: a chance to tell my story my way.

To my friend and one of my biggest supporters, and the one who initially encouraged us to write this book, Ken Kokin. Thanks for all your help.

To all my friends who have stuck by me throughout the years—coming to visit me, writing to me, and helping me out when I needed them while doing my time.

To Dee Dee, thanks for always being my friend. Your loyalty has been a constant source of strength. I could always depend on you.

To my mother, who stood by me and always taught me to stand on my own two feet and accept responsibility for my actions. Those lessons would later define my life.

To my sisters Paula and Maureen for their support and for taking care of my mother while I was away.

To Richie Egbert, who, besides being my pit-bull lawyer, has always been a true friend. To Tony Cardinale, one of the finest criminal lawyers in America, who has been my friend and confidant for many, many years and whose friendship I cherish more than words can adequately express.

To George and Michael Hogan, guys who epitomize friendship—never hesitating when I called them or asked them to help me out. Whether driving my mother down to visit me or helping out in any way to make my time a little easier, they were there, no questions asked.

To my boyhood friend Billy Mahoney, who came to the airport with me when I left to report to prison, I thank you.

To Penelope for loving me. It is better to have loved and lost than not to have loved at all. I'll never forget you. To your mother for the love and kindness that she has always shown me. The novenas she sent me were a constant source of faith, especially in tough times.

To all the men I befriended while doing my time—thanks for being stand-up guys. This book is dedicated to you and all the other guys like us in the world. There are still some men of honor left on this earth.

To Mark Wahlberg, who, above everything, is my friend. His support has been truly incredible. When they say someone has not forgotten where he came from, they must be talking about my man Mark. This is a guy at the top of his profession who has never forgotten or stopped helping the guys from Boston, and for that I am eternally grateful. I have a friend for life and Mark has one in me. God bless, my brother.

To Michael Coffey, who helped make this story what it is. His collaboration with Fran and me in writing my story made for a perfect mix. His writing style, more like poetry than the typical autobiographical style, helped capture my voice and make the reader feel what I felt. His is a truly special gift and I appreciate it now more than ever. He is a true poet. It must be all that Irish in him.

Last but most important, my friend, my brother, Fran Hurley. This book would never have been written without him. Who knew that when we started writing in his law office on Broadway in Southie that he could so eloquently and ably tell my story, but more importantly, bring my voice to life on these pages. Not just for writing this book with me, but more importantly being my true friend. We are, in every sense of the word, family. He and I are brothers to the day we die.

INTRODUCTION

BY MARK WAHLBERG

I first heard about John "Red" Shea about ten years ago from a Southie friend. Recruited as a teenager by Whitey Bulger, the boss of the Irish mob in Boston, Red ultimately had become his protégé. I was immediately fascinated by Red's story and by some of the similarities to my own childhood. At that time Red was serving twelve years in federal prison. While there, he became a sort of "gangster priest," counseling men ten and twenty years his senior to stay strong and not to rat on their friends. Even as a young man in jail, loyalty, honor, and integrity were more important to him than anything.

I wanted to meet Red. After he got out of prison in 2002, I got a call saying he was willing to talk to me. At our first meeting, I kept thinking he looked like an altar boy. The way people talk about him, I was expecting someone hard-looking, with the banged-up face of a boxer. He was nothing like I had imagined, but I could see that this was a very serious guy. When he talked about Whitey, his eyes became hard. "All that talk—all those years—about rats and being a stand-up guy. And he was the biggest rat of all." To Red it was an enormous betrayal.

Red believes in doing the right thing, no matter the consequences; his code of honor is unshakable. So here we are, after all this time, and Red finally gets to tell his life story to the world. It's a good story.

RAT BASTARDS

1

RELEASE

I walked out of federal prison on August 7, 2002, into a perfect summer day. The first thing I noticed was the air—it was clean and warm, like fresh laundry just out of the dryer. After being in the joint for so long, where all you smell day after day is sweat and vinegar and bad food, I felt the air hit me like the most beautiful scent. And this is New Jersey we're talking about. Fort Dix, my home sweet home for nine long years. Good-fuckin'-bye.

Last time I'd been a free man, I was dressed in an Armani suit, a Calvin Klein shirt, and Bally shoes. I even had Armani underwear. That was nearly twelve years ago, when I checked in to the federal prison in Milan, Michigan. Now, one welcome transfer later, my time was up. I got sentenced to twelve and I did my twelve, technically for drug trafficking. In truth, I did my time because the feds wanted Whitey Bulger, the boss of the South Boston Irish Mafia. Because I was Red Shea, Whitey Bulger's young apprentice, I was supposed to be the weak link, the kid, the guy who would flip. They were dead fucking wrong. I was never going to be rat. I'd rather be dead. So they hit me with some heavy time for a first bit.

An Officer Kennedy—a nice guy, a good guy, he showed me respect: *How ya doin', Shea? What's goin' on? How're your Red Sox doin'?* and so forth—led me out of the administration building and down toward the checkpoint. Dix isn't your average prison, being a former army base, with checkpoints and whatnot, not to mention softer bunks. I wasn't in Armani no more, but Levi's and new sneakers sent me by the guys.

I said to Kennedy, "Smell that?"

He said, "What's that, Shea? You like that?"

"Yes I do, Officer."

I took some deep drafts of it. Even though I was looking at a perimeter scarred by barbed wire and fences and double fences and was walking on dusty ground, I could look up: "Nothing but blue skies, motherfucker."

"Watch your language, Red," he said "And your ass. It's bumpy out there."

I shook his hand. My eyes were watering, from the smells. I had just turned thirty-seven years old, and I'd gotten my life back.

Beyond the checkpoint were some familiar faces waiting in a car: George and Michael Hogan, sons of one of the guys I'd been indicted with, and my attorney and friend, Fran Hurley. Handshakes and a quick hug all around. We were Southie Irish guys, not given to a lot of emotional stuff. But we were Irish, and the Irish have a sentimental streak for sure, going back to the Famine, I guess, and having to leave the Old Country. The old Partin' Glass and whatever. They were happy to see me, and I sure as fuck was happy to see them. I sat in the front seat. We talked about the Red Sox—they were sucking in August, no pitching whatsoever after Pedro and Derek Lowe. I turned the radio off—in no mood for gangsta rap, no offense. The traffic was bad, and soon the smell of paradise gave over to the smell of the turnpike and, like Springsteen says, the swamps of Jersey. We could see a waterfront with containers stacked high just like in Southie. Newark, I guess, with tall ship-container cranes soaring over everything, which prompted a discussion about work.

"There's the longshoremen," said Frannie. His dad had been a long-shoreman back in the day when they did most everything by hand and guys got maimed and killed regularly. Either from the work or from the fights during and after work, with the metal hooks they all carried. Most of the longshoremen were either from Southie or from Charlestown. Frannie, as always, was trying to be helpful in his gentle way. He was sug-gesting I work the Boston waterfront. George mentioned all the con-struction going on in downtown Boston. And, also as always, the Big Dig. Work, work, work.

"Fuck you guys!" I finally had to shout. I wasn't boiling over or noth-ing—but first the joint, then the fucking union hall? Give me a break. The only thing I wanted right now was a good fuckin' meal.

"You're right," said Frannie. "We've got better things to do." He popped in a CD. Van Morrison, *Moondance*. The guys laughed, and so did I. Frannie finally found the tunnel to Manhattan.

They'd booked a suite at the Hilton on Fifty-third Street—living room, little kitchen, big fucking bed, and an attached bedroom. We checked in, and I was starving, so I said, "Let's go to Smith & Wollen-sky's," my favorite steak house in New York. Back in the day, when I was on top, I got used to the best—in Boston, New York, Montreal, Miami Beach. I stayed in the best, ate like a king. Two-, three-hundred-dollar bottles of wine. I ordered a steak that night, rare, with baked potato and creamed spinach. We had some wine. Rothschild. We got mellow. We didn't talk about work anymore, thank God.

"How's my mother?" Frannie said she was good, doing well, she was living in an elderly apartment complex just off the expressway in Dor-chester. It's only a short bus ride to her job at a Southie nursing home. My mother was getting on in years. I knew from phone calls and letters that she was as feisty as ever and hanging in there. She's a tough woman. She raised me and my three older—much older—sisters, with no man around, my father having been thrown out just after I was born. She did everything she could for us. She worked two, three jobs at a time.

Cleaning homes, anything she could to make ends meet. But she was harsh, very harsh. I'd see her as soon as I got back.

How was Penelope? Frannie said he didn't know. Penelope Howard, the olive-skinned, dark-haired, brown-eyed love of my life, which I fucked up. Of course Frannie knew, so I knew she wasn't good or sure as hell wasn't waiting there for me to pull into town. I didn't push it.

I knew eventually someone was going to bring up Whitey. George, in his straightforward way, said it all: "All those years he was preaching to you never rat on anyone, Red? Then you find out that cocksucker Whitey was the fucking king of the rats?"

There was a silence at our table. These guys had their hands on their laps. I was sawing into my rib eye, the blood running out of it. How about that fucking rat motherfucker, eh?

James "Whitey" Bulger, who'd run the Boston mob for thirty years, who was like a god to me, a father, mentor, teacher, and protector all these years, had disappeared, just like that, back in '95. We all thought it was great back then, even us guys doing time for him. He'd ducked out, made a clean getaway, outsmarted the feds. Pure Whitey. But now we knew the truth about Whitey and his right-hand man, Steve "The Rifleman" Flemmi. These guys, all along, were working with the FBI, with a scumbag agent named Connolly. He was protecting them in return for Whitey exposing his enemies (I mean Italians) and giving up his guys as need be. Including me. Whitey, the blue-eyed, white-haired fucking genius of crime and psychology, was nothing but a fucking rat, now living somewhere—the Caribbean, Ireland, London, out west? No one knew where—in violation of the most important code of our life: You don't rat on anyone, ever.

I finished my steak and sopped up the blood with a roll.

"What would you do if you saw him across the room there?" asked Michael Hogan.

I stared at him. I let a few moments pass for effect, as I'd thought of this question a million times since I found out what Whitey'd done. I knew what I would do. I'd had a dream about Whitey practically every night for the last three years.

I avoided answering Michael's question directly.

"What he did he did," I said. "I know one thing: I walked into prison a man and I left a man. I'm better than him. I'm more of a man than Whitey Bulger will ever be."

I guess that's something I've wanted to be since I was a kid. A respected guy. A stand-up guy. In my world that is the highest compliment.

We walked back to the hotel. What's a guy want after he gets out of prison? A good steak might come in second.

We saw some whores getting out of a limo on Sixth Avenue, followed by some pimp with a small dog. We looked at each other. Back in the room, there was to be a little surprise in store for me—a gift from one of the Jersey guys I had done time with. To be accurate, two gifts actually. "Have fun," said one of the Hogans, then they all split to see the sights.

There was a knock on my door. I was trying to call my mother at the time, so I had to hang up. There they were, two Oriental girls. One a little bigger than the other, a little older. The younger one skinny as a rail, but nice. Both of them in short red satin dresses.

"Hi, mister."

"Hi, mister."

They wanted to get down to business, but I was in no rush.

Twelve years without a woman. Not easy to do in any walk of life.

They were naked in a second. So I had them massage me for a while, work our way into it. I played with them a little. They put on a little show for me. What's better than seeing a couple of women going at it? Nice. It was good for an appetizer.

Of course, after a bit I'd had enough of watching them and had to get into it. I worked on the older one first. After a half hour of that, I switched to the smaller one. She couldn't take it. She couldn't quite take me. I couldn't believe it. She was screaming like I was killing her. The other one said, "Too big for her, mister. Too big." The small one said, "Me Chinese, you too big." She tried to squirt this lubricant, and I knocked it away. I just continued to slam her. She was grimacing in pain, but she finally stopped screaming and yelling, "Too big, too big!" I was slaughtering her. Fast, slow, hard, soft, it didn't matter. I thought, What did they send me, a virgin whore? She was just too small.

I gave her a break. She got out of the bed and staggered to the bathroom. She looked like she had just gotten off a horse. She was in the bathroom for over twenty minutes.

I remember my older sisters, when I was a little kid. They used to pull my pants down. "Look at your little dick," they'd say. Real nice sister shit. *Look at the little dick!* I'd curl up in a ball, scream and yell. They thought it was a big joke, but it wasn't a big joke. I guess God must have rewarded me for that torment. I'm pretty lucky . . . for an Irish guy.

I went back to the bigger one and worked her over again. This went a lot better. She had been around and knew what she needed to do and how to do it. All those years of sexual frustration. It doesn't go away easily, but this was a start. I appreciated the thought from my friend from Jersey.

After they left, I called my mother. I could hear the relief in her voice, but just a little fear, too. Like, *Here comes Johnny, back on the streets.* I told her, "Ma, you got nothing to worry about. The streets are full of rats. It ain't the same no more. I'll see you in a couple of days."

The guys had come back. They'd actually been listening in on some of the fucking shenanigans from their room, which adjoined mine. "You were killing that girl, John! 'Too big! Too big, mister!' " They were all laughing and talking at once. We settled down for a bit. We watched *SportsCenter* and then crashed. It had been a good day, a great day.

That night I had that dream I'd had countless times. I'm walking in New York City. I see Whitey Bulger step out from behind a tall column. He sees me. He comes over to me and tries to explain why he did what he did. Before he can get out three words, I snap his neck.

We fucked around the next day—four guys from Boston not on your regular holiday. Went to Times Square, which was nothing like I remembered it—the triple-X movie marquees, street-corner preachers, and hawkers were long gone. Now it was like walking around in some pinball game, all bells and lights and fake smoke and theme restaurants. We went to ESPN Zone, upstairs where they have a big game room. I couldn't get enough of the boxing machine, where you put on the gloves and fight a simulated bout. All the old footwork came back, the combinations, bob and weave and left hook, bang-bang-bang, the slip and the straight right hand, over and over. I worked up a lather, remembering every fight, from the time I first put on the gloves in McDonough's Gym when I was five years old till I fought as a pro. All the discipline, the heavy bag, the speed bag, the crunches, the roadwork, the sparring, the great fucking camaraderie of the fight game. I thought I was going to make it. Boxing would be my highway to heaven, my escape from the streets, my road to the big time. Bang-bang-bang! I almost made it, like lots of guys almost make it. It's a tough business. I had the stuff, but I got sidetracked. There were easier ways to make money, and for a while I fucking made it. Lots of it.

I lost it, of course. Lost it all. But boxing, like my education with Whitey, gave me something that was crucial to my survival. It gave me mental toughness, and mental toughness is what gets you through prison, as well as life. Focus, discipline, integrity.

On Sunday we headed back to Boston. It was brutal going north on I-95. Construction all through Connecticut. Sundays are hard enough, with half the world on its best behavior and nobody wanting to return to work or school or what-have-you. And it's torture in a traffic jam, with every asshole on a cell phone, which was something new. In my heyday I was one of the few guys with a mobile phone, necessary for business. The thing cost me a thousand bucks. Now ten-year-old kids had 'em in the backseat.

It was just me and Frannie awake, with the Hogans snoozing in the back. I was going to live with Frannie for a while till I got on my feet. He was from Southie, like me. When I was indicted and needed a place to live, he was there for me. We were friends before that, but after that we became like brothers. His friendship was a source of great strength during this time. He always said loyalty breeds loyalty. It was a way of saying I could always depend on him no matter what. And if the time came, I'd be there for him as well.

The Hurleys were good people. Frannie had a stable home life, with a father and all. He'd gone to New England School of Law at night. He was making it. But he was still neighborhood. We talked a little about job prospects. We found the Red Sox game on the radio. Then his phone rang. "You won't believe it," he said, handing me the phone. It was a friend of ours calling on behalf of a local guy made real good, Mark Wahlberg. He was interested in my life story. Hollywood was calling.

But I could definitely believe it. I knew I was destined for something, I just never knew exactly what. But I'd been schooled by the best. I'd been schooled by Whitey Bulger to be a man. Turns out I was more of a man than he was. I had one-upped the king. He was on the run. He ratted on his friends to save himself. He had killed people and gotten away and fed us to the DEA in order to maintain his carte blanche deal with the feds. Except I didn't accept the slaughter. I wouldn't become like him, like many of them. There had been fifty-one of us rounded up and indicted while he looked the other way back in 1990. Some of them ratted and talked and whined and made excuses for talking to lessen their own punishment for living the life they fucking chose, knowing full well what that life meant. But I hadn't. That's what our Hollywood guy knew. That's what all the rats knew but hated to admit.

I said a lot of yeah-yeahs on Frannie's phone, playing it cool. We agreed to set up a meeting back in Boston.

"Why me?" I said to Frannie, trying to act humble but really feeling totally vindicated.

"One reason and one reason only," said Frannie as the traffic started to lighten past New Haven. "You're the last man standing, the last stand-up guy. It about time they told a story about a stand-up guy, John."

"Yeah," said one of the Hogans, waking up. "Just ask that Asian girl."

2

CHILDHOOD

I was born in Boston City Hospital, August 12, 1965, and came home to a small two-bedroom apartment in a three-family wooden row house on I Street in South Boston. There were me and my three sisters, Paula, Claire, and Maureen, and of course my mother, Mabel. Maureen was the oldest; she was already a teenager when I was born. Claire was about eleven, Paula around nine. Ma brought us up by herself, at least after I was born, since she'd kicked the old man out by then. His name was Al. He fixed televisions and had a serious drinking problem. That problem wasn't rare in Southie, as many of the fathers fell victim to the Irish curse—a love affair with booze. He was all Irish, as far as I know. His grandmother was from Galway, I believe. My mother was a Van O'sdol, with Dutch and English and Irish in her. She looks like me—blue eyes, reddish hair once upon a time.

I was the baby of the family. You might think I got away with everything. You might think I got away with murder. Not true. Not with my mother, I didn't. She was the boss. It was her house, no matter where we were. Under her roof whatever she said is to be done is done. Or else. When I was late for dinner, she'd chase me down the street, screaming at me, yelling at me, grabbing me by the hair and dragging me up the street because I wasn't on time. But that was the era. They were all like that, the parents. That's how *they* grew up, that's how they were taught. She'd use belts, a broom, a spatula. Amazing the household items that could become enforcers. She was strict. I certainly wasn't the only one getting it from a strict parent, but I have to say I never saw other kids getting it as bad as I got it. Then again, the other kids weren't exactly like me. I wasn't bad once in a while. I was in trouble all the time. I was full of energy and aggression—a bad combination in a child.

I don't know if the era quite explains why my mother was like she was. My sisters said my mother's mother was a nice woman, gentle and calm. My father couldn't have helped the situation. My mother had it tough, all on her own. The pressure was enormous. Getting the food, finding the apartments, cleaning, schooling us, keeping a wild boy like me in line. She also lost her first child, a little girl who passed away at two years old. Meningitis and tuberculosis. Something my father brought home, I believe I heard. Her name was Betty. We had some pictures of her. She was a beautiful baby. She had beautiful blue eyes with dark hair like my father. My mother says that all the time: She had beautiful blue eyes.

Southie was a very tough part of town, about a mile square. To look at it, you might not think it was so bad—it sits on Boston Harbor, but it runs back west and north to the border of downtown Boston, where the rich live. Mayor Curley built three low-income housing projects in Southie—Old Harbor, D Street, and Old Colony—back in the Depression. The projects were in the part of Southie called the Lower End, and that's what it was. It kind of hung on the underbelly of the harbor area, which was called the Point, named after the City Point section of Southie, where the big fort sat, protecting us all from the British. The Lower End was the lower end of the pecking order, too. If you were middle class at all and from Southie, you probably lived in the Point section. If you were like us, you were Lower End, and you were likely from one of the projects. Nearly every one of my friends in my life early on was from one of the projects.

We moved from I Street to G Street, which is only two blocks away, when I was four years old. It was while living on G Street I realized that most of the kids in the neighborhood were not quite like me. I was wilder and much more aggressive. Most of them had two parents and at least some money. We were very poor, always just getting by. Most of the neighborhood was either poor or borderline middle class. No mansions in Southie. My best friend in the G Street neighborhood was a kid named Sean Long. He had a big Irish family. Bunch of brothers. His father ran a vending-machine business and did pretty well. I remember that, even though the Longs were a big family, they always had a lot more than I did. Sean's brother Danny was a pro fighter, and I remember looking up to him. I wanted to be a pro fighter just like him.

Growing up was tough. It was like a war, but for us kids, it was like a *game* of war. The parents might have seen it differently. There really were two wars going on—among ourselves in Southie and with outsiders in general. Among ourselves . . . well, the kids from the projects were always at it with the kids from the Point. We had nothing—shitty clothes, shit apartments. The kids from the Point called kids from the three housing projects D Street dirtballs, Old Colony rats, Old Harbor dustheads, depending. They had hockey equipment and better baseball mitts and were the ones always with the sticks and pucks. But if it came down to a problem with kids from outside Southie—Dorchester or Charlestown kids, say—we all stuck together. Kids from Southie were legendary around Boston for their fighting ability and their balls. Kids from Southie would fight you all night long.

I couldn't have known it when I was really young, but just about everyone in Southie was into something or other. The adults, who themselves had probably grown up in Southie and were more than likely Irish, were no different from their kids. They fought each other, but when they had to, they fought together, against the outsiders. And compared to the normal misbehaving of kids, the grown-ups were into more serious business of one sort or another, sidestepping the law if not breaking it. There was gambling, drinking, there were drugs, fistfights, murders, stealing, hijacking. You name it, it happened in Southie. It was like the Wild, Wild West in an urban setting. Guys carried guns and knives. Everyone had a baseball bat in his car, and it wasn't to play Little League. Parents were harsh—with the tongue, the fist, and the belt. Even the nuns in Southie were vicious—they might wield a pointer or a long wooden yardstick, and they knew how to use it. Some people called it one of the last urban white ghettos. We called it home.

For all its lawlessness, though, there was one cardinal rule that you learned and followed in Southie before you even knew what it was: You never ratted on anyone. You never rat or run to cops with your problems. You take it or fight back. This was especially so if you were a boy or a man. This is what made you a man, in fact, your ability to handle yourself, to fight and fight back. This was passed down from grandfathers to fathers to sons in Southie. To take care of your own problems and get what was yours. Someone breaks into your house, find out who it is and beat them to a pulp with a baseball bat. But never, ever run to the cops. Or you will be labeled a rat for eternity.

I was born with that Southie attitude. That was clear pretty early. When I was five years old, I got myself beaten up by a couple of bigger, older kids. I got pummeled and left in the gutter, my clothes all wet from the filthy water running through it. To add insult to injury, they spit on me as I was lying there. I was bleeding and soaking when I got home, but I wasn't whimpering. I was fucking enraged. I was possessed. My youngest sister, Paula, was home. I told her what happened, and she marched out into the street and looked up and down. She couldn't have been more than fourteen herself. She asked a neighbor, Mrs. O'Brien, if the account I had given was true, that I'd been beaten up in the gutter. She must have gotten some kind of confirmation, because she headed down the street, and the next thing I know, she's flushed out my two enemies and chased one of them, the slower one, up the street and into the front hall of his house. I followed. Paula proceeded to smash this kid with the end of a coatrack, pinning him in the corner and spearing the thing into him, screaming, "You'll never spit on my brother again, you fucking piece of shit!"

I still couldn't get over what those kids had done to me. I'd been beaten. Okay. But spit on me? Even at the age of five, I knew that was unacceptable. I appreciated, I'm sure, my sister's intervention, but I believe I sensed even then that this was my score to settle, not hers. Maybe if my father had been there to do something, or maybe an older brother, I could have accepted it. Although what Paula did was probably no different from what any older brother would have done, it was still my teenage sister fighting my battles. And old Mrs. O'Brien as the informant. To say the least, that didn't sit well, not with me stewing. I was in a rage for over an hour. When my mother got home, there was no way she could cool me down. Paula neither. It was then that she convinced Ma that I should learn to box. And so began a long apprenticeship with the fight game. It would take me a long way over the years. I'd learn an awful lot—about life and the art of boxing, the sweet science, from some great men. It would damn near almost get me out of Southie. But not quite.

I had a lot of problems with anger growing up. I guess I was born with it—a very bad temper, a hatred for authority, and an independent streak. My mother was always doubling up the belt on me or grabbing me by the hair and throwing me across the room. If I tried to hide under the bed, she'd come at me with broomstick, poking and poking till I had nowhere to go. *Where you goin' now, John? Where you goin' now?* My sisters said she was worse on them, but I beg to differ. I was more dangerous than they were, and my mother knew it. She tried to show me limits, teach me discipline, but it did no good. She'd have my sisters take me to visit my father once in a blue moon. I have a vague memory of it. It was like, Hello, good-bye, as far as I remember. He couldn't do nothing.

My mother worked cleaning office buildings. She put me in a Catholic school when I was six, St. Peter's, hoping the nuns could do something for me, but I was the class clown. I'd sleep on the desks. Sister Claudia, I got into it with her. She stood me in the front of class, and I started smirking, and all the kids were laughing. She whacked me with a three-foot ruler, right over my shoulder, and the thing broke in half. I laughed right in her face as if to say, *That didn't hurt.* More laughter.

She finally put me in the coatroom, where you'd just stand amid the coats in the dark. When my mother heard this, she went into a slow burn, marched down to St. Peter's, and tore into them. No one hits her son. They expelled me.

I did better in the public school. The main reason was some great motivation—a beautiful red-haired teacher in the third grade. Her name was Miss Cooney. I can still see her with those boots up to her knees like Nancy Sinatra. She was strict, but she had a soft spot for me for some reason. It must have been my red hair, like hers. She had style, too. She drove a white convertible. A Triumph or a Fiat, I can't remember. But she was cool, for a teacher, and I had a huge crush on her. I was calmer in the public school, and I did better. Beauty was calming the beast, at least for a while. There weren't nuns in your face all the time, swinging by you in the aisles with their black habits flapping at you and you couldn't do a thing.

My mother tried, God bless her. She got me a private tutor, since I was pretty hyperactive and didn't learn too well in a big group. She encouraged me to play ball—T-ball and hockey, though we couldn't afford the equipment. I got into fights. I got thrown off a football team before I'd even made my First Communion. Somebody'd block me, I'd punch 'em in the face. I'd wrestle the tacklers. I just wasn't into those team sports things. I was more of a one-on-one sort of guy. That's why I took to boxing so well. You could stand there in front of men like Ed Kelly and Red Cochran and Tommy Connors and they would tell you what you had to do to defend yourself. Not someone else. Yourself. It was simple. It was profound. I was still a kid, but I knew.

When I was seven, eight, nine, a couple of days a week I'd go down to the gym, walking by myself through the streets of Southie. I loved the gym, the smell of it, all the sweat and resin and liniment. It went right to your head. The sound of leather popping the canvas bag, the rhythm of combinations, the rat-a-tat-tat of jabs, the scuffling sound of good foot-work. And the laughter. Men hollering encouragement or instructions. Jokes and curses. I was wide-eyed, however skinny and small and freckle-faced, with fair skin and red hair. I felt there was a beast inside me, and I knew these guys could show me how to tame it and use it.

Southie had always been its own kind of island. We had our own people, our own schools, our own culture. People seemed to love life or at least eat it up with gusto. From the harbor back to Four Point Chan-nel, that was us. Across the channel was Chinatown and then downtown. They could have it. Out to sea was out to sea. But right here on these streets was a rough kind of home. It was hard, don't get me wrong. But it had charm, which is more than you can say about a lot of places. In the shops in Southie and on street corners, the men all talked excitedly about one thing or another—a ball game, a horse race, a boxing match. The Red Sox, the Bruins, the Celtics, Suffolk Downs, Ali. And they'd get even more excited talking about the local fighters, the local trainers. And the local politicians. Lots of people out of work or drinking too much, the teenagers all fucked up, stoned, violent at times. The tired guys com-ing home from the factories, like Gillette, or the construction workers or the guys from the docks. Then there were the guys you knew were up to no good, who always had something to sell.

It was our own world with our own cares, however poor they seemed. It wasn't like Ireland, it wasn't like New York. It wasn't even like Boston. It was Southie.

When I was nine years old, things took a turn for the worse, somewhat in my life and more so in Southie. First off, there came a knock on the door at our apartment. My mother was told that my father had died. Cir-rhosis. It didn't change much. It didn't change anything, really. My father was already gone, as far as my life went. Now he was officially gone, as far as his life went. Later that year, 1974, forced busing began. Suddenly our neighborhood was on national TV. A federal judge had ruled that there was an unbalanced school system in the city of Boston, and he determined that schools that were all black were worse than ones that were all white, so he figured he would change the mix and improve the schools. But in our part of town, none of the schools were that great—whether the all-black schools in Roxbury or the all-white schools in Southie. They were both poor. And busing poor black kids into a poor white neighborhood was one of those ideas that still makes you scratch your head, especially when that meant poor white kids couldn't go to the school in their own neighborhood, but had to be bused to a poor black neighborhood. Well, Southie was having none of that.

In September of that year, most families in Southie boycotted South Boston High School, which was right around the corner from my house and three blocks from my elementary school. I could look out my window and see the chaos unfolding every day. When the buses arrived with the black kids, the white parents and lots of us kids were on the streets. The local men were throwing stones and bottles at the buses. I joined in just like everyone else.

Boston's Tactical Police Force was out in full strength with shields and clubs, and they would beat the fuck out of you if they caught you. I saw a black man dragged through the streets. There were fires and overturned cars. It was like a war, and frankly speaking, for a kid, it was fun as hell, and exciting. Here was the whole neighborhood fighting to protect itself, not only from the blacks but from the Boston police, the white liberal politicians, and the country as a whole. We were saying, This is our town, get the fuck out. I missed about two months of school. It was great.

One day I was in the middle of a rally to block the blacks from using Carson Beach. I was nine, or maybe even eight. I was right outside Billy's

Pizza across the street from the Old Colony Projects. Everyone was meeting there to march over to the beach. There were hundreds of people lin-
ing the sidewalks and spilling out onto Old Colony Avenue. The traffic
was slowly moving past the crowd. I noticed a small car with a black guy
inching up to the stop sign at the rotary. As soon as he stopped, his fate
was sealed. The car door was ripped open, and he was dragged out. He
was no more than ten or fifteen feet away from me. He tried to stand up,
and all you could hear was a loud crack as a wooden baseball bat smashed
across his forehead. It looked like the top of his head came off.

Everyone knew that lots of inner-city schools had kids from poor
families in them and that the schools didn't have a very good graduation
rate and had lousy facilities. But this they blamed on the fact that all the
poor black kids were together in one school and all the poor white kids
were in another? Like if they mixed 'em, things would get better? Far
from it! What about the all-white schools in the suburbs, like out in
Newton? They had things better off but were just as segregated. Why
weren't those schools subject to forced busing? Because they were the
schools where the politicians' kids went, that's why. Boston figured they'd
make a big liberal show to make it look like they knew the virtues of in-
tegration and that they would force it, if they had to. They had some
guilt complex, about housing patterns being a result of whites wanting to
live with whites and blacks wanting to live with blacks. Why feel guilty
about that? It was the result of neighborhoods making free choices. It was
natural that Southie was the way it was, because it was full of the people
who wanted to live there or who lived there and couldn't find a life for
themselves anywhere else. Same with Roxbury. Busing wasn't natural.

When things got really hot, one of our Southie politicians stood toe-
to-toe with the police commissioner, an Italian. The police commissioner
was there to ensure that the blacks could come peacefully to South
Boston High. Our politician was up there in front of the school saying
no way. He jabbed his finger at the commish. He told him to go fuck
himself. That was Billy Bulger, our state representative.

One day I overheard my Uncle Larry telling some of his friends about what was going on at Southie High. He was holding court outside of the Heights Tavern. He was saying, "Billy told 'em to go fuck themselves. The cops better watch out for Whitey."

A lot of people in Southie thought that Whitey Bulger was all-powerful, too. That the mayor and the police commissioner and even the Kennedys—who supported the busing, by the way—would be sorry they tried to mess with South Boston. And I agreed: Yeah, Yeah, Whitey'll show em. But we were wrong. We were making the same mistake that the people of South Boston would make for the next twenty-five years, thinking that Whitey had our interests at heart, that he was looking out for Southie. Don't get me wrong: Whitey hated blacks, and he always hated the idea of busing. In typical Whitey fashion, he instructed the kids from the neighborhood what to do. All the while he was using them to keep the cops busy. Because if the cops were busy protecting the buses and preventing a full-scale race war, he was left alone to ply his trade and run his operations with impunity. He just wanted the cops occupied.

Little did anyone know that at that time, Whitey, along with Stevie Flemmi, Korean vet turned killer, who grew up in Roxbury, was making a deal with a rising FBI agent, another Southie guy named John Connolly, that would affect my life and the lives of nearly everyone in South Boston.

3

WHITEY

I knew who Whitey was without knowing. He was, somehow, The Guy. Kids would spot him being driven in a car somewhere, white hair combed straight back, steel blue eyes, dressed in a windbreaker or leather jacket. We figured he was moving around taking care of everything in Southie. I heard grown-ups say that—Whitey will take care of it. When I was eight or nine, I think I figured Whitey was like the mayor of Southie. The boss, like at my mother's job. Then I thought he was guy who could do anything. I was partly right, as I found out when I was a little older. He was indeed a boss, the boss of the Irish Mob in Southie, and the top Irish mobster anywhere. He was also the older brother of the then president of the Massachusetts Senate, Billy Bulger, one of the most powerful politicians in the state. You could say he was connected.

Whitey had been a punk, like me. He was no different. He came from a large family of tough-luck Irish. His father had lost an arm in the squish of two railroad cars and didn't do much after that, supposedly, but walk the neighborhood and leave the raising of the family of six to his wife. He did get the family into the Old Harbor projects, the first of the public housing set up in Southie back in the late thirties. Whitey, born in

1929, the year of the stock market crash, was five years older than Billy, who'd go on to become the politician. Billy did everything right—studied hard, stayed clean and out of trouble. I've heard that he is what they call a Triple Eagle, because he went to Boston College High School, Boston College, and Boston College Law School—and the BC mascot is an eagle. He took time off his education to go to Korea. He went on to law school, married his sweetheart, also from Southie, and ran for office in 1960, the year JFK sneaked into the White House. Billy was representing Southie in the House of Representatives at the age of twenty-six. At thirty-six, he was elected to the state senate, eventually becoming president of that body, a position he would hold for seventeen years.

Whitey, on the other hand, took a different route. When he was a teenager, he was known as a vicious football player by the other kids but as something else by the police and the shop owners: a criminal. Like us when we were kids, Whitey was into it early, tailgating trucks, which has always been a profitable and exciting pastime in Southie. You find a truck making a delivery, one guy follows the delivery guy into the store, and the other guys grab and run from the back of the truck bed. Whatever you find—cigarettes, newspapers, soap, cans of food—you could sell. In a poor neighborhood, where no one has much, there's someone to buy anything, if the price is right. And because it's Southie, they won't say a word. Perfect.

Whitey got busted at thirteen, for stealing. He got beaten up more than once by the cops, who got sick of following his crazy antics around town. This guy was fucking insane. My Uncle Larry told me that one night Whitey stopped and picked him up in a car. As soon as Larry's ass hit the seat, Whitey gunned it around the heights and down Telegraph Street, which is one of the steepest hills in Boston, at eighty miles an hour, and scared the daylights out of everybody, scattering old folks and moms with baby carriages. Larry almost shit his pants. That was the last time he ever took a ride with Whitey.

Like me, Whitey wasn't a big guy—about five-eight and lean. But he had a swagger, all right. Like me, he wasn't cut out for team sports, shall we say. They used to play kind of a sandlot football—no pads, of course—and supposedly you didn't want to get Whitey mad. But he was always mad. At the drop of a hat, he would beat someone senseless with his fists or a weapon if it was needed. In a word, he was brutal.

He joined a gang, The Shamrocks. Back then, in the 1940s, organized crime as we'd come to know it was just getting started. There had been a big showdown between the Irish gang of South Boston and the Mafia, and the Mafia had more or less won. The Irish ran their errands for them. Only thing is, Whitey Bulger was nobody's errand boy. So he freelanced. Jewelry-store hits, smash-and-grabs. And then he graduated to cowboy stuff, with a piece—gimme your diamonds. He got nailed for a bank robbery out in Indiana. I believe he was in flight from a sex rap—though he'd never talk about that—and ended up, at twenty-seven years of age, getting sentenced to twenty years in federal prison.

Whitey hit all the big spots and did a lot of hard time. Three months' solitary in Atlanta. Alcatraz. Leavenworth. Lewisburg. He took part in a government LSD experiment, which I don't imagine bothered him any more than the time in the hole. Whitey was tough-minded. He was like a machine. I often thought he worked like a machine, with a machine's tooling. It could do one thing, inevitably, perfectly, over and over. And nothing else. And nothing could get in the way. Not even jail. While in jail Whitey was taken care of by Donald Killeen, the leader of the Killeen Gang, and by Hank Garrity, owner of The Pen, a bar on Broadway. They sent him money and helped him get started when he first came home.

Like me, Whitey did his time—nine years for him—and came back to Southie looking for work. His brother Billy, by then a state senator, found him a job as a janitor in the county courthouse. I don't think Whitey came back with the idea he'd be a janitor. I don't know if he resented this "gift" from his brother. I imagine he took it and used it to do his one main thing: crime. It really didn't matter, because Whitey was fired due to his criminal record. A former political foe of Billy Bulger's had found out. That same person was eventually dismissed from his position and put into permanent political exile. Payback.

Whitey was a smart guy. His brother was proof of good genetics, and Whitey would eventually prove his brother's equal; it's just that he was walking on the other side of the street. Or actually both sides. He didn't waste his time in prison. He read voraciously. One of the things Whitey would give me is a love of good books, good storytelling. History, biography, war. He wanted to know how people led other people, how they made war, how they won and how they lost. Whitey got right back into it.

There were some new gang elements in Boston. Whitey began to work for Killeen, who made book, loansharked, took various kinds of action. Their Irish rival in Southie was the Mullin Gang, which was led by Tommy King. Tommy had a connection to the Winter Hill Gang from years of dealing with them, selling them loads of cigarette or booze that was hijacked. A series of bar fights and turf battles and bad tempers had led to a key Mullin Gang member's getting his nose bitten off, which sparked a long campaign for revenge between the two gangs. It was always all about money. Whether it was over a woman or an insult or a legitimate beef that was a reason to pop someone, it didn't matter.

Tommy Ballou, the then head of the Winter Hill Gang from Somerville, and his right-hand man, Howie Winter, set up a meeting at the Bay View Pub in Southie to mediate the dispute. Whitey, Tommy King, and the others agreed to settle their differences and become partners. Tommy and Whitey would be the bosses. Everyone agreed that it was time to stop fighting and start making money. Whitey quickly aligned himself with the Winter Hill Gang, which by this time was headed up by Howie Winter. Tommy Ballou had been shot to death in a drunken barroom brawl. Winter recognized the value of a fierce and disciplined guy like Whitey. Some folks think that spelled the end for Donald Killeen. In any event, Killeen was at home one day for his kid's birthday party. Killeen got a phone call that trouble was on its way. He told his wife he had to go out to his car. The reason he went out to his car was to grab his gun, as he never kept a gun in his house. He went out, got into his car, and got blasted with machine-gun fire in the face as he sat there behind the wheel.

At the time no one knew who did it. But it is known that a few days later a man drove past Killeen's brother Kenny's home, fired a shot as he stood on his porch, rolled down the window, and told him that business was over; there'd be no more warnings. The messenger was Whitey Bulger.

Now Whitey was with Howie Winter. The Killeen Gang was done. The Mullins remained, but not for long. Six bodies later Whitey ruled Southie. Tommy King, Paulie McGonagle, Billy O'Sullivan, and Buddy Leonard all ended up dead. Respected Southie guys known for their ambition and balls. Character traits that inevitably got them killed. Buddy Leonard shot to death in his car with a machine gun. Hundreds of rounds fired to make sure the job was done right. Billy O'Sullivan shot in front of his home. Tommy King and Paulie McGonagle disappeared, never to be heard from again. Or so Whitey thought, until many years later a little rat told the feds all the secrets and led them to the makeshift graves of Tommy, Paulie, and others.

Now Whitey was right where he wanted to be. He had it all.

But he also got himself a partner—or rather partners plural.

The rogue hit man and former U.S. paratrooper Steve Flemmi, who freelanced his services to a variety of employers and whose mother lived in Southie, had gotten in serious trouble. A favorite of New England mob boss Raymond Patriarca Sr., Flemmi was offered made status in the Mafia but declined in order to continue to work on his own. He got indicted for attempted murder, though. Turns out Patriarca had almost made a mistake. This was no guy to bring into the family. With the heat on, Flemmi took a phone call from an FBI agent named Paul Rico. Somehow the murder charge went away. Rico was a guy working both sides of the street; he was helping the criminals who were helping him—

a typical career move in law enforcement. He helped the Winter Hill Gang locate a guy who had killed several of their members in a spree of revenge, and who was then killed. That was back in the early sixties. Frank Salemme eventually had to go underground because he was wanted for attempted murder in a car bombing. Years passed. When the time was right, Flemmi, who knew where Salemme was, gave him up to a new FBI guy once Rico had retired to Florida. The new FBI guy was another Southie lad, John Connolly. He grew up right next to Whitey and Billy. He was a young agent with a lot of ambition. Flemmi gave Connolly a tip, it is believed, as to the whereabouts of Mr. Frank Salemme. Amazingly, in a city of millions, Connolly "recognized" the wanted Salemme on the streets of New York and made a dramatic, heroic arrest on the spot. Instant promotion for Connolly and a triumphant return to Boston from his post in New York. Flemmi had another fed in the bag.

Flemmi, who had been on the run, living in Montreal, returned to Boston. He and Bulger began working together. John Connolly made the same phone call to Bulger that Paul Rico had made to Steve Flemmi years before. Whitey made the same deal—to provide information to the FBI in return for certain kinds of protection. Whitey and Stevie became partners, a match made in hell. This was in 1975, when I was about ten years old and cheering on the Red Sox, working my way up through amateur boxing, trying to find two fucking nickels to rub together. I wouldn't know the truth till twenty-five years later, a lifetime later. When I found out—found out that Whitey Bulger was an informant, the worst species of human being, a rat—my knees buckled as if I'd been hit square on the chin with a vicious left hook.

4

EARLY BOXING

Boxing was everything to me when I was a kid. I was obsessed. When my sister dragged me to the gym to learn how to box, I found a world I could relate to, a world where people valued self-protection and admired violence as long as it was controlled. Here was a place—the boxing ring—where there were rules, like everywhere else, but within these rules you were allowed to zero in on a guy intent on hurting you and you could hurt him back. It was brutal, and I loved it.

I also found a world full of great men living what I thought was a great life. The gym and its old guys were a mystery to me at the start. I was just a kid. And of course there's nothing like a mystery to keep you interested, kid or not. Red and Tommy and the other trainers all had their ways—their sporty brimmed hats, their smokers' coughs, their worn sweaters, and the smell of booze coming off them mixed with a little Old Spice or Aqua Velva. But what they had to say was both so tough and so tender, telling you how to fight but also how to look after yourself, that I couldn't do anything except drink it in. It seemed like the ultimate wisdom. I felt as if I had entered the real church of Southie, where you learned true salvation. These guys really got it. Sure, the priests might be telling us how to prepare ourselves for the hereafter; my mother might be telling me—or trying to—how to prepare myself for the future.

But Tommy Connors, who eventually took me under his wing, was
telling me how to deal with today—hands up, jab, jab, step and hook,
right to the body, uppercut, left hook, and move. Run, squat, lift, work
the heavy bag. Eat right. Do a thousand push-ups a day. Run, run, run,
run, run. All of which I do to this day.

My first competition was in the Baby Golden Gloves. I was six years
old. I fought a kid named Brian Yanovich. I fought Brian all the time as
a kid. I beat him every time. At this point Ed Kelly and Red Corcoran
were my trainers—I wasn't old enough yet for the great Tommy Connors, who would work in the center ring with the older fighters. I was
skinny and narrow-chested. My hair was fiery red, my eyes a cold blue,
and I was vicious and driven, even then. Quite a few of the kids had their
fathers involved, and they pushed the kids to train. I had to push myself.

I fought on any boxing show I could. I fought every time I could
fight. It helped me deal with the anger I had for not having a father
around and with the resentment I had for my mother. For a long time, I
used to blame her for driving my father to drink, with her harshness.
Shit, sometimes I wanted to drink!

Boxing became a great source of pride for me. I liked it, and I was
good at it. One day my mother took me out of boxing because I was
doing poorly in school. Do you know what it's like to have your mother
show up at the gym and tell the men there that you're through, that you
have bad grades, that boxing made you worse, more violent? I pleaded
with her. This was my only joy, I said. I asked her to call my father. He'd
approve, I said, desperate. I don't approve of *him,* John, so what's that
supposed to mean to me, eh? He's gone, John. And you're coming home
with me. She tried to grab me by the hair. Instinctively my left hand
came up and blocked her. I grabbed a towel and headed to the locker
room to change. Tommy Connors was there, taping his own hand to do
some work on the heavy bag. As I passed him, shame turning my face a
deep red, he gave me a nod of the chin to get my attention, rolled his
eyes, and then winked. It was like a little sentence he was saying: *Look,*

kid, you'll be back. I appreciated it. And I came back, all right. I got into so many fights out of the gym and pestered her every minute of the day with, "Please, Ma, let me go back to the gym?" that she finally gave in. I ran out the door and right to McDonough's Gym.

I started working with Tommy Connors when I was twelve. He was an employee of the Boston Parks and Recreation Department. I can't say the city did nothing for us kids, but the parks programs were about the extent of it. And I took advantage.

Ed Kelly told me that Tommy was the best fighter ever to come out of Southie. He won the Golden Gloves many times and went to the national finals twice. As a pro, he was 30–2. He once knocked a guy out in thirteen seconds—and that includes the ten count—in the Boston Garden, a record. And nearly everyone he met was told this last fact, you can be sure.

Tommy said that if you were committed to boxing and had courage, you could learn how to box. Commitment was easy—Tommy could tell you what to do and how often to do it. And then do it over and over. But courage was complicated. It wasn't the opposite of fear. It wasn't fearlessness. It was a mixture of guts and smarts. This was a much more difficult lesson to master. It was acquired with time and experience. Learning how to size up the opponent, how to pace yourself, how to take your opportunities, how not to get greedy, how to wait for an opening, how to gamble when you had to, and to know when. Which guy to jab, which to hook, which to punish to the body. You could tell a weak chin by the set of the ears, he said. Look at Floyd Patterson, he would later say. Little ears, down low. Glass jaw.

Tommy loved the fight game, and it rubbed off on us kids, but no one more than me. I soaked him up, and I was far and away—if I do say so myself—his star pupil. He knew he had a tiger in me. And he took a liking to me. It really went beyond him being just a trainer. He was the closest thing I ever had to a father figure. If we went out together for a bite to eat, Tommy would tell everyone, "He's my kid." But he wasn't my father. He was my trainer.

Tommy was, and is, a true character. Five foot five inches tall, a buzz of constant chatter and hyperactivity. Tattoos of striped bass on his arm and across his chest, a large belt buckle with a striped bass on it across his gut. He loved fishing as much as boxing, but he loved sex, I gradually learned, as much as either. If he wasn't talking about this fighter or that, or this fish he caught or that, he was talking about girls. I'd have to say he taught me more than how to box. He told me how to handle women—for better or for worse, I can't be the judge.

I was a gym rat, always there learning as much as I could. I'd go down after school, climbing up the G Street hill every day with my gym bag over my shoulder. I'd grab a soda and a candy bar on the way. I'd say hello to the guys at the G Street Deli. They could all see that I was driven. I was all business. Even back then I was careful what I put into my body. I needed the sugar pick-me-up, and there was nothing around like today, with protein drinks and nutritional bars, so I made do. But my mother was pleasantly surprised to see that I ate my vegetables and told her I wished she'd get the whole-wheat bread and not those long, cheap loaves of white shit we usually had. And I had a handy place to get fruit and nuts—down at Lambert's. This is a true story, about how you had to do what you had to do to get along in Southie.

My Uncle Larry, God bless his soul, used to look after me quite a bit. He had no kids and wasn't really my uncle—he was my mother's cousin. He was a great guy. He may not have been our real uncle, but in every way he was an uncle to me and my sisters. One day he dropped me off early over on Morrissey Boulevard, in Dorchester. I was about twelve or so. I'm waiting for Bradlee's department store to open. It was Mother's Day. I wanted to get my mother a gift. But the only store open at the time was Lambert's Fruit. So I walked in there just to get a piece of fruit, and a guy in there, the owner, says to me, "Hey, kid." I say, "Yeah?" He says, "You wanna work here for the day and make some money?" I say, "Yeah, absolutely." I figured a few dollars would help.

He showed me the back of the place. He wanted me to clean all of it. Crates all over the place, squashed fruit, stinking, et cetera. Looked like there'd been an accident, and plenty killed. "Sweep it up, clean up the trash, wash it down," he says.

It was seven in the morning when I walked in there; eight hours later I walk out, dead tired. He comes up to me after dealing with every last customer he can wait for to shuffle up to the counter, and he leans over to me. "Now, what'll I do for you, my little man?" he asks out loud. "Let's see what we have." He goes back behind the counter. Waits on another customer. Then looks at me. I finally got in line. I'm next. He dings on the cash register to open it, looks inside. I figure I'm getting at least twenty-five bucks for busting my balls for Mr. Lambert all day. He hands me a ten-dollar bill. I couldn't believe it. If he had told me in the morning I'd get ten dollars for cleaning up the back of the store, I'd have done a different job on it. I broke my back for this guy. I just turned red in the face, and that's pretty red for me. "You look bushed, kid. Have an orange."

I took the money, turned around, and left, burning up. I was mad at him and mad at myself. I went over to Bradlee's and bought my mother a couple of those angel Hummels that she liked. When I told her about Lambert's, she was pissed, too, but she was proud that I did it, proud that I earned that money legitimately.

That didn't do much for me. But after that I made a promise to myself: Every chance I got, I stole fruit from Lambert's Fruit. I got all the fruit I wanted from Lambert's Fruit, and I dared that motherfucker to say something to me. Funny thing is, he never seemed to notice. I even took a plant once, to give to my mother. "Where'd you get that nice plant, Jay?" "Lambert's, Mom." "Oh, thank you, Jay."

Even today when I walk in there, I take something and walk out the door.

Have an orange! Yeah, right. That guy fucked with the wrong Irishman.

So did a lotta guys. I won the Junior Olympic Championship for the first time when I was fourteen. At fifteen I fought a kid named Steve Miranda from Fall River, for the title. This kid was as tough as they come. Because I had tennis elbow in my left arm at the time and couldn't jab, Tommy had me use short left hooks and right crosses. It was an epic battle between two evenly matched fighters. These were three-rounders, so the fights didn't ebb and flow. They kind of went in one direction and then they were over, though it could take the whole three rounds to find out where it was all meant to go. Miranda got a little frustrated because I played it so close and was so controlled. He got a little sloppy. He started really winging punches at me, and I noticed his mouth opening up. He was breathing hard. I came right down the middle and beat him to the punch, right on the button, his mouth open. That rattled his brain around, and the fight was over. Altogether, I won the New England Junior Olympic Championship three times, fighting at 106 pounds. I compiled a record of 60–6.

Southie loved its fighters. The *Boston Herald* loved to tell my story. "Little Red Shea Has His Opponents Seeing Red." "Little Red Victorious," with a picture of me, my arm being raised high as the winner by the referee, me screaming with joy. Interviews with Tommy Connors, interviews with me. "A life on the street seemed an inevitable epitaph to Red's story," they wrote. "A bundle of stored energy in need of an outlet, he found it one day at the mature age of five fighting in Southie's McDonough Gym. Now he's setting his sights on the Olympics."

5

OTHER BATTLES

When I look back on it, I was always fighting. Getting my ass kicked in a puddle when I was five, getting my hair pulled by my mother from whenever, getting the stick from Sister Claudia—it was one long steady brawl. In the ring I could make sense of it. There was a tradition, a way. Everywhere else was war, some big, some small.

Eventually I got bused. For high school I got bused to Roxbury, where there were a lot of blacks. It was tough. My head wasn't in school. I was dealing with my boxing, my mother, life on the streets. School was like a joke. Except it wasn't funny. I spent half my time in detention hall. Good spot. They'd keep an eye on us keeping an eye on the blacks keeping an eye on us. It was tense. All quiet, but the place packed full with I-don't-give-a-fucks. The administration kept us in check for the most part. They hired extra security, local toughs mostly—in fact, Kevin Weeks, who would become one of Whitey's guys, worked the halls in South Boston High School after he graduated. He should've stayed there.

I got fed up with the shit in Roxbury. One day I organized a little mini-riot in the auditorium, which was empty during second period. Most of the white kids were intimidated by the black kids. I had enough of the white kids getting bullied by blacks; it was time to take a stand. A few of us—me and a couple of other kids from Southie—cornered a couple of blacks there and let them have it. There'd been this little rift going on for too long. They were giving us a hard time in the cafeteria and in the school yard, outnumbering us, blocking territory and basically terrorizing all the white kids. "Not this table, motherfucker, don't even think about it." Or, "We're fucking playing here." "Are you? I don't fuckin' think so." They were bigger than us, for the most part. And they were most definitely protected by the administration, in my view. The administration didn't want to be called racist, no way.

Of course I'm not taking shit from nobody. So we go after these guys and punch the shit out of them, where the security guys can't see it and where the rest of the blacks are out of sight.

The next day I left school early in the morning. I slipped out a side door because the blacks were trying to corral me. I went down to see Tommy Connors. I told him that today was officially my last day of school.

"Why you doing that?" Tommy asks, in his way. Not prying, but you better have an answer. I tell him, "Because they'll be trying to corral me and fucking trap me."

"Why," he says.

I tell him about slamming those guys in the auditorium.

"And these guys have weapons," I add. And they did. Pipes, knives. They somehow kept them around the school.

He says to me, "Kid, you're gonna end up being stabbed. You ain't learnin' nothing up there. You're going to school to fight. You're gonna end up dead."

"Yeah," I said. "I ain't afraid."

He told me, "Red, you are better off leaving that fuckin' school and getting out of there. You're right."

So I did. I quit school in the tenth grade.

Ma didn't go for that, but I was stubborn. That was it. She tried to make me work, but I was working at boxing. I'm gonna be a champ, Ma. Leave me alone. Support me or not, whatever. Just let me be.

My mother got me a job at the nursing home where she worked. I was an orderly, washing and buffing floors. I hated the fucking job. I got fired for not showing up for work on Christmas weekend. It was like a Christmas present. Now I was free to box and work the streets. I made more money in a couple hours on the streets than working my balls off with those old folks all weekend long.

I agreed to get my GED, which I did. I also started to earn my degree on the streets.

I started out with shoplifting and tailgating. Waiting for the trucks to hit the store. We'd pop the lock with a crowbar—cigarettes, TVs, liquor. And we'd resell to another store around the block. Cheaper price than they could get them otherwise.

I loved it. Waiting, waiting, waiting, like stalking prey. Then bang!

After a while me and Johnny Baldwin used to go out to the malls. Ray Tallent would take us in his blue Cadillac. Maybe five of us—Billy Mahoney was always with us—all dressed in Southie style: Barracuda jackets with the collar up, Izod shirts, freshly pressed dungarees, green Gazelle suede sneakers with three white stripes. Every week we'd head to the mall in Natick for a shoplifting excursion. We'd steal clothes mostly, then sell them back in the bars in Southie. Celtics jackets, Bruins jerseys, packs of underwear, the gamut. One time security spotted us, and the chase was on. Me and Johnny Baldwin had to run about a mile through Natick till we found a toolshed we could hide in. We waited it out for a couple of hours, till dark, and then hitched home. It was great.

Once we stole walkie-talkies from a police car. Joey Purcell had the bright idea that we could sell them—back to the cops! So Joey and Johnny grabbed a pair off the dashboard of a cop car parked beside Billy's Pizza. We ran around to the back of a tire store nearby and huddled behind some dumpsters. The cops called on the walkie-talkies. Joey figured out how to use it. The cops wanted their walkie-talkies back. "See?" said

Joey to us. He then explained to the cops that we had just found them. And that we wanted some kind of reward. Pretty smart! The cops said they'd come over and get them and give us our reward. Yeah, sure. Then we heard the thing crackle, and we heard the cops calling in backup and planning to arrest us. We took off and left the walkie-talkies squawking under a dumpster.

Sometimes we got tired of all the heisting and hustling and just went out looking for trouble. Not often, but always on St. Patrick's Day. It was one day when you'd be sure to find a bunch of out-of-towners walking down our streets, acting like assholes. We always called them hicks. They were easy to spot—big stupid work boots, dungaree or bikey leather jackets, long hair. They stuck out like a sore thumb in Southie.

One St. Paddy's Day, when I was about fifteen, Joey Purcell and Walter Novicki, and I were walking along Old Colony Avenue when four men and a girl, in their early twenties or so, passed us. The men were wearing black leather bikey jackets. We could tell they were from out of town. They were pretty drunk. We stared 'em down. One of them said something fresh, like, "What the fuck are you lookin' at?" Joey said, "You got a problem, you hick motherfucker?" The guy made a little move, and Joey hit him with a right hand. The guy swung back, and they went at it. The other three guys jumped in, so Walter and I jumped in, too. The fight was pretty much a standoff. We were tougher, but these were big guys, all around six feet, two hundred pounds. We were skinny little Irish kids. Then I grabbed a lead pipe and began beating all of them. Three of them got away, but I began to viciously beat the last one. I lost it. I was screaming in the middle of Old Colony Avenue, "You motherfucker! You are gonna pay for what you and your friends said! Where are your friends now, you fucking punk?"

I beat this guy to a pulp—head, back, face. Then Joey yelled, "The cops are coming, Red!" So we took off. It was hard to run, I was laughing so hard, and I slipped and fell. Good thing. I rolled the pipe under a parked car. A cop came over to me. I then put on a great performance.

"Those kids beat up my friends and me!" I cried. "Go get 'em!" He took off after them. I ran in the opposite direction to my friend Frank "The Tank" MacDonald's place. Frank—a little older than us—was one of the best fighters at the gym. I looked up to Frank. He was heavily muscled and tough as they come. He lived up to his nickname. His house was always our refuge when we needed to get away from the cops. Walter and Joey were already there. We started laughing hysterically. I remember I almost pissed my pants. Then I said, "Let's go out looking for some more hicks."

It wasn't long after this that I had one of the worst days of my entire life. I've had a lot of them. I've seen a lot of bad things, done a lot of bad things, things I regret. I've seen shit I had nothing to do with that was bad, but this was the worst.

I was around fifteen or so. It was a Saturday, and my youngest sister, Paula, was getting married. I had to be there because I was giving her away, since my father was deceased by then. I was dressed up in a tux. It was the last place I wanted to be, but it was family. And Ma insisted. "You have to give your sister away, John." "I wish," I said, and almost got a crack, but Ma knew better by then. I wanted to be with my friends. There was some party or another.

These guys, all friends of mine, got in some kind of beef with some other guys. My friend Billy Mahoney, who drank too much since he was thirteen or so, passed out on the couch and didn't go. The rest of them all jumped in a car, and they were racing over to take care of business with these other people, some guys from the Point, I think. If I was available, if there was to be a confrontation, I would have been there. But I wasn't. I was squirming at the reception.

When I woke up the next morning, Ma said, "Jeez, there was an awful bad crash down at Andrew's Square last night." "Really?" I said. "Yeah, a car hit a city bus head-on. Terrible one."

A few minutes later, the phone rings. It's Billy Mahoney calling, giving me the bad news. Six in the car—two survived, Joey Purcell and Moses Michael Mulane. Johnny Baldwin, Bobby McCormick, Keith Miller, and Billy Welch, all dead. Some of them decapitated.

I met up with Billy later. He and I and Johnny Baldwin and Joey Purcell, who was injured real bad, were the best of friends. We were all friends. It was shocking.

The four funerals were all together. Blocks long, the procession. You've never seen a town in such mourning.

There was a lot of talk after about how now maybe the kids of Southie would learn something. That their wild ways were leading to a bad end. But all I thought was, Thank God I survived. I'm a survivor. I wish those other guys had made it, but they didn't. Winners and losers. Luck and bad luck. So I got a break. Good for me. I said a prayer for those guys, whose names are now on a big plaque along Columbia Road adjacent to Columbia Park, which looks out over the harbor. I've walked past that plaque many times and realized just how short life really is—and how cruel it can sometimes be.

Later that winter my luck almost ran out. I almost got fucked—not by some hick or some gangster or a speeding car but by my own fucked-up family.

It was my mother's birthday. My middle sister, Claire, lived in the projects, not far from us, on Pilsudski Way. She had two little girls, Erin and Paula. I loved those girls. I drop by, and Claire is on the phone with my youngest sister, Paula, who now is married. And them, not being so gracious in their asking me—coming from Southie, where the women can be fucking coarse, especially in my family—I hear Paula on the other end of the line, "Did he get Ma's birthday present?" So Claire turns to me: "Did you get Ma a birthday present?" Acting as if they already knew the answer. It was in their voices: Of course the prick didn't get his mother a birthday present. I said very calmly, "No. I'm on my way to

pick up some money from Louie Sasso. Gonna buy her something now."
Well, that wasn't good enough for the two of them.

It was brutal, growing up with those three and my mother. Listening
to them all my life. I was always the baby, but I wasn't babied, I'll tell you
that. I was yelled at, constantly. Do this, do that. You didn't do this, you
didn't do that. They never played with me. They never took their little
brother in their hands and held him. It's what they should've been doing.

"You don't have it," says Claire to me. "He doesn't have it," she says
to Paula over the phone. Now they're having a good fucking time. I can
hear Paula's shit from the other end. I see Claire standing there shaking
her head as if I am the biggest piece of shit she's seen in her whole life
and it's standing on her living room rug and she's disgusted.

So what do I do? I'm being attacked, I fight back. I start yelling, "I
told you! I was on my fuckin' way to getting some money. For Ma's present. Shut the fuck up!" Claire hangs up the phone and sits on her couch.
I take the offensive. "Don't you come up to Ma's house tonight, because
I'll stab you and your boyfriend, I swear to God."

She sits there and says, "You won't stab shit."

I go, "What?" Now she's fucking doubting me. Like I'm lying, like
I'm a coward, like I'm not a man. Her kids run out of the room and into
the bedroom crying, and they shut the door. I grab a knife out of the
kitchen drawer. I walk over to her on the couch. I make sure my left hand
is out, and I put it on her shoulder. I have the knife in my right hand. I
have her braced, so she can't do something stupid. I don't really want to
stick her, I want to scare her. If I wanted to stick her, I would have walked
over to her and just put it in her, period. But I have it back, cocked like.
What does she do? She reaches for the fuckin' knife, slowly. Not to grab
it, she's not gonna grab it from me. And she slides her palm across the
blade. She tries to slice her hand.

She's much older than me, and she's thinking law. I'm not thinking
law, I'm thinking fucking hotheaded argument. She's thinking of putting
me in jail.

I pull the knife back. "You're a sick motherfucker," I say. She just smiles. She says, "No, John, *you're* sick, and you're fucked." I took the knife and threw it across the room. It stuck in the wall, *twang!* "Don't come up to Ma's tonight!" I yell, and I head out the door.

Claire goes and calls Ma and tells her the story. Ma calls Uncle Gilly. He had a few connections, worked with the police on community stuff, worked with the Cub Scouts, the Police Explorers, a youth group learning about civic things. Bunch of geeks. But Uncle Gilly was all right. I go across the street. I'm waiting in Columbia Park to see what's going down. I see Uncle Gilly pull up. He goes in. I'm bird-doggin' the situation, scoping to see if the police come. Not long after, Uncle Gilly comes out. I run across the street. "Uncle Gilly, what the fuck's up?" "What's up?" he goes. "You're in fucking hot water. I can't talk to that woman. She said you tried to stab the kid and you held a knife to the kid." I told Uncle Gilly, "You know I wouldn't do something like that. You gotta be shittin' me." He says he tried to talk to her. "I can't help you on this one, kid. I told her that I will never talk to her again if she does that to her little brother."

And Uncle Gilly held to his word—he died without ever talking to Claire again.

I wait things out. The cops don't show. Maybe it's cool. I go up to Ma's house. "Hey, you want some hot dogs and beans?" "Yeah, Ma. Happy birthday. I'll give you your present tomorrow." I go sit on the edge of the bed, waiting for something. Here it comes: a knock on the door. Boston police. "Mrs. Shea. We're here to arrest John. Is John here?"

I'm standing there when they come in. "Yeah, what's up?"

Assault and battery, they explain.

They cuff me and bring me downstairs. They get me in the car. As we head toward the station, they're asking me questions. Do you know this? Do you know anything about that? Someone got shot in the projects. Somebody got clipped. And there was this black kid in the backseat with me, over in the shadows. I didn't even see him at first. Where'd he come from? He ain't from Southie, I know that. I know enough not to say nothing. And the black kid was all right. He gave me a little fucking check. He nudged me with his elbow, in other words, Don't say nothing. I wasn't going to say nothing, but I liked that, I appreciated that. Because I knew I was next to a guy who was gonna keep his mouth shut.

Down at the station, in Dorchester actually, after endless delays and time in a holding cell, I'm brought before a night judge, and they set bail. My family's got no money. And I am not calling them anyway. They got me into this shit. I call Tommy Connors. He pays the bail bondsman. I stay at Tommy's house for a few days.

Eventually the case fell apart. Not because Claire gave up. She pushed it so far, all the way to trial, that my sister Paula finally intervened and just asked my niece Erin, "Did Uncle Jay do that to you?" "No, my mommy's making me say it." I got a two-and-a-half-year suspended sentence. I would have gone to jail if not for Paula. She and I may have fought over the years, but Paula would never have called the police on me. She didn't want anything to happen to me, did not want to see me go to jail, especially over a lie. Paula tried to help me during this time, took me in and tried to protect me from going to jail. She ended up testifying at my trial and recounting her conversation with my niece and how my niece had been coached to lie by my wonderful sister Claire.

6

THE STREETS

Billy's Pizza, a small, cramped store situated next to a laundry and gas station on Old Colony Avenue, across from the Old Colony projects in Southie, was our main hangout since I was about twelve years old. It was right next to a Texaco station—ironically, later to become the South Boston Liquor Mart, which Whitey Bulger would take over and use as his base of operations, along with a variety store next to it. This was a busy spot, used as a cut-through from downtown to the suburbs south of the city. The avenue led you south toward Quincy and out of town, while Columbia Road swept to the left, eastward along the shorefront all the way out to Castle Island. I used to hang out there with Billy Mahoney and Johnny Baldwin, the Novicki brothers, and Joey Purcell. It wasn't *our* base of operations, by any means, but when you were just young fucks mixing it up, you needed a place where you knew you could find each other or get the word or at least have a soda and a slice. And it had an awning outside we could stand under out of the rain and from where we could see who was coming and going. Billy McCarthy's father owned the place. He'd say to us, "You fuckin' kids better be careful, you hear me?"

The car wreck changed all that. Or maybe it didn't, but there were too many ghosts around Billy's Pizza after losing those guys, too many shadows on the sidewalk. I went in there after the day of the funeral, and I couldn't stand the sound of the soda going up Billy Mahoney's straw. Inside, tables all set, with place mats and whatnot, and nobody there. That's what it seemed like. Now nothing seemed like anything, except the one undeniable fact that we had lives to live. And these other guys didn't. Johnny, Bobby, Keith, Billy: They'd always be sixteen fucking years old. We wouldn't.

I started to tag along with some older friends, guys I'd met at McDonough's Gym. Some of them not that much older than me, three or four years—Frank the Tank MacDonald, another MacDonald (no relation) nicknamed "Andre" after Andre the Giant. Six foot four, 220 pounds, and a vicious puncher. These guys were skilled, very tough guys, very capable in the ring, very dangerous on the street. And a guy named Paul "Pole Cat" Moore, about twenty years older than me, who was more or less their trainer. This began my long, long association with Paul Moore.

Frank lived around the corner from me in Old Colony. It was his house we ran to on St. Patrick's Day after beating up those hicks. The MacDonalds were a huge family, run by a crazy but wonderful mother. For all the good cheer she brought to the house and the neighborhood— she was known for going on whacked-out sprucing-up schemes around the apartment, once putting a new coat of paint on everything in the bathroom, including the tub, sink, and toilet, and for getting home late at night, throwing up the window, and shouting, *"Fuck the neighbors!"* and riffing on her accordion—for all that, the family got dealt a rotten run of luck. Davey, who was schizo, tried to fly off a roof and died. It was a hot August night, and the word went out—Davey MacDonald had jumped off the roof. Across from his building, he stood in the street, blood all over him, shadowboxing and babbling. People gathered around, tried to help him. It took forever for the emergency service people to get there; they took him away, but he didn't make it through the night. Kevin, who was a couple of years older than me, had been dealing drugs since he was about twelve—pot and mescaline. These were the days of the disco craze; everyone was getting high, the teenagers were running wild in the projects, and adults could be seen driving into the neighborhood to cop.

Kevin would do business out of his mother's apartment, in the hallway. He fancied himself a "made" gangster, claiming he worked for Whitey Bulger and making the most out of a ride he once got in Whitey's car, which at that time—the kid still had a newspaper route, for crissakes— was probably a serious fucking talking-to. And he was tricky with his stash. One night the cops busted in and arrested his older brother Frank, who was surprised to find hits of acid and a rifle hidden in his room. Frank never tried to pin nothing on Kevin, but it was Kevin, all right.

As bad as I felt for the MacDonalds about Davey and about the sister Kathy, who I believe was pushed off a building in the projects a short time later—and spent two years in a coma—I was more serious about my present. That's where I was gonna build my future.

I spent more and more time at McDonough's Gym, where Andre the Giant and especially Frank the Tank were making their mark. Frank was doing it right—eating right, doing roadwork, keeping clean. I looked up to him. Frank was a Golden Gloves champ, bound for the Olympics. He was a model in a sense of what I wanted to be. He was a hero around town—an undefeated fighter, well liked, with a flashy Lincoln.

I had a little more of Frank's little brother Kevin in me. Kevin was smaller than Frank. And Kevin, for all his blustery talk about Whitey connections, was actually out there working the deals. And if you were working the deals—showing up with a truckload of garments or TVs, or you were the man with a thousand hits of acid—you can be sure Whitey knew about it and approved. By which I mean he was getting his cut or some kind of tribute. Anyone who sold anything or robbed anyone, Whitey wanted a piece, or sometimes he wanted it all.

My mother and I were at odds at this time, because I wasn't working and I was keeping strange hours. Let's say I didn't look too productive. Sleeping late, working out in the day, hitting the gym, hanging about on the nighttime streets, figuring how to make a buck. Boxing, crime, whatever. I was working the angles I saw open to a guy like me. I would do what I was good at. That's how you make money. To be honest, that's how you take care of your mother in the long run, though it was myself I was worried about, first and foremost. When I'd say to my mother, "Ma, I'll buy you a house one day," she'd say, "You're fulla shit, John, just like your father."

Now she said, "Get a job or get out!" I didn't get a job, and true to her word, she kicked me out. I was glad she did, I have to admit. I couldn't stand all the fucking rules, and if I ate another fucking potato pancake with sour cream, I thought I'd puke.

So I ended up moving in with Paul Moore. I'd been introduced to Paul by Tommy Connors. Paul liked me because of my boxing ability and tenacity. He was very respected around town, one of the toughest guys in Southie. Good-looking guy, six feet, two hundred pounds, dark hair, dark skin, muscular. He'd gotten his nickname from a local boxing writer who saw a bout Paul had with a tough black guy in Freeport Hall in Dorchester. Paul was overmatched. The tall, rangy black guy was punching him around the ring, so Paul started running, hitting and running. The guys in his corner were going nuts. "Fight, you motherfucker, fight!" It was comical. At one point Paul slipped down onto his knees as the guy was coming toward him. Paul grabbed the guy around the waist. As Tommy Connors said later, it looked like Moorso was about to give that bonehead a fuckin' header. An article in the *South Boston Tribune,* written by a guy from Southie, Jack McDonough, said Paul Moore looked like a "polecat" in the ring. Hitting and running. A definition of a polecat is, they spray and they run. They spray and they run. Because a polecat is a skunk. Paul was so pissed off when he saw the article that he wanted to give Jack McDonough a beating. But Tommy Connors talked him out of it. He explained to Paul that Jack had a bad heart, and if Paul touched him, he might kill him. Once Paul heard the word "kill," he wanted no part of that. Of course I busted Paul's balls. "Aren't you going to give Jack a fucking beating? What are you, scared he might fuckin' die?" Fuck that!

I always wondered why Paul was so dangerous in the street but not in the ring.

So Pole Cat wasn't a boxer anymore. But he had plenty of women, not to mention a little drug business going on. He figured I might be of some use.

I had been traveling around with him for a few years, helping him out. We'd work out together, or I'd drive down to Plymouth with him so he could spend time with his daughter and work on his house. He was separated from his wife at the time. I'd help with the landscaping, fuck around with his two bullmastiff dogs. We'd run and work out down there before driving back. In South Boston he was living the life. A different girl every week. And he had money.

He'd take me to the bars before I was of age. He would drink very little, he didn't smoke, and we went from place to place—Triple O's, Streetlights, a bunch of other bars, all in Southie. I could see there was business being done. As discreet as it all was, he wasn't hiding it from me. He was showing me.

I learned that a lot of business was done in the bathroom. I learned that you locked the door if you could. I learned to note where the back door was and whether it was open. I learned you never showed money when it exchanged hands and that you didn't carry on your person once in the place or only a little that you could spare to ditch. I learned that you found a spot for the rest of your stash, somewhere inside the joint or somewhere outside. I learned how to roll joints and cut and bag coke in little envelopes with eight folds. Working with Paul, I got real good at math and with the scale and with

breaking up the product. I even started to make a little money of
my own.

But I was a boxer, and I wasn't giving up that dream.

I had turned amateur. Most amateurs begin in the novice class and gradually move into the open class, where you compete against anyone of
your weight class, no matter how seasoned he is. I went right into the
open class in my very first amateur tournament, the Golden Gloves in
the Lowell Memorial Auditorium. This was pretty big-time.

The place was sold out. The crowd was loud and raucous. I was only
sixteen; I still weighed only 106. And I was fighting men.

I won my first two fights and got to the finals. I was up against a
twenty-five-year-old Cuban kid. This motherfucker had won the Texas
Golden Gloves the previous year and had moved to Lowell. He and his
brother saw me down near the locker room before the fight, and they
laughed at me. They were looking at a cakewalk. They thought. I coun-
terpunched his brains in. He'd throw a punch, I'd step in and punish him
with three- or four-punch combinations. I was too fast for him and hit
him too solid. I won. I was the New England Golden Gloves champ.

Look at me now, Ma. Just like James Cagney. But my mother didn't approve of the fight game. She didn't approve of the people I was hanging
around to get there. Too bad, Ma. This was gonna be my ticket. At least
I had to try.

In the championship tournament, which would decide who went to
the Nationals, I fought a kid by the name of Troy Tomms of New Bedford. He was twenty-two years old and the number-two-ranked fighter in
our weight class in the entire country. I had Frank MacDonald and
Tommy Connors in my corner. I had no problems with this kid; I punished him like I did the Cuban. He'd land a shot, I'd land three, four. At
the end of the third round, Frank said to me, "You did it, champ."
Tommy was busy wiping me down. When he squirted water in my

mouth, I could see the proud smile on him. "Lou Duva will be calling you," he said, referring to the legendary trainer. And then I started hearing boos from the crowd. It kind of built from boos to a chant of "Bullshit!" Frank looked at Tommy. I stood in the corner waiting to have my hand raised. I couldn't believe it. Tomms was standing in the middle of the ring with his hand held high by the referee.

That's boxing. It's no fairer—no better or worse—than real life. I went out to the middle of the ring. Tomms came to me and raised my hand. "I'm sorry, man," he said. "You beat me."

I can't say this derailed me one fucking bit. There are tough knocks in life. This couldn't stop me. Tommy and Frank both knew I won. I knew I won. Tomms knew I won. I proceeded as if I did. Maybe I'd see Troy Tomms down the road.

I went on a traveling team to fight in Canada. I roomed there with a guy who was one of the best kids I ever met in boxing. His name was David Galvin, also out of New Bedford. David was very good fighter; he would eventually fight for the bantamweight title of the world and then call it quits. He lost the fight on a split decision by one point. I would get a chance to catch up with his life years down the road.

In Canada I easily beat the Canadian champion, Joe Gatti, brother of one of the great warriors of boxing, Arturo Gatti, who was trained by Lou Duva. I knocked Gatti through the ropes with a right hand, and then he spent the rest of the fight like Pole Cat, spraying and running. After the fight a Canadian boxing official came to my dressing room demanding to see my hand wraps. They found nothing but gauze and tape.

In '84, I was at the top of my game. This time I won the New England title again and also the Golden Gloves held in Lowell. Mike Tyson was the heavyweight champ in the Tournament of Champions. He was a fuckin' man-child. He was knocking everyone dead.

But there was something about all this amateur-tournament stuff that didn't sit right with me. I saw so many good fighters come and go; I'd seen so many "political" decisions in the ring. I'd seen guys get forgotten because someone was really grooming someone else, and that seemed to color everyone's view—the judges, the press, even the other fighters. And I was in too much of a hurry to trust the process. I decided I was ready for the Big Show.

7

CALIFORNIA

Around 1982 I went to California with a guy I'll call Eddie Flynn. Eddie had been a professional boxing manager and trainer for years in Southie. He had a gym, first on West Broadway and then in an old factory building on the outskirts of Southie, behind a bakery. One of the great things about going down to Flynn's Gym to work out was the smell of the breads and cakes baking. You walked into that gym hungry.

Eddie was the big guy in town for the professionals. Years back he'd worked with Paul Pender, onetime middleweight champion of the world, from Brookline. Pender fought them all—Fullmer, Basilio, Terry Downes. And he took a split fifteen-round decision against the great Sugar Ray Robinson. Like me, Pender had started out as New England champ. Eddie knew everyone around town very well, including Tommy Connors and most of the guys from McDonough's Gym. He'd followed my career, too. I'd had a long talk with Tommy. I told him I was through with the amateurs. I was ready *now*. Tommy said, "You got to work." He said he'd talk to Eddie Flynn for me. Eddie told him, "He's gotta work *and* fight." And though Eddie wasn't about to take me on as a fighter, he was of the opinion that if I was serious, as I said, and in a hurry, as I certainly was, and wanted to fight, I should go where the fighters were: California.

California was full of Mexican fighters in my class—lightweight now, 130 pounds. I was no longer the skinny fists-of-fury choirboy: I was bulking up across my chest and in my biceps. Running had given me legs. I was in tremendous shape and ready to go to war. And, being Irish, and I mean textbook Irish—guys like me, red hair, square jaw, white flesh, green trunks, had been a staple of the fight game since time immemorial—made me a good draw. Promoters liked a good Irish fighter with balls, skills, and a good chin—the people who loved 'em and the people who hated 'em would all show up. In theory. California dreamin', but why not? That's what boxing is about.

My mother could hardly believe it—her boy going to California. And my being under the wing of Eddie Flynn meant something to her, after I explained to her who he was. For once I think she thought boxing might be a good thing, though as usual she gave me no encouragement. "You'll be back, John. You'll be back here working on the docks like you should be." That's the thing about my mother—she was not much of an optimist. And my sisters, they just laughed. "Yeah, good luck, Jay!" But I know they were relieved that I'd be out of their hair, bound for another fucking failure. I was going to prove them all wrong.

Since I'd been hustling with Paul, I'd been able to put some money aside. I also got a little help from the guys at the gym and from Flynn, who was real good about it. Tommy even ran a benefit for me to raise money so I could survive in California for a while until I got situated.

We flew out of Logan into Los Angeles, my first time on an airplane. A piece of cake.

Things got a little weird pretty quick. Eddie Flynn and I checked in to the Hotel Figueroa on Figueroa Street, not a bad place. Had a certain charm and a great bar right out of Cuba—wrought-iron balconies, big wicker chairs, tropical plants all over, and some beautiful women like I'd never seen in any Southie bar.

There's a real good café right next to the hotel. Looks like a lousy diner, but you go in there and you can get mashed potatoes, gravy and meat loaf, good old American cooking. We went in there, and the food was inexpensive and good. I started to feel fortified, ready to go. This was it. Eddie told me of a long list of gyms and trainers he wanted to showcase me to, starting the next day. I wanted to get a good night's sleep, but Eddie liked to go for a walk after eating, and he reminded me that it's an aid to digestion. So we went for a long walk, a very long walk. I didn't know where the fuck I was, so after a while I had little choice but to go along. Plus, Eddie was talking about old fighters, the awkward Gene Fullmer, the perfect Basilio, and a good fighter I'd never heard of named Jimmy Saxton, out of Chicago. Then he told me about how Basilio could never win in Chicago and how Robinson could never win in Boston. It kind of made my head swirl. Boxing was a political game everywhere, amateur, pros, didn't matter. But I wanted in. Maybe California was a good fit.

Finally we get to this club. Eddie wants to go in. He's thirsty and has to take a piss. I'm not of age yet, and I don't want a drink anyway. I tell him I'll wait for him outside. It's a beautiful night, and in L.A. the air smells of all kinds of trees and flowers you don't get back east. So I stood outside, watching all the cars cruise slowly by, looking for movie stars. As I'm waiting, I see these guys come out of the club. "Hey, baby. How ya doing, baby?" They're looking at me. I take a peek through the window. It's full of fuckin' fags. It's all fags. I'm saying to myself, Why did we walk all this way? A weird way to walk. We go to this desolate bar on Sunset, no one else is walking. Everybody's driving their cars.

A half hour later, Eddie comes out. I'm fucking pissed. There was a big tree there. I kind of backed up to where the tree was. I kept my fuckin' back against it. I don't know why, but now that I think of it, I guess I do. "Where the fuck were you?" I ask him. "What the fuck took you so long?" He goes, "Why? Why? Why? What's wrong, John? You scared out here?" I said, "Fuckin' guys coming out callin' me 'Baby, you look cute' and this and that." He started laughing. He thought it was a big joke. I said, "I don't think it's funny." But I didn't push the issue.

As we head back through the night, I finally break the silence. "What are you doing in a fag bar? Are you gay?" He says, "C'mon, John. C'mon." Whatever that means. Now this guy's thirty years older than me, and I have my fate in his hands. So I leave it alone. But as we walk, me being a street kid, I see everything that goes on—anything and everything. No one was walkin' anywhere near us before, but all of a sudden we've got one big black guy, about six-three or six-four, walking across the street from us, going in the same direction, just a few steps behind us. I say, "Eddie. Fuckin' black guy over there, he's been followin' us for a while."

"No, no, no, no," he says. "No way, John. You're gettin' paranoid." I say, "Eddie, I'm fuckin' tellin' you."

I knew he must have gone into that club and picked this guy up. I decided to have a little fun with this one. I say, "Eddie. Don't worry. If he thinks he's going to try and rob us, I got something for him. I got something right here," and I pull out a knife. A knife with the knuckles on it, brass knuckles. I flip it open. "Don't worry. I'll fuckin' stick him if he comes anywhere near us. We'll fuckin' leave him right here."

Eddie fucking panics. "Jesus Christ! Put that away! Please, please, put that away! What are you doing with that thing?"

"I brought it from home. You never know when some six-foot-four-inch brother half a fag is going to come after you, do you?"

"Keep your voice down," he says.

By now we've walked I swear at least three miles. This guy's still with us. We're all the way back to Figueroa, and the guy stops at the fuckin' corner, stays there.

I don't push the issue anymore. Eddie and I go up to the hotel room. If Eddie's a fag, he ain't gonna touch me. That's why I showed him the knife. If he wants to suck some dick out here, where no one knows him, where it ain't Irish Catholic Southie Boston, what do I fuckin' care?

"I'm hittin' the sack," I tell him. "Big day tomorrow."

"Good idea, John. Why don't you get some rest. I'm still a little rest-less, you know, the time change and all. I'm gonna go out for a while, maybe have a drink at the bar."

"You do that, Eddie. Good night."

I looked out the window. I figured I should follow this story to the end, for the sake of the guys back home. For the telling. The black guy was still across the street, leaning against a light pole. After a minute he walks to the curb, looks both ways, and hustles across. Fucking disgust-ing and none of my business.

I went to sleep, trying to put together a run for myself for the morn-ing, out of the streets I'd seen.

Eddie started bringing me around the next day. He had explained a little of it to me on the plane. I was for sale. He said, "John, it's like a race-horse. You go down to Keeneland and look at the new yearlings, you see 'em move, you look at their breeding. You might become an investor. We are going to show you around; people will take a look at you, people who know the fight game, who are in the fight game. They know what an in-vestment is, they know what the possible payoff is. It can be big. And they are in it for the action, too. They look at you spar, hit the bag. They talk to you. They ask questions: who you trained with, who you fought, how you did. They check your jaw, your teeth, your wind. They try to figure out what your bad habits are, how you do your work. Then they might buy a piece of you. My job is to sell all the pieces of you and leave you with something. But someone has to pay the rent, feed you, train you, take you around, line up bouts, get you on a card. What we're look-ing for first is a trainer. Sometimes in a gym you run across a guy in a suit sitting there who wants to back a fighter, and he brings the trainer. But usually—and this is what I'm hoping for—we find you a great fucking trainer with good fighters. Maybe I'll manage you, depending. Or one will come along. Depending on the trainer. Then you look for the money. Everybody gets a cut, John, it's true. It's a tough game. You know the score."

I did. This was nothing I didn't know. It was like life, for guys like me. Unless you were born on the money end of it, you didn't have the ante to get into any game. But if you found something you were good at and then found someone to fuckin' believe in you, you had a shot.

So Eddie shopped me around. It was a new gym every day. And then we went to Joe Goosen's Gym in L.A., and there I met Pat O'Grady. O'Grady was the whole package. He was a very well known trainer, and he'd become a promoter. His son Sean won the lightweight championship of the world, beating Hilmer Kenty in a tough fifteen-rounder that is considered one of the greatest lightweight bouts of all time. Pat and Sean were the first father-son team to win a championship. I'd seen that Kenty fight, called by Howard Cosell on ABC back in '81. It was a war. O'Grady dropped Kenty early; he knocked his mouthpiece out, then got cut himself. They fought toe-to-toe for the last ten rounds, and Sean won a close decision.

But politics got involved somehow, and O'Grady was stripped of his title by one of the judges. That's when Pat formed his own boxing association and declared his son champ. I mean that's balls, that's loyalty. These were my guys.

At first Pat and I hit it off really well. He liked my style, he liked Irish fighters, and he could see the good left hand I had, just like Sean. Sean was a few years older than me and had a shitload of fights under his belt. But this guy was champ in his early twenties. Pat knew how to work the game.

I began training with the two of them. Great fuckin' sessions. My footwork had always been good—I had balance and leverage. Tommy had told me, you throw good punches with your feet. And it was true. But I learned from these guys that if I was gonna fight in California, I had to handle a lot of Mexican action—which is incredibly fast and fu-

rious. They walk right up to you with their head down and start fuckin'
flailing. The worse the fighter, the worse it is. You have to use your hands.
You have to be ready to push, push, push 'em away. "Don't worry about
hittin' 'em coming in," said Pat. "Push. Stop him. Then the straight right
hand. Bang. If you catch him good, step to the side and double up on
the hook."

Pat was a bigger-than-life character and bigger physically than his son.
He was all talk all the time. When we went out to eat, everyone had to
order the same thing—T-bones. It was a little controlling, but he was
buying, so what the fuck? He told me I should fight under a different
name. John is Sean in Irish, he tells me. "You should fight as Sean, and
we'll add the O back to Shea. Sean O'Shea." "Yeah, why not?" I say.

You couldn't tell him nothing, but he had the goods, so there wasn't
much reason to complain. This guy had a million things going on. Everyone wanted to talk to him at Goosen's—press, guys in suits, and of course
the fighters. But when he was with you, I think because he was so busy
the rest of the time, you got all of his attention. He told me my cheek-
bones were good, my brow was solid. Irish fighters usually cut. He told
me to toughen up the skin around my eyes with this vinegar solution he
had. It made the eyes burn, but the skin got tough as leather. One thing
he harped on, though, I just didn't like. It was my jab. I've always had a
good, quick, hard jab. It had served me well in the ring and on the streets
when I wanted to make a point. But Pat wanted me to turn it over, more
than over. He wanted me to twist my fist so that when I hit the guy, my
knuckles are just about parallel to the guy's nose. He said it did more
damage. I thought it took a lot of the jolt out of it. I didn't say nothing.
I did try to work with it. But it was almost like pulling my punch.

Pat put me up in this little apartment with an eighty-year-old lady,
near his house in Glendale. It was free. All I had to do was walk the old
lady's dog. I'd get my running in and then get down to the gym.

I worked with Sean there. He was a little fucking iffy on the jab tech-
nique as well. "That's the old man," he said when I asked him about it.

Sean had me over for dinner to his house. He lived right next to his dad outside of L.A. in a community of cookie-cutter houses—they all looked the same. Once inside, the first thing I noticed was a cabinet with his championship belts. They gleamed. He took one out of the case and told me to put it on. It had a great fuckin' feel. I put it around my waist, and it felt like someone hugging you. For a few seconds, I felt like the champ. Just like years earlier when I saw Frank MacDonald's Golden Glove robe, I wanted one of those for myself.

Once I saw Sean's wife, I forgot about the belts. She was gorgeous. A former Miss Oklahoma, she was the healthiest, brightest thing I'd ever seen—gleaming white teeth, tanned skin, a beautiful smile—and she and Sean both had that Oklahoma drawl, which on her sounded like some kind of very kindly invitation. Of course I knew it wasn't. We had a nice dinner, I thought. We had a few drinks. Sean seemed to let his guard down about this father. They'd had a real falling-out after the title was stripped, and Pat then founded the WAA and set Sean up with a big-punching Hawaiian named Andy Gannigan. Gannigan KO'd him in two rounds. So they'd had their difficulties.

I was bothered by something the old man had told me, so I decided to ask Sean about it. I told him that just the other day his father suddenly announced that I should get a job. That I should go down to the mall and apply for employment. So I had asked his father, "Where's the mall?" "Down the street," he says. "Walk down there, you'll see it on your right." So I say to Sean, "I walk down the street. And I walk and I walk. I walk for two miles, and there is no fucking mall." Sean's wife then says to me, "You must've missed it. Try it again," and she does so a little gruffly, like she's imitating Pat and his voice. And then she laughs.

"What'd you say to Dad?" asked Sean.

"I said *I couldn't fucking find it.*"

"What'd he say?"

"Well," I say, looking at Sean's wife, and now I get it, "he said, 'You must've missed it. Try it again.' "

Sean gives me a ride home, and he says to me in the car, "Listen to me, John. You're a good kid, and my father is a nice guy. But take it from me, you don't want to be with him. He ruined my career. Don't let him ruin yours, too."

I felt bad for Sean, because I knew that it was probably true, that his dad had ruined his career. I will always be indebted to Sean, because he told me the truth, and it must have hurt.

The next morning I'm on a pay phone to Tony Cardinale, a big-time criminal lawyer back in Boston who I know through boxing. "This ain't working out," I tell him. "Eddie Flynn did his best—I saw five gyms. But I'm no piece of meat."

Tony knows the ropes. He books me a ticket to fly home. "We'll try something else," he says. "Come see me."

8

THE END OF BOXING

Tony Cardinale was a guy I met at Eddie Flynn's Gym. We hit it off right from the get-go. He was a young lawyer, originally from New York City. He grew up in Hell's Kitchen, so he knew a lot of Irish guys like me—Westies, Southies, what's the difference? His father was a professional fighter, then a trainer, so Tony knew the fight game. His old man and a bunch of uncles ran Delsomma's, a restaurant in the theater district, so he knew something about the well-to-do. And Delsomma's saw its share of mobsters, so he knew his marinaras.

Tony'd come to Boston for law school—he went to Suffolk—and he hooked up with F. Lee Bailey, the famous Boston criminal lawyer. Bailey liked Tony's fire and knew he could make use of the Cardinale street smarts and charm. For certain cases that's crucial.

If you had a strike against you, Tony was a good guy to have in your corner, literally and figuratively. Jerry Angiulo, the head of the Boston Italian Mafia, facing forty-five years in prison, hired him; one of the three Irishmen accused of running guns out of Boston for the IRA hired him; some Boston cops accused of extorting money from liquor-store owners hired him. He would be a lawyer eventually for Frank Salemme, at the time the reputed head of the Italian mob in Boston, and he'd be part of the legal team for the infamous John Gotti. Guys went to Tony not just because he was sharp but because he had big balls. He would take on any case, anywhere, anytime, and not back down from anyone. Tony was a pit bull in the courtroom, and the world needs guys like Cardinale—no matter what you think of his clientele—because even the guilty have rights. Believe me, the cops and the law in general are breaking the law all the time—because they're lazy, because they're greedy, because sometimes they don't give a fuck and sometimes they're just stupid. End result: You can get railroaded in a heartbeat, whether for convenience's fucking sake or a vendetta or by accident, and you need a lawyer who'll defend your rights no matter what. That's the way it should be.

When I got back to Boston, I told Tony the situation with Eddie Flynn and what had happened with O'Grady. "So close, John," he said. "So close." I told him what he already knew: that I should be working and fighting those good Mexican fighters out west. I told him my dreams. Tony said, "John, I'd rather have you as my fighter someday than my client. You know what I'm saying? If you're serious, and I can see that you are, I am going to ask my brother Dennis to work with you."

That meant back to California. Dennis Cardinale, Tony's older brother, lived in San Pedro, not far from L.A. Like Tony, he knew the fight game, having grown up around it, and he was looking for a way to get a piece of it. He made his living dealing overstock and auction cars to used-car dealers. He could use some help in his business and had heard great things about me as a fighter. I thought, Why not?

Eddie Flynn got wind that I was back in California and working with Dennis. He had the balls to call Dennis one day and try to get some money out of him for my contract. Flynn said I was his fighter and he wanted to be bought out. Dennis told Flynn in no uncertain terms to go fuck himself. Flynn had no contract with me and had done nothing but try to sell me off. Fuck him.

Dennis met me at the airport. He looked a lot like Tony—dark curly hair, medium build. Didn't talk as fast as his younger brother, but nearly. I mean, a lawyer and a car dealer—those guys have to know how to talk.

I met his wife, who was really nice. They had no kids. They had a town house with a Jacuzzi on the rear deck. I would soak in the Jacuzzi after working out at the gym. His wife made me homemade yogurt and kept me on a healthy diet.

Eventually Dennis found me a basement apartment with a divorced woman who had a daughter and a son. It was in Palos Verdes, rich-people country, though these people weren't exactly swimming in it, taking in a boarder like me. But they were friendly enough and big fans of the TV show *Cheers,* so I was a little bit of a novelty to them. I told them the *Cheers* set was based on the Bull & Finch on Beacon Street—same oak bar and stools around it, with a seafood joint upstairs—but that the show was filmed a lot closer to them than Boston. They thought I talked like Cliff. They said, "Say 'Normie.' " Yeah, right.

The first day I'm there, the woman's husband, or ex-husband, shows up to look me over. His daughter is about fourteen or so. He says to me, not in so many words, *Don't touch her.* I thought, What is this, an invite? I wouldn't even think of it—she's a kid. I felt like saying, *Pal, if you're so fucking fatherly concerned, what am I doing here—an eighteen-year-old mick fighter from South Boston in your house?* I just smiled and looked him dead in the eyes. "*She* doesn't have to worry about me," I said. I just continued to stare him down. He got the message loud and clear. He never said another word about it.

Dennis took me over to the local gym the next day. I'm introduced to Jackie McCoy, a great Hall of Fame trainer who'd handled Carlos Palomino and four world champs. "Let's take a look at you," Dennis says, with Jackie looking on. So I get ready to spar with this black kid from South Africa. The kid comes over. He's long and lean, whippetlike. We say hello. He leans over and whispers, "Easy-light. Right? Easy-light." I nod, but I think to myself, I'm not falling for this. A guys says "We'll go easy," and as soon as you go easy, he hits you with a right-hand, left-hook combination, and that's it. Cheap move, of course. I let that happen to me before. Once.

"Okay," I say to the guy. I give him a wink. And I come out—bang, bang, bang. I'm looking to impress here. I've got Jackie McCoy on the ring apron, and I'm going to show him what I got. I'm moving and banging, and the kid can't get away. I'm going to show everybody what I got. I catch up to him, and he's covering up, trying to survive. I'm punishing him to the body. Everybody likes to see that. Then I rip him with an uppercut that almost takes his head off. I am all over him, both hands firing. *I'm going to punish you, motherfucker. I'm not Red Shea from Southie all the way out here on my own to take it easy on you.*

When it's over, Jackie goes, "Jesus Christ. He tried to kill that fucking guy." He says to Dennis, "He comes in here as a choirboy and he gets in that ring and he's a fuckin' assassin." But then he tells me what I don't want to hear. "My advice," he says, "would be to go back to the East Coast, because that's where it's happening now, because of Atlantic City, with the casino business and all. The West Coast is kind of died down," he says.

But my blood was pumping, and I wanted it now.

So even if it wouldn't be Jackie fucking McCoy in my corner, Dennis knew he had something. We settled in. I helped him at his work—driving cars around for him. Going on a few collection runs, where people owed him money. I'd just stand right at his elbow. He'd get paid, and he appreciated it. He paid me enough, enough to pay my rent and eat well. And I did plenty of training. I used to run along the coast, with a view of Catalina Island splashing out there in the Pacific. It was gorgeous.

Dennis took a real liking to me. He was about fifteen years older than me, and with no kids of his own, he seemed to like palling around with this eighteen-year-old kid. We used to go to Santa Anita—Dennis liked the horses—and we'd make the three-hour drive down to Caliente Race Track in Tijuana. Dennis owned a horse down there, and we would go down on most Sundays. The few dollars we might have left after the track went a long way in Tijuana. Everything was on the up-and-up, and it was a relief to be away from the Southie scene, the street life with Paul

Moore, the hustling and dealing. We had hardly a scrape. And though our luck at the track came and went, we stumbled onto a little score at a Denny's once, when I found a satchel on a newspaper box outside the restaurant. I looked around and took it real quick back into the car. It was full of tattooing equipment, some weed, and an envelope with about six grand in it. Then we realized there were cops around, so we split. We must've broken up a drug deal or something.

I said to Dennis, "How we gonna enjoy this shit thinking these jerks might come around the corner at any minute? We got to get rid of 'em."

"Whoa, John, cool it, man. Listen," he says. "We'll head down to the track. With your luck there won't be any money left anyway. C'mon, man."

"No, no, no," I say. "We got to get rid of these guys."

I'm fucking with him a little. I'm gonna play with him.

I'd already gone through the satchel. We ditched the weed on the parkway. Who needs it? But inside I found a hotel key.

"Let's go over and stake this place out. Here's the address right here."

"No, John, no fucking way. My wife's fucking right. You're a crazy kid."

"Dennis, let me show you something. And forget the wife. Let's just go over to this fucking place. No one's gonna get hurt. I'm just curious."

We sit in a parking lot across the street from the cheap dive of a motel—not a hotel by any means. The ones where you park in front of your room. I'd also found a pill bottle in the bag with a name on it—Hawaiian-looking. "Gimme a quarter," I say to Dennis.

He balks.

"Just gimme a quarter."

I go to a phone booth next to a garage. I ask for the Hawaiian guy. The call goes through.

I disguise my voice—a real low growl. I sound like a bad-ass angry brother. "You muthafuckas tried to set us up! You better get the fuck out of town right now or we're gonna fuckin' kill you, you fuckin' pineapple. There were cops all over that joint! We know where you fucking are!"

I went back to the car.

"What's up?" says Dennis.

"Watch," I say.

Three fucking chunky longhairs come scrambling out of one the units, jump into an old '57 Chevy with Hawaiian plates, and squeal the fuck out of there.

"Let's go to the track," I say. "I feel lucky."

Dennis set me up with a promoter, Harry Kabakoff, who worked out of the Redd Foxx Building in West Hollywood. And he got me my first professional bout, at the Reseda Country Club. This was a huge venue. It had concerts by U-2, Metallica, all the big bands. The boxing operation was under the control of Dan Goosen, a big deal guy who teamed with Steve Wynn promoting a lot of events. With Dennis in my corner, I made a splash.

I came out in my green shamrock trunks, a white robe with a green stripe on it, my red hair, white skin. These people were used to mano a mano, Mexican on Mexican. And here was this Irish rover.

I wasn't nervous at all. This is what I had come for. After a few months of working in California, I was ready. After eighteen years of fighting in one war or another, I was ready for a sanctioned bout with a purse.

I looked at my opponent in the center of the ring as we got our instructions. I swear he looked like the devil. He had a long pointy goatee, jet-black hair slicked back. He jiggled all around while I just stood there and stared, calm as a cucumber.

When the bell sounded, he came rushing over, rolling his arms around before he even got to me, like he was some storm brewing. At center ring I started the annihilation. I stopped his windsailing with a couple of body shots, and then two hooks to the head backed him off. Then I came after him. He was on the defensive, ten seconds into the round. After another minute I had him in the corner. I was running through combinations, everything perfect. A left to the liver, a right to the heart, and right-left uppercuts spilled him out toward the center of the ring. He was listing like a ship, half turned away from me, looking at the canvas. I caught him with a right hand on his jawline, near his ear, and to the canvas he went. He curled up there like he might be going to sleep. The fight was over: a minute and thirty-seven seconds.

The place went wild. The fans threw money into the ring. They loved me. I took that kid apart, and they loved it.

People were amazed. Someone told Dennis that I looked like I had twenty fights under my belt. They couldn't believe this was my debut. I have to say that that night was one of the best moments of my life. I could see it all in front of me. The limelight, the money, cars, a home for me, a home for my mother. Pride. Fucking exoneration. Respect. Women. I could leave the street life behind.

I got five hundred bucks for the fight. It felt like a million.

Of course I worked even harder after the fight. I trained with a new confidence. This was serious. Like I had always thought, I had the stuff. Unfortunately, things started to go sour with Dennis. Not that he had a problem with me. In fact, it was because things were now starting to cook with me, as his fighter, that his wife got a little concerned—about how much time and energy he was spending with this kid Red Shea. Dennis was great to me, and he was straight with me. And I have to respect a guy who makes a decision on behalf of his wife's wishes. What am I gonna say? But very soon after that first fight, Dennis isn't training with me anymore.

Physically it didn't bother me. I did my roadwork, I got to the gym, I sparred. But mentally it was a different story. It's like you turn around and there's no one in your corner. It takes the edge off somehow. Mentally I began to drift.

Kabakoff got me a second fight—and Dennis was there for it. No excuses, but I was mentally off my game. Dennis wanted to help me as much as he could, and he wanted to earn his cut. But against this black kid named Wilkins, before I know it I get tagged with an overhand right. It smashes my nose. I'm eating blood, and it ain't pretty. It was the hardest punch I've ever been hit with, in or out of the ring. But this guy was in for a fight, whether I was ready or not. It was a four-round bout. Rounds two and three were toe-to-toe, head-to-head. I was giving as good as I got. In the last round, I came on. I had him rattled, but I couldn't put him away. The judges gave him a split decision. I was proud of myself. Even when I didn't have it, I gutted it out.

I looked at Dennis. "No excuses," I said.

I had no complaint over the decision. I was disappointed but not broken, not by any means. After the fight, the actor Kevin Dobson—Crocker on *Kojak*—sent his bodyguard over to say Dobson wanted to see me. I was brought over to his seats in my trunks and robe. He introduced me to his wife.

"I like how you fight, kid," he said. "You've got guts." He knew a little bit about South Boston, as he was a New York Irish kid. He mentioned Southie's reputation as a tough Irish neighborhood. "You certainly lived up to it, kid." He grew up watching Friday-night fights. He loved the game. He gave me his phone number and invited me to his house for dinner some night. I thought, Maybe this guy wants a piece of me, too. But I never made the call. I went home a week later, back to Southie.

9

BACK TO SOUTHIE

L ife smacked hard back in Southie.

I didn't have my tail between my legs, though my mother had that look of "I told you so." I said, "Ma, I wouldn't even be here if I didn't need some of my clothes." But we sat down at her apartment. I'd been away six months. She looked a little older, a little grayer. Otherwise the same. She started to tell me how my sisters were doing, but I tuned her out. I had to plan my next move. She fried up a piece of ham, and we had dinner. I watched a little TV with her. I told her during the commercial breaks that I'd done very well out there in California. I gave her fifty bucks. I think I determined then and there to continue fighting. And dealing drugs—that was my last fifty bucks.

I moved back in with Paul Moore. He'd heard of my tough luck out there and could see that my nose was a little the worse for wear. "You come back ugly," he said. Big heart. He expected me to work. I was ready to work, but not for long for him. So I stayed with him for a while in his little apartment next to Triple O's, a Southie bar on Southie's main drag, West Broadway. It was Whitey Bulger's place, owned in name by Kevin O'Neil, who fancied himself quite the businessman. He was Whitey's money guy. Lots of action over the years would go down there. Paul of course was right on top of the action. I didn't care much for sleeping on his couch, but a roof was a roof.

I was living there when the news came about Frank MacDonald, Frank the Tank. A Golden Gloves champ like me, a guy who was like an older brother to me. I learned a lot from Frank, though I could never be like him. He had the even temperament; he was respectful in all situations. He was a handsome, easygoing guy from a hard-luck family. Boxing helped him get out of himself. He became somebody through the local fight game, drove a nice car, had respect in the community, did an honest day's work for a moving company located in Southie, Casey & Hayes. But the dark side of Southie got ahold of him. And eventually destroyed him.

Frank had had a little coke habit along the way. In fact, it was Frank and his younger brother Kevin who got me fucked up on coke for the first time—and the last time. I was only sixteen or so. Frank would have been about twenty-one or twenty-two and Kevin maybe eighteen. We started out snorting coke in Frank's apartment in the afternoon and did it all day and night. We hit the bars, we did coke in the car. We were high as kites. I'd never felt anything like it. I was flying. These guys were pros, though, compared to me. At some point they actually decided it was time to eat. What was food? We went to a Chinese restaurant, and it couldn't contain me. I was so wired I was talking to the kitchen help. Probably in Chinese. They got me out of there, and we drove all the way to Quincy. I don't think they wanted anyone to see me. We went to Kevin's place, and they took me upstairs. I was just like in a pinball machine—here, there, bang, bang, didn't matter. Talking a blue streak. At some point Frank tried to explain to me how fucked up I was. I just laughed. They gave me Nyquil to bring me down. Frank said they couldn't take me home like this. I drank two bottles of Nyquil and lots of water. Frank and Kevin went back out to continue partying. They told me to get some sleep. Sleep? I was fuckin' bouncing off the walls and paranoid out of my mind. I had to get out of there. Somehow I got a bus and made it back to Southie. I needed help—of what kind, I didn't really know—but I didn't want to go to Tommy or Paul. I went to see Jack Leary, a probation officer. "I can't go home, Jack. I don't want anyone seeing me like this." He took me to his house until I came down. He never asked any questions, just helped me. He gave me a place to get my head back. That was the first and last time I ever used drugs.

It took my head on a wild run. I didn't like it. It was like being in some electric storm. A few days later, I confided to Tommy Connors about the shit. He was livid. Frank told me Tommy went to him and tore him a new asshole. "This kid's mind's not strong enough for that," Tommy told him. "He's just a kid. He could have committed suicide or something. Use your fuckin' head, Frank."

I don't think Tommy approved of Frank doin' the shit either, but Frank was a man, and to Tommy I was still a kid.

For the most part, Frank was making it. Everybody was happy for Frank. So he wasn't going to be a professional fighter—he had backed out of what was to be his professional debut a few months earlier. He'd been the best that Southie had, in the light heavyweight division, and he still worked as a sparring partner for the Irish fighter Sean Mannion, who lived in Dorchester. But he wasn't around the gym much anymore. So I can't say I was shocked when I walked into Triple O's and heard that Frank had been involved in an armored-car heist out in Medford. But I was devastated to hear he was dead. It was as if I had lost a brother.

The wake at Jackie O'Brien's Funeral Home was huge. The entire neighborhood came out. At the funeral mass, at St. Augustine's, there were feds across the street snapping pictures. Whitey and Stevie sent flowers to pay their respects. Just to set the record straight, they had nothing to do with the armored-car robbery.

As was the way in Southie, forces moved to take care of people in tough times, or at least make them feel better. In this instance I had a hand. It was decided that, in Frank's honor, the party at his mother's house after the funeral would not feature a barrel of Guinness or a case of whiskey, but cocaine, mounds of it. I provided. There were detectives there, I have heard, looking out for the accomplices in the heist. The detectives spoke to Mrs. MacDonald, telling her what they were up to. She wanted to know who Frank had been involved with, too.

Mrs. MacDonald saw Whitey on the street one day, and she took him aside and asked him if he had anything to do with it. He told her no. And he told her that Frank was a stand-up guy. Just as I had always known.

A few days later, word got around that somebody should do something to help the MacDonald family with the funeral expenses. A collection was taken up from guys around the town. I went looking for Frank's older brother, Johnnie, who was home on leave from the Navy SEALs. I found him at his grandfather's place down at the Point. I gave him an envelope with ten grand inside. Johnnie looked at me with disbelief. Like, this is what Frank's life is worth? I couldn't argue. After I left, Johnnie fisted up the money and threw it in the bay. Or so I am told.

Boxing was still in the mix of what I wanted to do. It says something about who I was and where I was that it didn't seem like a choice was necessary. Boxing and dealing drugs seemed to be part of the same thing. It involved a lot of the same people in all the familiar spots. I trained, I boxed, I filled my pockets at night. I had to be tough, focused, aggressive no matter what I did. Everything was about the same skills, mental and physical. No difference. It says something about how old I was that I didn't see the difference. I realize now that some of the choices you make are the choices you don't make.

I went to see Tommy Connors shortly after I got back. He was glad to see me. He asked me straight if it was over with the boxing. I told him, "Absolutely not. I'm good, Tommy." He said, "I know, John."

I had six more fights, with Tommy as my trainer. After Eddie Flynn and Pat O'Grady and Dennis Cardinale and Harry Kabakoff, it was good to have a steady guy I knew very well in my corner. I fought in Boston, New York, and Atlantic City. In one fight in a Boston nightclub—a long way from the Reseda Country Club, I admit—I threw so many left hooks at this guy with a very soft breadbasket that they called me a fiddler crab in the papers. I knocked him down countless times; the ref finally stopped it. At Freeport Hall in Dorchester, I put my hands down by my side and stuck my chin out. I let this kid hit me twelve, thirteen times, and then I beat him senseless.

Tony Cardinale was watching my progress. He felt bad about how things had worked out with his brother, but I told him, "No hard feelings. Dennis was great to me. One of those things." Tony then spoke to Lou Duva, the legendary trainer, about me.

Duva goes back as far as Joey Giardello. He trained a Hall of Fame roster of fighters but was mostly a big-time promoter, the founder of Main Events, which he ran with his son Dan. He had a great young fighter named Vinny Pazienza, from Providence, and Lou agreed to take a look at me down there and have me work with Vinny.

Duva would promote an entire card of his fighters, and although it was hard for me to make a living and devote myself to boxing, I did my best. With Paul Moore I started moving up, selling not only grams of coke but eight-balls, which went for three hundred dollars. It was really no riskier, if you did things right—carried light, stayed cool, knew your customers, or at least the turf. But the money rolled in faster, and you moved product faster. In that respect it was safer. Not as much shit around in little fucking envelopes.

But I put in my time. I thought I could work things both ways—a little dealing, a little boxing. I went down to Providence for a few months. I got to like Vinny Paz—the Pazmanian Devil, they called him—a lot. He had decent ability and a great work ethic. And he had the best who owned him—if owning can ever be good—in Duva.

Duva seemed to think I had potential. He told Cardinale so. And he was using me to spar with Vinny. I had to be careful there, because I found I could easily hit Vinny with overhand rights but didn't want to get my ass shotgunned out of there. So don't we end up training in Passaic for an Atlantic City card? Duva's Johnny Bumphus is the main event; Vinny and I are both on the undercard. When we're training, another good Duva fighter, Rocky Lockridge, slices Vinny's eye open with—guess what?—an overhand right. Duva's not happy, so he shuts Vinny down for a bit to let him heal. Vinny and I kick back at the motel, around the pool. Vinny starts fucking with some asshole who's at the pool with his wife and two kids. This guy just has a strut, what can I tell you? But he has his headphones on, listening to music, fucking oblivious, and Vinny's making fun of him. I warned Vinny, "Be careful, this guy might hear you." Doesn't the guy come over and take his headphones off and say to Vinny Pazienza, "Who the fuck you talking about, you guinea fuck?" I say, "Whoa, fella. Can't you see this guy's cut? You want something, you can talk to me."

He wants to step outside. This guy doesn't know he's talking to two fighters. Either of us would put him away with one shot, but he doesn't know that. He also doesn't know that we'd be crazy to take him up on his offer. Duva would have our asses. So we toy with him, send him outside. He comes back. "Hey, relax, I'll be right there," I say. "Can't you see I'm putting on my shoes? You'll get your beating soon enough." He goes out. He comes back. His chest is all red with rage. He spits when he talks. He's so fucking mad he looks like his head is going to explode. "Can't you see I am putting on my shirt, dude? I'll be right there." This fucking idiot walks back outside again. Vinny is on the ground in tears, he's laughing so much. Finally the guy comes back, and he finally gets it. He starts laughing, too. He went back to his family and sat back down on his beach chair and put his kid on his lap. Smart guy!

When I get to the gym the next day, Duva is all over me.

"Where the fuck were you yesterday? You were supposed to be here. You're working with Paz."

I remind him, respectfully, that Vinny has the cut. "Vinny's shut down, right? So I'm with Vinny at the motel."

"No fuckin' excuse," he says. "You work for me. Fuckin' don't miss a day."

I tell him I don't work for him, I don't work for anyone. And I ain't his fucking slave.

At the fight Bumphus wins, Vinny wins, I win. I beat a tough kid from Philly like a stepchild. Some of Whitey's crew came down to watch the fight. After the fight I had dinner with them at Bally's. One of the guys gave me a gold bracelet with my name on it. It was just like the one he had on his wrist, with one big difference—his name was spelled out with diamonds on it, mine was blank.

That was my one and only fight for Lou Duva. No one yells at me like that.

Things got worse in Southie, worse for the MacDonalds again. Kevin, the wild one, had a hard time dealing with his brother Frank's death. When you're so wild so young, when you're a criminal so young, growing up at superspeed in many ways, you also *don't* grow up. Kevin was always Frank's little brother, and now his big brother was gone. Not long after Frank was buried—making it yet another MacDonald in the St. Joseph's Cemetery, which was filling up with them—Kevin got involved in a jewelry-store stickup with a buddy from D Street. It was out in Framingham. The jewelry-store owner locked the doors on them and pushed the buzzer that alerted the police. The owner was shot, paralyzing him. Kevin somehow took one in the leg and ran through Framingham. He managed to get a cab and hid out in Southie for a while, but with his leg and all, it was only a matter of time. The cops found him at home and grilled him about the stickup and about the Wells Fargo robbery—they still didn't know who Frank's accomplices were. They grilled him hard. They told him they had him on videotape but needed a confession. They told him the tape exonerated him from the shooting of the owner and that they would admit the tape in court if he confessed. Who knows what they had? But Kevin talked. He was sent to Bridgewater State Hospital, a psychiatric hospital, for a month or so. He was sent back to await trial in the high-rise jail in Cambridge. A few weeks later, he hung himself.

He and Frank were blood. Frank was killed in that robbery; if he'd survived his gunshot wound, he never would have talked. But he never got a chance to do the honorable thing. Kevin did get the chance, and he failed. He got scared, and he violated the code. To his credit, he couldn't live with himself. He gave himself the justice all rats deserve. That's harsh, I know. Southie harsh.

10

IN BUSINESS

I started selling ounces and grams of coke on my own. I was sick of making short money, I was sick of living with Paul Moore, a cheap and greedy motherfucker. He put the cheapest gas in his car, he ran an extension cord to the hallway light socket to save on electricity. When he cut up the money, I got shorted. And I was tired of sleeping on his couch in the apartment above Triple O's and then tired of the apartment with no heat we moved to up on the Point. He was making the real money, and this fucking place was like a prison cell. He had a bed, and I had a fucking lumpy couch.

Although I wasn't making a lot of money, I could see the light. I'd done enough with Paul—and on my own—to know how it was done and that I was good at it. Smarts, guts, determination, discipline, and intimidation. Just like in the ring. Boxing might be over, but not the dance. And I knew the steps.

I hustled my ass off and got enough money to move out to a nice apartment on East Fifth Street. I was selling marijuana, pounds and ounces, and coke, which was where the real money was. A good gram business, you can make out very well. I could get fifty grams out of an ounce of good coke, really good coke, primo stuff, stepping on it, making it last. Back then grams were going for a hundred apiece. That's four thousand dollars profit. I could make that in a night. I could do that every night. That's what I could see. That was my business model. The better the coke, the better the price, the more money I could make.

Like Paul Moore, I was working on my own. But no one truly worked on their own in Southie, not in this business, not with Whitey in charge. There wasn't much that went down without his knowledge and approval. The lone wolves were rare and living dangerously. That's the way Whitey liked it.

But I was ambitious, and I didn't give a fuck. I didn't want to be another runner who sold his ass to someone else, who took his orders from someone else, who took all the hits for a little scrap, in hopes of one day just being a little bit of a bigger sucker in the scheme of things. I had balls and street smarts. I knew that was all I had, but it was something. It was rare, and it was respected. In fact, look where it had gotten Whitey Bulger.

I had known about Whitey since I was around nine years old. Everyone knew who that guy was. People reported his sightings. *Whitey did this. I saw Whitey there. He was taking Theresa Stanley, his girlfriend, here or there.* He was a celebrity. He had risen from the ashes of the Killeen gangs, when the Irish mob was completely disorganized, and he now ran the shop. And it was tight and powerful. He was the king of kings, the don of dons. The Irish Godfather. The Italians may not have liked him, but they certainly respected him. He was one of the most dangerous and cunning guys around, and they knew it.

I was introduced to Jim "Whitey" Bulger when I was about fifteen. I was hanging out at the D Street Deli. Older guys were there—Paul Moore, my trainer Tommy Connors, George Hogan, Kevin Weeks. We were all on the corner fucking around, and I see these other guys talking on the opposite corner. Always a wise mouth, I say, "Hey, that guy there's got some tight fuckin' pants." No one says anything to me. The guy with the tight fuckin' pants turns around and walks toward us. It's Whitey Bulger. Kevin says, "Jim, this is Red Shea."

"How you doin'," Whitey says to me, his voice smooth and confident, his white hair slicked back. He wore a nice light jacket, and his open shirt collar was crisply starched. He looked trim and powerful.

"Nice to meet you," I say, and I shook his hand and gave him a good fighter's grip. I wanted to keep the conversation going.

"You grew up with my uncle, Richie Kelly," I say.

"Now, that guy had a ton of balls," he says to me. "I'd go over to your uncle's house in the morning and wake him up so we could go out to work."

I was trying to look right at Whitey as he spoke. Once I did, it wasn't hard. I could see his eyes behind his sunglasses. They looked cold and dark, but steady. He was relaxed.

"Your uncle and me, we'd go stealing and robbing anything not tied down," he said. Then he laughed.

I appreciated his candor. I appreciated his humor. It relaxed *me*. I was very impressed, but poor Uncle Richie. He ended up on the short end of a fight with a gang of blacks in downtown Boston. He froze to death in a snowbank. I appreciated Whitey Bulger remembering him.

After that, Whitey always spoke to me. He'd see me at the gym or at the deli. "What are your plans for the future?" he asked me once. "To keep fightin'," I told him.

Whitey started to talk to Tommy Connors about me, even when I was young, and of course Tommy would tell me about it, as Whitey knew he would. "He has big balls, but he needs guidance," he told Tommy. He said I reminded him of himself when he was younger—wild and uncontrollable.

Whitey surely knew I was tailgating and nickel-and-diming around town. He didn't miss anything. But at one point, when I was about eighteen, he learned something about me he might not have known yet. That not only was I fearless, I wasn't even afraid of *him.*

I'd had a few too many drinks in Triple O's one night. I was talking to Deirdre, the bartender. Deirdre was a smart, tough lady, about ten years older than me. She was good-looking and knew what was what. And she liked me. We had a little thing going on, in the sexual department. I was drunk—it was a slow business day, the painting of the Seven Dwarfs that ran along the wall looked particularly stupid, so I was just waiting for Deirdre to finish her shift when I saw this guy there that I'd seen at the bar a little too often lately. I got jealous.

"What is *his* fuckin' problem?" I say to her. "What is he looking at? He your new boyfriend? I'll shoot him right here right now, if he thinks he's a tough guy."

I had a .380 automatic on me. This guy was standing at the bar ten feet from me. I could see Sneezy over his shoulder. I was standing right where Whitey usually stood. Right next to the door, so you can see who comes in and out. I could see the fear in this guy's eyes. Deirdre barked at me. "John!" She motioned to me with her head. Okay, I figure, what's she have to say about this fuckin' prick? She says to me, in essence, that if I acted up, Whitey would take care of me.

She shouldn't have said that. Not to me.

"Fuck Whitey Bulger," I said to her. "What am I gonna do, cower? Am I a fuckin' coward? And what the fuck does Whitey have to do with this asshole over here?

"I'm not afraid of anyone," I tell her, and I pull my jacket back so she can see the gun tucked in my waist as I look over at her friend, or whatever he is. "Do not doubt me, Deirdre. Ever."

Needless to say, the asshole splits. I keep drinking, but I'm not cooling down one bit. Deirdre takes me to my apartment on Fifth Street. I'm hot. What is she gonna do, fuck me? She still has this cocky attitude when we get there. We argue. I pull out the gun and start shooting up the apartment. I shoot through the doors. Deirdre is sitting there, covering her ears. The place is ringing like a fucking bell.

"Are you fucking crazy?"

As she ran out the door, I asked her, "Where you going?"

I slept this rough night off. I ended up sleeping all day. I didn't really want to see the holes I'd shot in my own place. By the time I got out of bed, it was getting dark out. I decided to go for a run. I took my usual six-mile jog along the beach, around Castle Island, up and down the hills in Southie. I saw Tommy Connors on Broadway and stopped to shoot the shit when Paul Moore comes around the corner in his Bronco. He pulls over. "Whitey's looking for you."

Paul looks scared. "What'd you do wrong, Red? What the fuck did you do now?"

I tell him, "How do *I* know? And so fucking what!"

Paul says, "He's hot, and I think you should go see him. Right now."

Then around the corner comes Whitey's blue Ford LTD. Stevie Flemmi and Kevin Weeks are with him.

Paul whispers to me, "Don't do anything crazy."

Tommy Connors says, "Don't worry, he's not stupid."

Whitey, who's driving, pulls over. He gets out of the car and walks across the sidewalk and stands with his back against the wall. I stayed where I was. Kevin Weeks got out and stood next to him.

"Red, come here, I want to talk to you," says Whitey.

I say to him, cocky, confident, "You want to talk to me? Sure." I walk over to him.

"Let me ask you a fuckin' question," he says. This time he has no sunglasses on. His eyes are not cold and dark, they are burning like blue laser beams. "You got a fuckin' army? Have you got a fuckin' army, Red?"

This catches me off guard. "No," I say.

"Well, Red, I fuckin' got an army. And last night you threatened to shoot some kid, and that kid's father is a friend of mine. When my name was mentioned, you said you didn't give a fuck, is that correct?"

I stepped up closer to Whitey. I was dressed in running shorts and

shoes. Nothing else. I said to him evenly, firmly, "First of all, I had a little too much to drink last night, but that's not an excuse. I was told that
you were going to come after me. I was threatened with you. And I said,
'So let him come after me.' No, I don't have an army, but I didn't threaten
you, and they used you to threaten *me.* My mother taught me to stand
on my own two feet and defend myself. This had nothing to do with you,
and yet someone's calling you in."

I held my ground. Whitey was looking me right in the eye. I looked
right back at him with my own blue eyes. And then his tone changed
completely. He said, "If that ever happens again, you tell them you're my
friend. You understand. You're my fuckin' friend."

As he walked away, he said, "Set up a meeting with Deirdre, and I'll
straighten this shit out."

He had a smile on his face. This eighteen-year-old kid stood toe-to-
toe with him and didn't flinch. He fuckin' loved it.

Paul Moore stared in awe. Flemmi and Weeks were looking at me
from the car as Whitey tore out of there.

Yeah, I had fucked up: got drunk, got angry for no good reason, shot
up my own fuckin' place. Yeah, a temporary loss of control. Not good.
But I was right to stand firm when the almighty Whitey was invoked. I
showed no fear. In my world that's what mattered. And as a result I was
Whitey Bulger's fuckin' friend.

11

KILOS

In the mid-1980s, Southie's own Raymond Flynn was running the city of Boston as mayor, Billy Bulger was running the state senate as president, and Whitey was running Southie as boss. Some kind of Irishman was in the White House. It was feel-good time. The busing bullshit was a thing of the past, so was Yaz, so was Freddie Lynn, on to the Angels, the fuck. Now the Red Sox had a phenomenal young pitcher named Roger Clemens and a great lefty named Bruce Hurst, my favorite, and the best pure hitter in Boston since Ted Williams in Wade Boggs. And I was running my own life, finally—out on my own, money in my pocket, girls when and if I felt like it. I wasn't rich by any means, but I was a long way from Lambert's Fruit and Vegetable.

It was a good time to be doing what I was doing. There seemed to be money everywhere, and especially in the hands of yuppie types who couldn't get rid of it fast enough—buying cars, condominiums, and cocaine, plenty of cocaine.

I was thinking strategy. I wanted to do better. I wanted to figure out how. I was on a mission. And I wanted to be smart.

Now, it's not as if you can go around Southie getting career advice. Of course there's always plenty from the women—get a job, clean up your act, watch your mouth, grow up. From the men you might get just talk. You talk with people you know, people you trust, people who know something. And you listen. And you can learn a world of good from the older guys, the old-school guys who won't steer you wrong. It's up to you to pick and chose. No fuckin' lecture. No ultimatums. This is this.

I spent a lot of time with Tommy Connors. This guy taught me to handle myself, literally, in the ring. A guy does that by looking at you, listening to you, and, I think, caring. He gives you his view on what you can do and what you better watch out for. Strengths and weaknesses. A guy who talks you up all the time is going to get you killed. And a guy who never does is gonna lose you. Tommy never lost me, and he never got me killed. Not yet anyway.

I'd meet him at the gym, where I still went to work the heavy bag, spar a little. Shoot the fuckin' shit, catch up. We'd go to the movies once in a while, have dinner once in a while. Sometimes we'd go to Squires, the strip club across the street from the movie theater, and watch the girls shake their titties. But what I most enjoyed was watching the fights with him on HBO.

In '85, Tommy had a bunch of us over to his house for the Tommy Hearns–Marvin Hagler fight. Two great fighters with opposite styles— Hagler was a fierce, bald-headed, wicked puncher with devastating hooks from either hand. He was the middleweight champ and a local guy, of course, from Brockton. Hearns, from Detroit, was a welterweight coming up in class, a long, lean artist with a great ropy jab and the kind of right hand that earned him the nickname "Hit Man." They'd both handled Roberto Duran, Hearns in a couple of brutal rounds, Hagler in fifteen.

There were a few other guys over. Tommy had beer and whiskey and ordered in a few pizzas. I got there very late, but, as usual, the undercard took forever, and when I arrived, it was still the guys in the tuxedos talking. Tommy made room for me on the couch. I glanced around and actually looked for Frank MacDonald. I don't know why. He'd been dead for over a year. Maybe it was because his brother Kevin had been dead only a few weeks. They both would have been there. Or *should* have been there.

It's kind of perfect, talking about life around a boxing match. You're sitting there with a reminder of how violent life is, how important skills are, and guts and know-how. And opportunity. Some people might get reflective staring into a fire. I liked to watch a fight.

"I don't know, Tommy," I said to him.

"About what, John?"

"I've gotta do something."

"Well, I've been thinkin'," he said.

We watched one brutal fuckin' bout. The greatest three rounds ever fought. Marvin came out smokin', loading up on every punch, but Hearns, looking skinny and pretty vulnerable, would step to his left and thunder back. After one round of total war, Hagler was bleeding from his forehead—Hearns had cut him between the eyes. But Hagler would not quit. He won the second round, and you knew if he didn't get Hearns early, he'd never make it; he'd have blood in both eyes, and they'd stop the fight. Hearns gave as much as he got. In the middle of the third round, the ref stopped the fight for the doctor to check on Hagler's cut. We were fuckin' booing. But the doc let him go on, and he ran all over Hearns. Hearns turned his back on him to get away, and Hagler hopped up and nailed him in the side of the head. The Hit Man hung there like a fish out of water, and Marvin hit him again. He went down in a heap. Somehow Hearns got up, though he was definitely on Queer Street now. The ref held his gloves, looked him in the eyes, and then waved his arms. Fight over.

The three or four other guys at Tommy's went nuts. Me, I wanted Hagler to win, him being from Brockton and all. It wasn't the same as having a guy I could relate to more, like a Sean O'Grady or Vinny Paz or Sean Mannion. Guys like me. But I admired the artistry of these guys. Tommy shook his head.

"Great fight," he said. "Hearns is no middleweight, though. Like Billy Conn was no heavyweight."

I said, "C'mon, Tommy. He took a shot. He took a shot!"

"Yeah, John. But a guy's gotta be smart. I've been thinkin'."

We went to the kitchen. We sat there among the empty pizza boxes and a sinkful of beer bottles.

He tells me, "John, you took *your* shot. You gave it your all, in this game. Duva, O'Grady, Cardinale, the rest. In boxing a fighter needs help. He needs people. But people are gonna take. Take their piece. That's the fight game."

"Yeah. Like I'm a piece of meat," I say.

"But this, now, is different."

"What's different, Tommy? What are we talkin' about?"

"You're out there doin' all the hustling, right? You have customers, right?" Tommy knew what I was up to, with Paul and on my own.

"Right," I said.

"A guy moving his own product is taking the same risk, but for a better payout. In boxing you can't promote yourself."

"And on the street, you can, right? Listen, Tommy, I don't have that kind of money."

Tommy then gave me the name of a girl and a phone number, in Florida.

"You can get kilos cheap down there, John. Less than twenty grand. That's like thirty-five ounces, right? Think about it. What would that cost you here, getting it from the guys? And pure shit we're talking about."

"Yeah?" I say. "Yeah."

"You're running the risk, John. Make it pay at least."

Tommy didn't say it, but he didn't have to. The last part of what he was telling me was, *Make it pay, John, or get the fuck out.* In other words, *Be smart.*

"I hear you," I said to him. I took the phone number from him. And then, like on cue, my beeper rang. I'd figured there'd be a postfight rush of business, and I had to go.

A lot of people at the time thought that Whitey Bulger was antidrug. They thought he was an old-style gangster—numbers, extortion, stolen goods, hijacking cases of liquor. Like it was the 1950s. But it was the 1980s, and just like Willie Sutton went where the money was, Whitey went where it was, too. That's not to say he didn't use his head: When angel dust was big, he wouldn't touch it or let any of his people deal in it. It made people crazy, and crazy people are dangerous. He stayed away from heroin, too, because it made people desperate, and desperate people are dangerous. Heroin also killed. Not great for business. But coke was gold.

I knew I was taking my chances trying to go out on my own like this. Whitey's mob had punished plenty of people for just this sort of thing—dealing on their turf. But, truthfully, I didn't give a fuck. I'd play it smart, continue to buy a little from the organization, keep them happy. But if I was going to finance my own runs, I was gonna sell my own product to my own customers, and fuck the rest of them. I was gonna be the lone wolf.

The Hagler-Hearns fight was in April. By June I've got about nineteen thousand dollars cash on me and a round-trip ticket to Miami.

Tommy's contact, a girl named Marina, is living in a trailer down in Key Largo. "She's got a little coke habit, nothing too bad," says Tommy, "but she knows people, she's good people, and she's set the whole thing up." Tommy tells me, "Dress like a college kid, not some mick from Boston looking for trouble." No problem. Light bag, Bermuda shorts, baggy T-shirt, sunglasses, a plain white baseball cap—one of the good guys.

Marina picks me up at the airport, and we drive Route 1 out to the Keys. The sun off the water is almost blinding. You almost have to close your eyes till you get used to it. The air is beautiful, tropical. And the women everywhere, gorgeous.

We get to her place, right on the beach. Of course the Keys are all beach. She tells me the guy—she calls him "the Captain"—is coming by shortly, so stick around. So I walk down to the water, but the coral is so sharp my feet can hardly take it. There are barracudas fuckin' flyin' by, and I want to get this over. I've got nineteen grand on me, and a knife, and I don't know nobody here but Marina. And I don't really know her, but a friend of Tommy's I can trust.

And there's the fuckin' Captain; he comes around the corner of the trailer, a white guy, mid-forties, sure enough a white-and-blue sailor hat on. We're introduced, in a manner of speaking. And he doesn't like the looks of me, I can tell. And then he tells me straight off.

"You look like a cop," he says.

"Yeah, I know," I say. And fuck you.

But I know he's right. My hair is short, my skin is white, very white for Florida. I've got the Southie tan.

Marina suggests we go inside. It is broiling out.

The Captain says, "Marina, come here. We stay right here. This guy can use the sun."

"I'm no fuckin' cop," I tell The Captain. "And I didn't come down here to be called one."

"Easy, then. Give me the money," he says.

"Where's the fuckin' product?" I look at Marina with a look of, *What the fuck is this?*

"If you're not the law," he says, "you'll give me the money. All the money."

I look at Marina. "Is he good for it?" I ask. She says, "He's good for it."

I get a zipper bag out of my luggage and hand it over.

"I'll be back in an hour," he says.

Marina says she's gonna take a nap. She looks wasted. It's late afternoon, and I'll wait out the Captain. I go back down to the shore. It's a different ocean from the one that laps up at Carson Beach in Southie—

a different color, a different smell, a different sound. You can hear the whole thing churning in the Keys. It's fucking vast.

I wear my sneakers this time; the shells are too sharp. I don't see any more flying fish, which is all right with me. It would make me miss my gun, which of course I didn't bring on the flight. I could really see pot-shotting those barracuda as they flipped out there. But maybe it was too hot for them, too. It had to be ninety degrees out.

I killed an hour, and nothing. No Captain. I went back inside the trailer, which was suffocating. I set up a beach chair under a tree and waited. I whittled away with my knife on a piece of driftwood.

I woke up Marina. "Where is your fuckin' guy? You told me he was good for it!"

She told me not to worry. I tried not to think beyond what was in front of me. He had my money; I hope he had my product. I took a nap in the lawn chair.

I was woken by the sound of a helicopter. I thought this was it. Fuckin' SWAT coming in. I ran inside. Marina said to calm down. She made me a drink. I don't usually like rum, but this was nice smooth Cuban rum.

After a few drinks, I thought about fuckin' her. Maybe that would make me feel better, take our minds off this situation. She was Italian, with olive skin, dark hair and eyes. She was close to my age. She must have sensed that I needed to be calmed down. She came over to me as I sat on the couch in her trailer. She sat on my lap, face-to-face, wrapping her legs around my hips. Within a minute we had taken off each other's clothes. She began riding me, grinding, grinding. I didn't hear the heli-copter anymore. If shit was coming down, let it come down. I had an-other drink, and we went at it again. My plane didn't leave till tomorrow. There was still time.

By midnight I figured I was beaten for my money. I actually gave it till midnight, and then I sat Marina down and said, "Somebody's gonna pay. Either I'm gonna find your friend the Captain and kill him, or some-body is gonna pay. Him, some other fuckin' friend of yours. Or of his. I ain't leaving here empty-handed. Someone is going to pay one way or another. Clearly there ain't no fuckin' product coming."

Marina pleaded with me to give it a little more time. The Captain would come through, she assured me.

I knew it wasn't Marina's fault. It was my fuckin' fault, for involving a woman in business. I can't take it out on her. This was a one-shot deal. She would get a little for herself, that's it. She's not in it to fuck me over.

I was just about ready to fall asleep and wait for daylight to make a plan when the Captain shows up. It's 1:00 A.M.

I wanted to break his fuckin' face, but I was so happy to see him. He shows up with a kilo, my first kilo ever purchased, all wrapped up in newspaper with tape around it.

The Captain was all business as usual. He said it took a while to get it, and he wanted to make sure I wasn't a cop.

"Did you see my helicopter?" he says with grin.

"You motherfucker," I say.

"I wanted to make sure you weren't fuckin' law."

"Okay," I say.

Truthfully, I was pretty impressed.

"Well, here it is," says the Captain.

I opened it up, peeling the tape back, carefully removing the Spanish newspaper from around the product. It was the real deal. All fuckin' flake, a beige tone to it, a whitish beige tone, with sparkling colors, like mother-of-pearl, like blues and grays and golds catching the light. The most fuckin' potent cocaine I ever purchased. I knew I'd have to cut it, maybe by half. I was doin' the math.

I gave Marina a taste. She howled. I shook out a little shake for her and wrapped it back up. And the Captain was gone.

The next day Marina drove me by car along the Keys across U.S. 1 to Miami International Airport. Dangerous spot. This is the 1980s, *Miami fucking Vice* time.

I had snapped the kilo into two biscuits. A good kilo snaps. And this one wasn't broken from transportation. I loved seeing those seashell flakes along the edge, the pink and blue pearl. It was beautiful. I took the two biscuits and wrapped them in the plastic, and then I took a rubber sweat belt I'd brought with me that wraps around your abdomen. And I wrapped it around me as hard as I could with the biscuits inside, one in front, the other in the small of my back. I wore a green baggy Hawaiian shirt, green for good luck. Shorts, sneakers, and a hat. I looked like a fuckin' regular young guy. Didn't fit the description of a drug transporter at all.

I never was scared. That's the funny thing about it. I never was scared. It was a little nerve-racking, but I was never worried about bad scenarios. I didn't think about going to jail. I thought about making it to Boston, cutting my product with inositol, which I knew I had enough of at home. I knew just what to do to preserve the crisp of my kilo: After breaking it all up, I'd spread it out on the table and spray it with gin from a spray bottle and let it set. It brought back the rock to coke. I already knew a few tricks.

As for the airport, I'd done my research beforehand. I was timing everything. We got there just in time for my flight. You don't want to sit there long, because if you sit there in the lounge a long time, they have dogs—and I mean it could be a little fuckin' Chihuahua that a woman is walking around. And she'd be an undercover agent, and the dog would be fuckin' sniffing wherever it felt like sniffing, sniffing out anybody who was traveling with drugs, walking the whole terminal. Why sit there long enough to have that dog come over and piss on your fuckin' backpack? Get there, get to the gate, get on the plane. Gone.

Walking through the airport, Marina was clearly paranoid. She had been doing coke throughout that day. Three state troopers were walking toward us, and she was staring right at them. She couldn't take her eyes off them. Her eyes were wide and panicked. I grabbed her arm and gently spun her to face me. I said gently, but loud enough to be heard, "Baby, aren't you going to miss me?" "Yes, of course," she said, a little surprised, just as the troopers walked right by us. Then I pulled her closer to me and whispered in her ear, "Don't ever do that again—stare at the law. Just look at me. Talk to me."

That first kilo I got from the Captain was so strong that once it hit the street I had to cut it again, and once more—three times I stepped on that coke. I'd struck gold with this guy, but never again. When I called Marina to set up another run, she told me the Captain had vanished. "He's done," is all she would say. "Sorry." But she told me things were changing for her, that she was moving to Miami. She'd call me. Sure enough she did.

"You gotta meet Jerry," she tells me not more than a week later, over the phone. "We're living together." It's clear to me what's up. "Same deal," she says. "Come see us."

This time I changed my appearance. I darkened my hair with dye. I went a little far—I wore a fake mustache. I suppose I just looked weird—freckles and dark hair and a 'stache, but I don't think I looked like the law.

The cheapest flight was to Fort Lauderdale, and the safest. I didn't care much for Miami International. I rented a car and drove the half hour into Miami. Jerry had a big house with a pool in a Cuban/Colombian section of town. He lived there with his teenage daughter and now Marina. Risky, I realized, a Latin section of Miami, but Marina said it was safe. She was right before, so I trusted her again. But Jerry, he was another thing altogether. This fuckin' guy thought he was Tony Montana. He wanted to party, be a friend, go out to clubs. He wanted an amigo, not a customer. And he was a sleazy, greasy fuck. I couldn't see what Marina saw in him. Still, that first night we did party. We went to one of his joints, where he was treated very well. I think he did this to impress me and to show me he was a respected guy. He got a little too fucked up.

I wanted to keep it strictly business, in and out as quick as possible. This fucking maniac wanted me to stay at his house and party with him.

He offered me women to fuck, drugs—anything I wanted. I just wanted my coke and to get back home to do my business. I stayed with him for the next two days. We would hang out at his pool, and he would drink, do coke, and rant and rave about this or that. He introduced me to his friends. The first day I am sitting by the pool, and this young girl shows up. I am guessing she was eighteen or nineteen. She walks by me and sits next to Jerry and gives him a kiss on the cheek. Jerry introduces me to her. It's his daughter. This girl is fuckin' gorgeous. Long jet-black hair, dark eyes, and golden brown skin. That day and all day the next day, we hung out by the pool, and at night we went out to eat and then to a club. Me, Jerry, Marina, Jerry's daughter, and some of his friends. Jerry was throwing money around like he was printing it. Champagne, the best food. Whatever you wanted. Over those two days, his daughter and I began to flirt. She pushed me into the pool. I got out and picked her up and threw her in. She knew I was interested, and so was she. She rubbed sunscreen on my back and made a joke about how white I was, and my freckles. *Muy blanco!*

The second night we were out late. When we got back to Jerry's house, he still wanted to party. I begged off and told him I was leaving the next day and needed some sleep. I slept in a nice, cool bedroom with a view of the pool. I went right to sleep. Then I was woken up by a splash in the pool. I looked out. There, in the moonlight, was the daughter, standing naked on the diving board. I decided to click my light on. She knew I was watching her. I went back to lie down when I hear the bedroom door squeak open. There she was, wrapped in a white terry cloth bathrobe. As she walked toward the bed, the robe fell to the floor.

She crawled in, wet and cool and naked. She climbed on top of me. She spoke Spanish only. I am not exactly sure what she said, but I loved the way she said it. The sound of her voice and her passion was intoxicating, and I was drinking it all in. She rode me and rode me and looked at the ceiling. She did what she wanted. We made love all night long, I swear. It was daylight when she went back to her room. I thought, Well, I'll sleep on the plane. A part of me didn't want to leave the next day. I wanted more of *la chica,* but I had to keep my mind on business. The funny thing is, I think this guy knew I fucked his daughter, and he didn't care.

12

ON MY OWN

I made half a dozen trips to Florida, dealing with my wild Tony fuckin' Montana. I enjoyed this guy's daughter each time and learned a few choice words in Spanish, not only from her but from the crazy company her father kept. These guys—Cubans, Colombians, and I don't know what else—were fiery, hotheaded, and loud, but they sure loved life. It was one big party down there, money and coke and women and guns everywhere. I just trooped through it like a serious man. I kept my head about me at all times. I could see that they felt protected in the neighborhood. I wore disguises and got in and out quietly. I let the craziness swirl around me. I kept my hand on my money and fucked *la chica* and brought out product, real good product. Primo coca.

I got myself a burner and kept it down there. When the product came out—Tony Montana would draw all the blinds and turn the music off and conduct business in silence for once!—I'd put a spoonful of the powder on a glass slide connected to the burner and fire it up. Consistently the readout read 87, 88, 89 percent. Sometimes 90. Gorgeous, flaky, sparkling, crisp. I'd strap it on, drive back to Fort Lauderdale, or sometimes to Orlando, and fly from there to Logan. When I'd get home, out would come the scales. I got help from a few people at my apartment after I did my cutting and spraying. We'd make up ounces, eight-balls, and grams. All evening. That night I'd hit my main customers and then hit the bars for some gram action.

With money and coke in your pocket, you're on top of the world. You are necessary. There are plenty of women that come with the territory, but you had to keep your mind on the business. Business it was, but I have to admit it was fun. It really had its moments.

One night me and Paul Moore—and there were lots of nights like this, believe me—we walked into the Bayside Club. I was light then, heavier than my boxing weight but not near the 160 I am now. And Paul, of course, is six foot two, a little heavier than he had been, at about 215. And I see this stocky motherfucker with a PUG'S PUB T-shirt on. Pug's is a pub in Roxbury, and this guy is wearing it in Southie. Strange. Now, even though I know the guy who owns Pug's—a real nice guy named Jimmy Farrell—I didn't know this asshole. So maybe I looked at him the wrong way or something. He was drinking, I was not. He should have known better.

The place is basically pretty quiet and pretty empty, and somehow this guy, who must've weighed about 250, manages, out of all the space in there, to brush against me. I look at him, and he has his arms crossed like I'm supposed to be impressed by his forearms.

"You could say excuse me," I tell him. "Didn't your mother teach you any manners?"

And just as he is going to respond to this . . . well, I'll never know what his response was going to be, because I hit him with a right hand. And just as I hit him with my right hand, Paul hits him a shot right over my shoulder, and we catch him good. We both catch him at the same time. And then I see something I never saw before in real life. This stocky, heavyset guy goes right out into a sitting position midair. Then he hits the fuckin' brick wall and slithers down to the floor—like in a cartoon. Two bangs simultaneous, and the guy is sitting in the air, and then *wham, thump!* Wow. I am so amazed—and surprised, because I wasn't expecting Paul to take a shot like that—that I'm not watchin' and I get cold-cocked by this other guy I hadn't seen, who must have been the fat fuck's friend. Now I'm flying through the air and landing on *my* ass. For a second I'm amused.

Now the guy is backpedaling. *Well, guess what, pal? You underestimated me.* I get up. This guy was Paul's size, but in a split second I go right at him. I barrage him. I hit him body to the fuckin' head, head to the body. I'm barraging him like a fuckin' buzz saw. Paul comes from behind again and hits this fuckin' guy with body shots from behind. And while I'm buzz-sawing this guy in front, Paul is destroying his kidneys from the back. And the fat fuck gets up and wades in, and Paul and I take him apart, too. We beat the shit out of these two guys, stomping 'em, spitting on them. Pouring drinks on them. We stopped short of pissing on them.

All this over a push from Pug's Pub.

No one said a thing. It had turned into a silent execution, except we showed some mercy. No one calls the cops. No one does anything but call these guys a cab.

No one touches us, me and Paul. Not a fucking soul touches us, because they know better. And they know one other thing: not to say anything to anyone. Or they'll get it a lot worse than those two got it.

Another time, same place, I'm on my own, moving my own product— as I said, I still dealt with the organization, too, but more and more I had my own to move. So I'm starting my work, about 9:00 P.M., selling ounces. It's a Friday night. Going to make some money. And I'd just got done training. I was in high spirits. I am not looking for trouble. There's no sense looking for it when it's always there, potentially. And this guy I don't know decides to move a chair for some girl to sit in. And he moves the chair hard and hits me in the back with it. I spin right around.

I say politely, "You could have asked me to move if you wanted the chair."

He stands up right next to me, right in my face, and says, "Fuck you!" He clearly wants to show off for these two douche bags he's with.

Now this guy is ready to fucking go. He tries to hit me. Why? Because he was a fucking asshole and wanted to impress these girls? Stupid fuck. They were going to be impressed, all right, but by another guy: me.

It didn't have to be this kind of night. I wasn't looking for a beef. I was just trying to do some business and chill out.

Having just finished training—hitting the bag and everything else— I was sharp as a fucking tack. I hit him with a left hook, right hand. Two-punch combination. He hits the floor. I can tell I've broken his fuckin' jaw, and his nose is splattered. Two punches.

One of the guys that works in the club opens up the back door. I see the cop who's moonlighting coming down the bar from the front door. This guy is bleeding on the floor like a stuck pig, his legs shaking like he's having a convulsion.

I calmly walk out the back door, up the stairs to the function hall that was on top of the Bayside Club, and then I'm out the door, to East Eighth Street. I get in my car and leave. I've got other customers.

A couple of weeks later, I see the manager of the Bayside. He says, "John. Some cops came down here, they wanted to know who the guy was that fuckin' put the guy in the hospital. He's still in the hospital."

I say to him, "What guy? I've been away."

"That's what I told him," he says. He says he told the cops, "I never seen the guy again, whoever it was that did that. You know how it is, tourist season."

That's the way it was in Southie. That's the way it was meant to be. There was no reason to talk. There was every reason not to. Southie looked after its own. We didn't like outsiders, wise-asses, or people who thought they were better. We didn't like the busing, we didn't like the fags marchin' on St. Paddy's Day, we didn't like yuppies coming into our town. We took care of ourselves and each other. Who else was gonna stop any of that shit? Not the cops, not the politicians, not the church. That was our job. These other fucking people were our enemies, they had their own agendas, not ours. And we could do whatever we wanted, take whatever means we needed, to protect ourselves, and if everyone just kept their mouths shut, there was nothing that anyone could do about it. If a community keeps its trap shut, the law has no chance. That's what we were taught as kids, and it was the rule of the street, the code. It was what Whitey preached, but it was preached long before him. It was preached to him and back before that to the day that Irish gangs sprang up from the despair of the times. It's the code wherever and whenever you are at war.

13

RECRUITED BY THE MOB

In Southie and in the world of crime, information is power. Whitey Bulger wanted to know everything about everyone. And because, like any good businessman, he had on eye on the future, he clearly wanted to know more about me. Every time I ran into him now, I could tell he was sizing me up, trying to get a good read on me. He was interested in me, not only because he liked me but because he liked the way I handled myself. He could see how ambitious and driven I was. And I already knew a lot about him.

He was in his early sixties. He worked out every day in his home. He had equipment in every house he stayed at. He ran on a treadmill and did weights every day. He also ate very healthy meals. His business partner, Flemmi, was the same way. They both were into vitamins, juices, and healthy living. Whitey was organized, prepared and surrounded himself with like-minded people. He did not like excessive drinking, no drugs, and he wanted guys that took care of themselves.

He had a number of girlfriends. The majority of the time he stayed with Catherine Grieg in her home in Squantum. But he would often go to South Boston at night to have dinner with Theresa Stanley at her house. He also had another one, a young blond girlfriend who lived in a condo on Fourth Street in Southie. I'd see him driving with her on occasions. He loved blue-eyed blond women. He never was married, to my knowledge; no kids either. Whitey liked to travel light.

His management style was also a thing of legend. He was always in charge, dictating what was to be done. Flemmi would give him the information, tell him what was going on or relay him a message. But in the end Whitey would make the decision about what to do. He rarely came out in the daytime. At night he came out to prowl. He liked to eat good food and drink fine wines. He was a chameleon. One minute he could be at ease in a fine restaurant picking out a four-hundred-dollar bottle of wine, the next minute he could be chastising someone with his unique style and making them piss their pants. He always thought about what he was going to do before he did it. Contemplating every move and how it would play out. He never did anything on impulse.

So Whitey was watching me, but I was watching him as well.

Whitey could see I had money, that I wasn't struggling by any means. I had a nice leather jacket, three-hundred-dollar shoes, a black BMW. Like him, I took care of myself—he worked out every day on a treadmill, I ran six miles. But most important, I didn't cower in his presence. I didn't lick his fuckin' shoes. Those kinds of people annoyed him. Even though ultimately it was a sign of respect that people feared him, I don't think he could trust people who were afraid of him. But he *could* use them. And use them he did. When I'd see him around town, he'd always ask how I was doing. "You need anything, lemme know," he'd say.

Of course he knew that I was dealing with his organization. And knew that I was operating on my own. I think he respected the balls that took. But Whitey was smart. He could see that a guy like me could be counted on. A guy with no fear, with ambition. He knew something about recruitment.

At the time a guy I'll call Mickey O was running Whitey's drug operations. Paul had gotten his supply from Mickey, and so had I, until Tommy Connors gave me the nod to Florida. Mickey took notice after a while. One day I'm walking off a hard run down by the Point, and he pulls over in his car. Gets out. "Hey, Red, we used to see a lot more of you. Where you been? What you got? You not shopping with us?"

I had nothing to hide, not from this prick. I told him what he already knew. "I got my own connection," I said.

I could see he had some other guys in the car with him.

"We're not good enough for you now, eh? You think that's gonna pass?"

"Mickey," I said to him calmly, "this is a business. I have my own connection, my own customers. What's your fuckin' problem? I gotta go. I'm getting a fuckin' chill here."

"Nothing, nothing, nothing. Relax, Red, relax. Listen," he says, "why don't you come in with us? You can work for me." He goes back to his car and opens the trunk.

Of course this didn't make much sense to me. Work for this fuck?

"Mickey, why would I do that?"

He said, "C'mere."

I go over to the back of the car. The trunk is up. Mickey unzips a gym bag for a moment. I see it is stacked with cash, hundreds.

"Here," he says. He zips it back up. "Lift it."

I decline.

"That's one hundred grand, my friend. You want to go to Florida with that?"

He wanted a partnership. He wanted to take advantage of my connections—finance some big purchases.

"Whitey likes the way you handle yourself," he says.

I went for it. With that kind of money, I could make five times what I am making now.

So I dealt with Mickey O. I made two very lucrative trips to Florida. I'd fly down with over a hundred thousand. Then it'd take me a few days to round up seven or eight kilos. The organization had a lot more customers than I had. It was hard work, but the money got very, very good.

Mickey loved the product I was bringing back. But this guy, who had a Ph.D. in fucking over everybody he ever dealt with, didn't exactly surprise me when he proposed a little side action.

"Listen, Red. You and me, we become partners, right? You and me."

We were sitting in some bar downtown, where no one knew us. Mickey was acting weird. He ordered a beer, a Tuborg. Who the fuck orders a Tuborg?

"You take a chunk and sell to your own customers, and you can split it with me. I'll help you. It'll just be you and me."

I told him right there, "Mickey, this ain't right. It's not my style. It's a scumbag move."

In effect Mickey was fucking over the other guys in the chain of dealers—taking cash from the organization, distributing the product back for sale, but keeping a chunk for the two of us to sell on our own. This involved stepping on the product a little heavy. But Mickey was running the show. He was my boss. I went along. Though I wasn't happy.

I paid a visit to Tommy Connors at the gym. We talked back in the office, where the coffee was so bad you had to cut it with Jamesons.

"Fucking Mickey is a snake," I told him. "This ain't right."

Tommy was street-smart and knew all the players. "If they find out," he said, "Mickey is gonna put it on you. So all you say is, 'I was just following orders, Mickey is the boss. If you have a problem, go see him.' "

Sure enough, guys started to complain. One of the guys calls me on the phone and asks me to come down to the corner. "Red, this product is being fucked with, and we know you're fucking with it."

I said, "Go talk to Mickey. He's the boss."

"I just did. He said maybe it's you."

I said, "Get back in your fuckin' car, pal, before I take your head off. This is a serious fuckin' charge. I don't fuck my friends, and I never will. You go back to that fuckin' snake and tell him what I said."

Instead this guy went right to Whitey. I got word that Whitey knew right away that I had no part in Mickey's scumbag move. He said straight out that Red is a good kid, would never fuck his friends or his partners, but Mickey on the other hand is a scumbag that would fuck his own daughter and already did. He ordered Mickey to come back to Boston from his place in Florida.

I decided to get out of town. I'd take my girl at the time, Gail Crane, to Montreal for the weekend. I trusted what Tommy Connors had said to me. He said, "Whitey knows this Mickey is greedy. Mickey will try to put it on you, but Whitey won't believe that piece of shit. But it's better if you get out of town for a few days."

As we are moving through Logan Airport to our gate, every fuckin' guy with his eyes on Gail, who looks gorgeous, with tight jeans and a great ass, who do I fuckin' see but Mickey? He's all fuckin' panicked. I couldn't believe it. He comes running over to me. I turn Gail away. "Get me a newspaper, will you?"

"Red, Red! Whitey fuckin' wants to see me. What's up?"

"What's up, Mickey? Everything all right?"

"Weeksie called," he says. "Whitey wants to see me. Do you know what going on, Red?"

"I have no fuckin' idea," I say to Mickey. "I'm going up to Montreal with my girl for the weekend. We got to get going to catch our flight. Take care, buddy, I'll see you later."

I left him sweatin' there. I knew what was up: He was out. Fuck him. I hope it's the last time I see that greedy fucking scumbag.

Tommy Connors and I ran into Whitey at Triple O's when I got back from Montreal. He came into the bar with Kevin Weeks. Weeks traveled all over with Whitey. He was a tough guy in the street. I knew him from the gym. He was all right back then. Years ago he'd been hired to work the door at Triple O's but handled himself pretty well, showed himself well, dealing with some rowdy customers, enforcing what needed enforcing. He was six foot, stocky, good with his fists. He had graduated from the door of the bar to working for Whitey. Whitey would tell him what to do, who to talk to, and Kevin would do it. No questions asked.

Since Whitey hardly drank at all—he was on that regimen of health food and vitamins—his close associates were careful about drinking around him. Whitey knew that drunks were sloppy and dangerous and vulnerable. He didn't like it in his men. Anyone who wanted to impress Whitey didn't do it standing at the bar with shots or chugging a pitcher of beer. You had to be careful.

So, being a wise fuck, I bought him a drink.

"How you doing, Jim?" I say. To Deirdre, who was working, I say, "Get us a round, will ya?"

Whitey nods, says hello. Comes over. Not all the way over, but he makes like not to head somewhere else along the rail.

"You're doing good there, Red," he says.

"Not complaining," I say.

"No one's listening anyway," he says, and he looks up. I can't say he smiled, but one eye narrowed a bit. A little challenge.

I take a step back. I say, "I ain't askin' anyone to listen." I finish off my beer and put it on the bar, and I look at Whitey. He stands there, hunched at the bar, his hand touching both sides of his longneck Bud. He doesn't look up, but I can hear his leather jacket creak. He rolls his shoulder.

"Have another drink," he says. "On me."

We bought each other round after round. We drank slowly, easily, as the crowd filled the joint, although Weeks sat there nervously eyeing the place, hoping nothing would upset Whitey. He kept replacing Whitey's coaster with a fresh one.

All in all, with Whitey sitting at the corner of the bar at Triple O's, it was a special night, not your usual. A few people ventured to say hello. A few old-timers shook his hand. Funny how the older people could relax a little around Whitey. They'd seen it all, of course. And they were the ones maybe who enjoyed most the little services that Whitey provided— the gambling, the numbers, the help with a funeral—and thought it contributed something good and solid to the Southie way of life. Having a horse gave a little hope to the day, made the beer go down a little easier, which made the gambling loss go down a little better, too. A full circle. And Whitey ran it all.

Eventually I had my fill, and I had a couple of women on my hip. They wanted some coke, then some cock, so it was time to go. I slapped a hefty tip on the bar, gave a pinch to Deirdre's cheeks, and shook hands with Whitey.

He leans over and says to me, jabbing his finger on the back of my hand for emphasis, " 'The wise man does at once what the fool does finally.' "

"Really," I say. "Is that for me?"

"No," he says. "But I want you to know that your man is gonna find another line of work. In another town."

"I'm glad to fuckin' hear it," I say. "He'd fuck his own mother, you know."

Whitey nodded. "No," he says to me. "He'd fuck his own daughter." Okay, then.

"I better get moving," I say. I take a look at Weeks, who's nodding like he knows what's going on.

I leave with the couple of broads, jump in my BMW, and wonder what's in store for Mickey O.

A few days later, I run into Connors, right back there at Triple O's. It's a Friday night, I'm working, but I also got time for Tommy. We sit at the bar.

"Whitey was talkin' about you," he says.

"Oh, yeah? What's he sayin'?"

"He says you got a ton of balls."

"He's got that right, don't he, Tommy? He's got that right."

Tommy says, "Whitey said, 'Most guys are trying to break out of jail, but that kid's trying to break in.' He said you remind him of how he was when he was young. He said, 'He needs guidance. Have him talk to Kevin. Get close to Kevin. They are closer in age, and he will be able to relate better to Kevin.' "

I pause to tell some asshole to fuck off, some guy who wants to fuckin' commiserate about the poor MacDonald family. There's too much of that shit in Southie, drunks crying about this or that. Giving their own life meaning by sorrowing over something you couldn't do nothing about anyhow, especially now. "Get the fuck out of here. I'll make you fuckin' weep," I say to this guy who says he used to watch me fight when Frank the Tank was in my corner. Frank this and Frank that. "Do me a favor," I say to the guy. "Go suck your own dick."

"See?" says Tommy.

We go to a back table in the corner, where it's quieter. When I go back there, I'm not working and nobody bothers me. I'm far from the bar, far from the stupid Seven Dwarfs. Deirdre knows to tell people to leave me alone.

"Tommy," I say, "Whitey is calling me in. Into his circle. Why else is he giving a shit what I am up to?"

"What makes you think he gives a shit?" he says. "Whitey don't give a shit. He might find you useful."

"Well, he might be useful to me," I say. "You ever fuckin' think about that?"

"It gets hotter," says Tommy. "You think you have heat on you now, wait until you are close to that guy. He's hot as hell."

"What do I fuckin' need him for?" I say, not knowing what I think, really.

"Nothing, John. You don't need him. Not unless you've got ambitions. In which case you do."

I knew exactly what he meant. If I was happy staying small, I didn't need Whitey Bulger. If I wanted to be big, I did. And I wanted to be big. Tommy knew that from seeing me in the ring.

So Whitey is watching me, seriously. I am definitely intrigued. I'm still thinking about his quote—"The wise man does at once what the fool does finally." It's Machiavelli, of course. And I realize what Whitey meant: He's gonna banish Mickey now before it's too late. I realize what too late would mean—he'd have to kill the motherfucker. Who wants that? It's messy. It gives you certain problems. Bad idea. But who would replace Mickey O in Whitey's organization? Because he was fuckin' gone.

14

PENELOPE

At this time, just as I was on the verge of what felt like a recruitment into the upper echelon of gangster life, I also fell in love.

I met Penelope Howard (not her real name) at a birthday party in Dorchester. I was twenty. I'd just dropped by—I was out prowling that night, dressed all in black—black leather jacket, black pants. My on-and-off girlfriend Gail was there. She was the first girl I ever loved, but she was older than me and more experienced, and she fucked me when she was with another guy, so I didn't exactly trust her. I had already slapped her on a dance floor when I caught her dancing with some asshole, so we were more off than on at the time. But I don't think Gail gave a shit, to be truthful. I said hello, and she said hello and then introduced me to this old girlfriend of hers, from Dorchester, who'd moved away but had just moved back. I'd already noticed this beautiful girl across the room who I'd never seen before. I spotted long black hair swaying and brownish arms. When she turned around and I saw her face for the first time, I have to admit I could not take my eyes off of her. I never believed in love at first sight until I looked in her eyes. And when Gail brought her over—"John, meet Penelope. Penelope, this is John Shea"—she extended her hand to me. I saw those liquid big brown eyes turn up to me, and I looked into them and at her full lips. She had a gorgeous build on her, I could tell, as she stood there in a blouse and nice pants. Right away she was warm and yet confident. She had an Italian woman's manners and grace but was no pushover. She was all gentleness and warmth, with that Italian passion and fire. She wasn't like the other girls I knew from Southie, who always seem to have a coarse exterior, as if they had some kind of armor on. This Penelope, I could see, wasn't afraid. She was open, gentle, strong. She was the full package, a real woman.

We talked for a short time at the party. She liked my sense of humor, and she liked my manners. I could be very courtly around women. I don't know where I learned that from, fighting with my mother and sisters all the time. Maybe it was that every other woman I met gave me a chance to put all that Shea family bullshit behind me, not to deny it but prove that there was another way. That I wasn't a pig and a fuckin' bum and a little prick of a brother. I was a man, a gentleman.

I didn't see her after that for a while. In fact, I was on again with Gail, till we had a fucking fight. I forget what it was about, but she said, "Why don't you call Penelope? She thinks you're cute. Go fuck someone else." None of this was said nice, and I'll skip my mood. Let's just say I was mad enough to take her up on her suggestion. I made her give me Penelope's phone number, more as a threat than anything else. But the next day I called her.

Being a classy girl, she had a little problem accepting me calling her—she was Gail's friend. But I assured her that Gail and I weren't serious and that Gail had given me her number. That she could check it out with her. So she agreed to go to dinner. But the day of our date, I had worked out hard—a long jog in the cold, some racquetball, worked the weight room, then wolfed down the steak tips they served at the Bayside Club. At which point I realized I was sick.

So I had to call Penelope and cancel. I spared her the details but left it at food poisoning. I guess I'd caught something, with the working out and the cold weather, et cetera. But Penelope figured I was standing her up and let me know it. I said, "C'mon over, then. I'm just lying here, and I'm sick as a dog."

So she did. She comes up to my apartment with a beautiful white coat on and a red scarf. I loved the smell of her perfume. She has with her a big shopping bag. She's brought dinner—lemon chicken piccata that her mother had made and a bottle of ginger ale.

I stayed on the couch while she found her way around my kitchen, warming up the food. I ate a little—it was delicious. We sat and talked for a while, an hour and a half maybe. And then she went home.

As she left, she said, "No one's ever stood me up before. I want to keep it that way."

I said, "Let's have dinner on Friday night. I'll take you to David's, my favorite Italian restaurant."

And that was the beginning of something beautiful.

We started seeing each other every day. It was instant chemistry. After our dinner at David's, we came back to my apartment. We opened a three-hundred-dollar bottle of red wine. I kissed her for the first time. We made love.

Within two weeks I had bought her a pair of one-carat diamond earrings. Her mother heard about that and told Penelope she wanted to sit down and talk to me.

I went out to their house. Penelope introduced me to her mother, a nice lady, lovely like her daughter, with no nonsense to her whatsoever. Penelope then left, and I realized this was a real important meeting.

"Sit down, John," her mother said to me. We were in the kitchen, where real family business gets done. You don't have the kind of conversation we were gonna have in the living room.

"Listen," she said, "this relationship with Penelope. It seems to be getting serious very quickly. You bought her diamond earrings. They ain't cheap. I know."

I smiled. I was proud. I started to speak, but she wasn't done.

"She is my daughter, and I want to protect her. So I asked around about you. Who is this young guy from Southie buying my daughter expensive diamond earrings? You know what I was told?"

"Mrs. Howard," I said.

"I was told you were with the Irish Mafia, one of Whitey Bulger's guys. You are considered a very serious guy."

She had both her hands on the table. They were like Penelope's. They were caring hands.

"I heard the reason you was in California wasn't just for boxing but to get away from a shooting you were involved in. So you tell me who this Irish fellow John Shea is."

Holy shit, I thought. This was serious fucking stuff. She's a serious fuckin' woman. Looking out for her daughter like this. And I liked that.

"Mrs. Howard," I said, "with all due respect, I cannot answer your question about the Irish Mafia. And I didn't go to California for anything else than to box. And as to your daughter, I give you my word"—and I put my right hand upon hers—"nothing will ever happen to Penelope. No one will ever bother her, and I can guarantee that."

She thanked me for that, removed her hand from beneath mine, and asked another question.

"If something happens to you, can you promise me you'll just walk away?"

I took a deep breath. I looked straight at her. "I can't make that promise, Mrs. Howard. All I can tell you is, I promise nothing will happen to Penelope, ever."

She smiled. "Call me Carla, will you?" She got up. "And help me set the table."

I appreciated Carla being frank with me and getting all this out of the way from the get-go. That family wasn't a complete stranger to the other side of the street. A close relative had been in some rackets or another. I wasn't dealing with a Beacon Hill crowd. When Penelope returned, we sat down and ate about six or seven courses of food, all Italian, all delicious. And Penelope came home with me.

Penelope's mother was a pretty good detective. She had gotten some good information. I was in Whitey Bulger's circle, unquestionably. But the story about running off to California because of a shooting was total bullshit. I went to box, period. I told Kevin Weeks about my encounter with Penelope's mother. Kevin tells me, "You should have said yes when she asked you if you were in the Irish mob."

I couldn't believe it. "Are you fuckin' kidding? No fuckin' way I would ever admit that to anyone."

What could he have been thinking?

I realized that now, with Penelope in my life, fidelity was an issue. AIDS I didn't worry about, because I always had rubbers on me. Being with one woman is hard. I was starting to realize that I really loved Penelope, that she made me feel like no one else. It wasn't just in bed, it was everywhere else, her voice in my ear, her caring. My caring. That's not about fucking. Still, I loved the gangster life. Part of being a gangster is being tough. Part of being tough is that you don't exactly get sentimental. It's all business. Being with one woman can be a little sentimental. It can also be weak: There's something you want, you can have it, but you don't take it because you're afraid of what some woman might say? Or how she'll feel? That can be considered a weakness. And one thing you can't show as a gangster is weakness. So fucking other women is part of the job.

I did think a lot more about things with Penelope. If anything, it made me more ambitious. I had one primary goal, to be the boss. And I was definitely boss of my own life. I had my own connection, and I was making real money. I moved into a nice apartment in Marina Bay. I had the best stereo, brand-new furniture. I was living dangerously, for sure—

running coke from Florida, dealing in Southie and with Whitey. But I was living large and doing it right. I still handled some product from the organization. I was still in business with them, with Paul Moore. But I had something better going than they had. And they fuckin' knew it.

As for Penelope, she went to work during the day—she had a job with the city—and stayed with me at night, most nights. We had nice dinners, she had the best of clothes. She never asked about my business. She knew not to. She never crossed that line. She knew that the more she knew, the more she was in danger, and a danger to me. The less she knew, the stronger we were.

She was loyal to me, and how much of that did I have? It was addictive. She had a temper, no doubt, and a bit of a domineering attitude. We clashed at times. She liked to control what she could control. How I looked, what I said, how we did what we did together. She didn't like my temper, and I didn't like hers, but we were equals in that way.

One night we went to another favorite restaurant of mine, the Julien, in the Le Meridien Hotel downtown. Penelope wore a nice silk dress that I had bought her, a dark flower pattern, beautiful, and she looked great in it. I had borrowed a friend's Jaguar for the evening. We had reservations. I parked in front of the hotel. The doorman came out. I tipped him enough to keep the car in front. We went up. It was very exclusive up there. We sat down. I ordered the wine. Penelope was hot because she had found some lingerie in my house. I guess that's why we were at the Julien. I told her that the bra had nothing to do with me. That I had let one of the Hogans use my house, because occasionally he did fool around with some of the girls from the neighborhood.

She says, "Oh, yeah?" With a lot of attitude.

"Yeah," I say. "It was Hogan."

Of course she didn't believe me. And she had all the right in the world. After her first glass of wine, she started getting into her feelings. We were talking about other things. She bitched about her work, and I listened. We talked about going to Montreal. Too cold, she said. She said the Jaguar was too much like a pimpmobile. I listened. Then I changed the subject.

"This is a nice evening. This is a nice wine," I say. "It's great to be here with you."

But it was too late. She goes, "I deserve this," and drains her glass. She pours herself another from the ice bucket.

I let a few beats pass.

"You deserve what?"

"This," she says, throwing back another gulp of the best wine in the house. "You're making up for what you did. I deserve this dress and this wine and this dinner. And you'll do what I say."

I put my hand over her wineglass.

"Oh, really, Penelope?"

"Yeah, you're my slave. You're my slave, and you *should* do this for me."

I took my palm off her wineglass. Her hand was on the stem this whole time. "What did you say? I'm your slave?"

"Yeah, you're my slave, and you'd better do this."

I say, "Oh, I'm your slave, and I'd better do this?" And I said it loud. I made it so everybody could hear, and they looked, the people around us from the other tables looked at us. And now in each hand I had a glass—water and wine. And I hit her with the wine and hit her with the water, right on the chest. I stood up, I put four hundred bucks on the table and I walked out. I walked right out of that fuckin' restaurant.

I went outside, and I was hot, and I said to the guy, "Give me my fuckin' keys." He saw that I was hot, and he knew I had just gone upstairs with the young lady. I gave him a twenty. "Call the lady a cab when she comes down."

Penelope phoned when I got home. I was in my bed, in my house, fuckin' not happy, and she called me and said, "Was that necessary?"

I said, "Well, was it necessary for you? What do you think? I'm your slave? I'm a piece of shit? You think you're better than me?"

"Well, no one throws water and wine in my face. All over my new dress. John, what were you thinking?"

"Just don't abuse me at the dinner table. Show me some respect in public."

There is silence on the line.

"Listen, I'll tell Hogan to find another place."

"I'll see you tomorrow night, John." And she hung up.

15

THE TEST

There's like a low siren going in my head. It's a Whitey fuckin' buzz. I detected for the first time a weakness in Whitey: his greed. One of my guys has told me he's gotten the shakedown from Kevin Weeks. That Whitey wants his share. His pockets get ripped off his pants. Weeks takes his money. They want to make a habit of this—shaking my guy down?

I'm furious, furious not with Weeks, who just does whatever Whitey tells him to, but with the big fuckin' guy himself. I don't make a lot of noise around town. But I don't fuckin' like it. I tell Weeks, "It better not happen again."

"What, John? What?"

"You fuckin' know what I'm talking about," I tell him. "I've got guys dealing for me. I tell them I can protect them. Now you show them I can't protect them? What do you need from me? Whatever you need from me, you come to *me* for. You don't shake down my people, you understand?

I figure I'm in Whitey's sights, but I've stood up to him before, and he respected it. And I'll do it again. But that siren sound keeps blaring in my head.

I drive by his compound—the Rotary Liquor Mart, which used to be the Texaco station at the bottom of Old Colony Avenue. I'm looking for

Whitey's black Chevy, but he doesn't seem to be around. I'm wondering what's up, what's next for me? Then I get the call. Right at my house, late afternoon. It's Weeks. "Come see Whitey."

"When?"

"Now."

Whitey's open for business.

I drive down Old Colony Avenue, and I have a bad feeling. I don't know what it is. The sky is overcast, a solid gray. Here I am, not yet old enough to drink, but making it. I've taken care of my mother a little; she's a little better off, and things are gonna get even better for her. My sisters I don't give a fuck that much about; they're on their own. I have a thriving business. I have Penelope. Things are good. But maybe I got too close to Whitey. Should I be walking into his basement office?

I pull into the parking lot next to the liquor store. I lock my car and wonder if I'll be the one to unlock it.

I walk through the store to the back. Weeks meets me. I say, "What's up?" He says, "It's cool." But he's not looking at me.

Together we walk through the back and down to the basement office. The door is open, and I walk in. I hear the door slam behind me, turn around, and Weeks is standing there with an Uzi in his arms, and Whitey steps out of the shadows. Another Uzi.

Whitey walks toward me. I'm waiting for one of these fucks to point his Uzi at me, and I'm gonna tell 'em, *If you're gonna point it at me, shoot me.* But they don't.

Whitey talks. "Red, tell us about your friend. Where's he keep all his fuckin' money? He's holding out."

"Who? What friend? What are you talkin' about?"

"Connors," says Whitey. "That fuck owes me."

"Tommy fucking Connors?" I say. I'm incredulous.

"You know this fuckin' guy, you know his house. I want to know where he keeps his money. His business is my business. Now I want to know what you know."

Weeks tries to cock the Uzi but can't quite. I look at him. I shake my head. *Oh, yeah, tough guy here,* but keep it to myself. This could blow. Whitey could snap. I don't want him snapping for nothing. I'm being careful.

I look Whitey right in the eyes. They are cold as ice. "He's got nothing," I tell him. "He's done nothing. Do what you gotta do."

Whitey is steaming now. He shakes his head slowly and breathes deeply.

"Go on," I say. I say it to him and to Weeks, and I say it calmly. I say it like I'm speaking to a baby, instructing them on how to clip me. "Pull the trigger," I say. *You're not gonna get nothing out of me. You take from him, you're taking from me. So do what you gotta do.*

Whitey cocks his weapon, neat—*chu-chuk*. Seconds pass. I think, If I get out of here alive, I am going to come right back and kill them both. They can't see it, but I'm in a rage. I know better than to show my rage, though. A few tense seconds pass. All the while my eyes are locked right on Whitey.

Whitey raises the gun but then turns it away. He uncocks it and smiles. He looks at Weeks.

"It was a test, Red," says Whitey. "You passed. You got fuckin' big balls. You're loyal. You're one loyal fuckin' guy."

I let out a breath.

"Now you're with me," he says. He looks like a proud father. I, however, am one pissed-off son. My mind was racing, but I did not want to show him anything. All I could think about was coming back later and blowing their brains out. But I played it off and laughed. I thought later that day about coming back, even though it was "a test." I didn't like anyone holding a gun up to me, test or no test. I understood in some ways the reasoning behind it, but no one was ever going to test me like that again.

Whitey jokes around, relaxed. He and Weeks talk about the last guy they did the test on, who actually shit his pants. They have a good laugh.

I'm not laughing, but I'm alive.

The next day Whitey made me boss of the drug business for the organization. I'm twenty years old.

16

THE PROTÉGÉ

Now I had guys working for me, older guys, experienced guys with street smarts, customers, connections, brains. Jackie Mack, Eddie Mac, Jackie Cherry, Andre the Giant, even Paul Moore. Still, Southie looked the same to me. I could walk it with my eyes closed and knock on any door and know who would answer. My mother was living with my sister Paula in Charlestown. Paula would still call me once in a while, though Maureen I never heard from and Claire was smart enough to stay clear. I still picked up my dry cleaning every Saturday on Broadway, got my hair cut by Walter Berry at the shop on I Street. I worked out at the Boston Athletic Club, took my runs down by Columbia Park. I had dinner with Penelope at all our favorite joints. I still had Penelope in my bed and pretty much in my heart, all the time.

The difference was that there were a few people from whom I had new respect. The guys who answered to me, of course. But, more important, the guys at the top—Whitey and Stevie Flemmi and the two Kevins, Weeks and O'Neil. I was with them. I was entrusted with the serious shit: the drug operation, which was the biggest revenue stream. I was running the biggest risk—interstate drug trafficking, moving large cash and big weight. Drugs were my part of Whitey's turf.

This was where my education with Whitey really began. It was half philosophy, half street tactics. Some of it was very general: *Don't do anything in haste or anger.* Some of it was very specific to me: *Get rid of the green Jeep, John. It's too fuckin' brash.* Or, *No more jumping on the hood of a cop car or calling them morons or shakin' your prick at 'em.*

But most of it was purely tactical: *Always have the radio on when talking business. Dress inconspicuously ("Not like the fuckin' Italians"). Have your fun out of town. Put your women in white cars so you can spot 'em.* And some of it was the most important thing to learn as a gangster: *Don't do anything someone can hold over you.*

What he never had to say was, *Don't ever rat.* We grew up with that. It was like the First Commandment of Southie.

Still, Whitey had his hands full with me. But I'll say he was there for me. He kept an eye on me and was ready to intervene. He was investing in my education.

I was under a lot of pressure for a twenty-, twenty-one-year-old guy. I had money to handle, runs to make, product to package and distribute, debts to collect, tribute to pay, guys to keep in line. Early on, I was volatile, ready to blow. Sometimes at the slightest thing or the wrong thing. One time I'm pissed off over a side mirror that's broken on my car. I'd had an altercation outside a restaurant with a guy who used to see Penelope and who decided to talk to her as we were leaving. I scared the shit out of him, and he cracks the mirror as he's backing away. I was in a rage, but I took no action in haste, as Whitey would have counseled. I went to him the next day and "ran it by" him, as he also counseled.

"I'm gonna kill this motherfucker who messed with Penelope. I'm gonna wait for him at his apartment and shoot his face off."

I tell this to Whitey. We're driving around in his Chevy. He turns the radio up. Now it's like Joe Castiglione, the Sox broadcaster, is in the car with us.

"Cool it, John. She's with you, isn't she? You gotta know when you're in control. Don't be stupid."

So I was cooling. He was right. But as we are sitting at a red light, don't I see this other piece of shit Manny Rose, the jeweler, walking with his wife.

This guy's got some chains of mine and a ring to repair. Every time I stop by to pick them up, he's closed. Now I've heard he's closed the shop entirely and a lot of people are missing shit. I'm ready to kill this motherfucker right here.

"Pull the car over," I say. "There's fucking Manny Rose."

Whitey hit the button that rolled down the car window on my side. Manny, who was walking down the street with his wife, slowed down. Whitey said, "You come here," and he pointed and motioned for Manny to come over to the car. Manny and his wife both started to approach the car, but Whitey, leaning down a bit so he could speak through my window, said to the wife, "I didn't call you, I called him. Now get back over there." She did as she was told.

I sat back and let Whitey handle it. Whitey said, "Do you owe this guy some jewelry? Do you have his jewelry?"

Manny mumbled, "Yeah."

Whitey said, "Do you know who I am?"

Manny said, "No," although I knew Manny must have known who he was. That's when Whitey changed gears and began screaming at him.

"I am fuckin' Whitey Bulger, that's who I am! I'll blow your fuckin' head off if you don't get my friend his stuff back, you understand that, you cocksucker?"

Manny was visibly shaking. He could barely speak. Almost inaudibly he squeaked, "Yes."

Whitey said once more, "You understand me?"

Manny was shaking worse. He was quivering. Then I saw his trousers darken, and then a puddle of his own piss form at his feet.

Whitey buzzed up the car window and we drove off, laughing.

My jewelry was dropped off at the Liquor Mart the next day.

The whole thing was simple, vintage Whitey. He'd calmly get the story, make a decision, and act with swiftness. As if he were a super-attentive CEO. Sometimes, though, it was more complicated than the jeweler screwing you.

I had a very serious problem one day with a guy, and this one wasn't so easy to cool.

One night, Paul Moore is giving me a ride home. We'd done a night of work, it's late. But I notice across the street this kid sitting in a car. I recognize him, despite the poor light. It's why you shouldn't wear the same fucking hat all the time. We called him "Darkman." Let's say he was dark Irish.

I say to Paul, "You know who that is right over there? He shouldn't be here. He's the guy who shot our friend in the leg. You remember."

"Not fuckin' Darkman?"

"The one," I say. "Well, I've got something for him." I pull out my nine-millimeter.

Paul says, "John, John, you need some help? Let me give you some help."

"No, no," I say, knowing that Paul isn't up for this kind of shit. Whitey told me, *Don't do anything anyone can hold over you.*

"You go," I tell Paul. "Now."

Paul's a nervous wreck as I load the weapon. "Let me help," he says. "I know this guy."

I say, "This motherfucker must be high on dust, and he's come to take me out. He thinks he's got balls."

Then Darkman rolls out of the parking lot with his headlights off.

"Go on, Paul. Go your own way. I'll take care of my own business. I'll just wait this motherfucker out."

"I'll help."

"No!" I finally shout, and get out of the car.

I go up to the apartment and turn on the light. I sit at the window and watch. Fifteen or so minutes later, Darkman returns. Parks in the same spot. Sits there.

I'm watching. I'm being like Whitey. I'm not acting hastily or in anger. I'm learning. I'm investigating, being intelligent. *What's this guy up to? Is he after me? If so, I got him in my scope. If so, of course I'll kill him.*

After five minutes the cars rolls out again.

I put on some coffee. This is getting good. I sit back down at the window and watch. I see him swing through the parking lot again, slow down, and then keep going. It's starting to snow. I see the flakes spitting though the cones of yellow from the streetlights. Darkman is a dead motherfucker.

I put on my gear—all black. Pants, jacket, gloves, black wool cap, black boots. Fuck the coffee.

And I went looking for him. As I'm driving by the D Street Deli, I see Kevin Weeks standing outside. He flags me down.

"What's up?" I say.

"Hey, how ya doin', John? Come here, Whitey's got Darkman. He's got him now."

I say, "What happened? How do you know? How the fuck do you know?"

Kevin says, "Paul came down and told us. Whitey's got him now."

Seems Paul had run down to the liquor store before it could close. It was just around the corner from where I was staying. Paul tells Kevin, *Red's out of his fuckin' mind. He's gonna shoot this fuckin' guy.* Kevin called Whitey, who was at one of his girlfriends' house.

Whitey said, *Let's go find this kid right now.*

So Kevin says to me, "Whitey's got him. And he wants you. You got a gun on you?"

"Nine-millimeter," I tell him.

"Leave it behind."

I don't tell him about the knife. No one mentioned a knife.

I see Theresa Stanley's white Pontiac come around the corner. Whitey's driving. Darkman is sitting next to him in the front seat.

"What the fuck is this?" I say to Kevin.

"Maybe somebody doesn't want you to kill some-fucking-body, John."

Me and Kevin get in the backseat. Kevin sits behind Jim. I sit behind Darkman. I wait for Whitey to speak. He speaks.

He says to Darkman, "Why were you sittin' out there in front of Red's place? You sitting on drugs or what?"

I notice the radio's not on. I guess Whitey figures his girlfriend's car is clean.

"You thinking of making fuckin' trouble for somebody?"

The kid cops an attitude. "I wasn't sittin' there waitin' for nothin'. I was drivin' around, and I parked. So fuckin' what?"

A tough guy, I figure. I know that his father knows Whitey, and maybe he thinks this gives him a free pass. Not with me. If I had my gun, I realize, Theresa Stanley would have a mess in her car.

But I didn't have my gun, thanks to Whitey. So I stayed very cool, calm, and collected. I just sat in the backseat and let him handle it. I could feel I was impressing him.

Then fuckin' Darkman turns around and says to me, "If I was sittin' for you and I was going to do something to you, you'd know about it. But I wasn't."

He turned back around and looked straight ahead, as if he has just proved something.

Since I had been addressed, I felt I could speak. I moved up close to his neck.

"Okay, then," I said. "Then that's good for you. We are done then, aren't we?"

From that, Whitey realized that the Angel of Death had just entered the car.

Whitey's head spun around, and he looked at me with his fuckin' cold blue eyes, and I looked straight back at him with mine. Then he turned to this kid Darkman and tore him a new asshole. "You fuck! This is my fuckin' friend, you fuckin' piece of shit! I'll blow your fuckin' brains out right now! I'll blow your brains out! You motherfucker . . ."

Whitey unleashed a fury at this kid that I can't even describe. It was incredible. He was nearly foaming. It was so intense that Darkman began to weep.

Then all was silent. Just the din of Whitey's rage ringing. Whitey hit the unlock button, and the kid flinched.

"Get the fuck out of here," said Whitey. And Darkman left with his tail between his legs.

I'm ready to go, too, but Whitey says, "John, stay with me."

And Whitey drives me and Kevin around for a while, to cool me down. Nothing is said for several minutes. During this time I realize that Whitey acted to keep this kid alive and me from murdering him. All in a night's work, I suppose. I felt good, though. I showed Whitey I could use restraint but that if a line was crossed, I would act.

Then Whitey spoke. "This kid wasn't waiting for you," he says. "Flemmi is fucking his girlfriend. She lives in Old Colony. That's what he was keepin' an eye out for."

I realized something else. What we'd found out that night was very good for Flemmi to know. Call it Whitey reconnaissance.

17

TURF

If you sold drugs on our turf, I would make you pay me back for not buying our product, and then you would have to buy only our product. One night I grabbed this guy selling drugs in Connolly's Café. I dragged him in the back of the bar and went absolutely crazy. "You motherfucker, I'll rip your fucking eyes out of your head! You don't sell in this fucking bar again unless you deal with me. Now you're going to have to pay me back for selling in here, and you only buy the product off me." The guy, almost in tears, replied, "Red, I'll buy the product off you, but I can't pay you any money. I don't have it."

Before he got out the last word, I smashed him across the face with a .38 revolver and put the barrel of the gun to the middle of his forehead. "I'll fucking kill you right here, you piece of shit." Jackie Mackie, one of my associates, grabbed me and pleaded nervously, "Red, don't go overboard with this one, please." I backed off, but the point was made. The guy came up with the money the next day.

Another time, in broad daylight, I grabbed a street dealer who was not part of our organization for dealing with one of my customers. I caught him on K Street and jumped out of my car. I hit him with a barrage of punches, ripping his face to shreds. Blood poured from gashes over both of his eyes onto the pavement. As he lay on the ground, I ripped his pockets open and took all his money. "You fucking piece of shit, if you ever try to steal my customer again, I'll fucking cut you up into small pieces!" The beating was interrupted by a passing cop car. I nonchalantly walked back to my maroon Lincoln LS and drove away.

I took my business very seriously. If someone tried to fuck me, I hunted them down. I learned this skill from one of the great predators of all time, Whitey. One of my street dealers owed me ten thousand dollars, and for a few months he wasn't paying up. I put out the word that I wanted my money and that he should come and see me. When he didn't come, I went hunting for him. I clocked him and knew all the places he hung out. I would park down the street from his house, where I could see him but he couldn't see me. I was always dressed in black jeans and a black shirt, wearing black Reebok running shoes, a black hat, and black gloves. Sometimes I sat there for hours, listening to the radio, listening to the police scanner, quietly waiting, patiently. In the gutter, halfway between where I was parked and this cocksucker's apartment, I had hidden a black wooden baseball bat.

I'm a very patient man when it comes to business. It was exciting, waiting like that. It was like a hunter waiting for the prey. I liked sitting there, knowing this guy was coming home soon.

I saw his car coming up the street and pull to the curb, about a hundred feet in front of me. I got out of the car casually and walked up the street. I bent down to pick up the baseball bat just as he was getting out of the car. Perfect timing. He glanced back at me, but nothing registered. I walked up to him, head down, bat tucked behind my leg, until I was right next to him. Just as he was stepping onto the sidewalk, I hit him right across his face with the bat. It was the same loud crack I heard years ago in front of Billy's Pizza during the busing trouble.

I didn't say a word. I just hit him. He moaned and put his hands to his face. I hit him again in the back of his head. He fell to his knees. I hit him three or four more times in the ribs. I left him lying in the gutter.

He had not uttered a word. I called that "the ten-thousand-dollar beating." It was worth every penny.

How would it look? Some guy owes me ten grand and he's not paying me back? Now everybody would think they could do it. That's not good for business. The point was made. He was out of business for good.

Sometimes it wasn't just straightening out someone outside the crew. There were times I had to make a point with some of my own guys, my own friends. One day I was on my way to New York. I was in a hurry, as I had to catch a flight. I stopped in to see Paul Moore for a minute at the deli. As soon as I walked in the store, Paul was complaining to me that one of my guys was selling in a place where one of his guys was selling. This particular guy was a real hustler and making a ton of money for me. Paul was whining that the guy was in his area and that it was hurting his business. I told him that I would have the guy move out of that place. But Paul didn't accept that. He kept pushing it. "Fuck him. Why should he be selling and making all that money?" He didn't want the guy to move; he wanted him out of business.

"Listen, Paul," I say. "I'll have him move, but he is one of my guys and he is not going to stop doing business." He obviously didn't like what I had to say.

"I'm not afraid of you," he says, and moves toward me. I immediately move forward until I am no more than six inches from his face. I look him dead in his eyes.

"Remember this, Paul. I'm definitely not afraid of *you*." As I say it, I can see the fear in his eyes.

"Oh, yeah?" is all he can think to say.

"Yeah, that's right. Now I have to go to New York, but I'll be back in a few days, and we'll straighten this shit out."

I cut my trip to New York short and came back that same night. The next morning, just before 6:00 A.M., I'm sitting out in front of the deli and waiting for Paul to open the store. I'm dressed all in black, all strapped up for business. I'm not mad about business or the money. I'm out of my mind because this friend of mine is trying to bull me, intimidate me, because he is a greedy and jealous fuck.

As I'm sitting in the car waiting for Paul to open up, I remember a story Whitey told me. Whitey was talking to this guy, and the guy was getting angry and clenched his fists. By the mere act of clenching his fists, Whitey explained, this guy was never going to be able to clench his fists again. Paul was clenching his fist to me, and he was going to have to beg or he was going to meet the same fate.

As I walk into the store, Paul looks up, sees me all dressed in black, and I can tell he is terrified. All the color drains from his face, and he gets grayish white in a matter of seconds.

Timidly, almost childlike, he says, "Can I please talk to you?"

"No. You are going to listen to me. You disrespect me? You're supposed to be my friend. I am in control now, so this friendship is over. Because you made your choice and made that move, you sealed your fate. I am going kill you right here, right now, motherfucker."

Paul sits down on a box in the rear of the store. He starts to weep.

"I know," he says. "I don't know why I did it. I'm sorry."

I had no more problems with Pole Cat Moore.

18

I-95

Tom Cahill was a well-groomed guy, with gray hair and a good charisma to him. He'd look right at home in a betting parlor with a copy of the *Racing Form*, which is just where he could often be found. Cahill was a Southie native and had been involved in this and that. A friend of Tommy Connors. He was older than me, old enough to be my father, God forbid, but he had some great old stories. I liked him. He was good company, good enough to take long trips to Florida with. Tom became my driver.

I now had a lot of cash to carry down, a lot of weight to carry back. Airplanes were out. You couldn't hide that much shit around your waist, and you couldn't carry a gun through an airport. I knew we'd have to haul. I met with Cahill down by Castle Island. We got coffee and doughnuts at the stand there and took a walk.

"Listen," I told him, "this is what we're going to do. We drive down to Florida. I'll give you seven grand to drive down and back with me. Each time. Sometimes you'll drive down alone and drive me back, depending. I'll provide the car. If things work out, I'll get you a car."

Cahill had a job with the state water authority. He said he'd have no trouble working around that. He had plenty of vacation and an in with the superintendent.

"I like the sun," he said, though he looked like he'd never had a tan in his life.

We would drive to the Fort Lauderdale area all the way down I-95 basically, about an eighteen-hour trip. We'd then leave the Massachusetts-plated car—whether my BMW or the Town Car I later bought him—and rent a small vehicle with Florida plates and drive on down to Miami.

I'd make a phone call to set it up. "Hi, how are you doing? It's John."

"Hey, John. How are you?"

"Good. I'm going to be coming down in about a week or so, all right, buddy?"

"Yeah. Yeah, things are pretty good, you know. Hopefully I get to run some mileage down there."

"That's good, man. I'm looking for six or seven of those Michelins. Whaddya say?"

At first I still had only my Tony Montana connection, but I had to make the most of it. Part of the reason Whitey had taken me on and told Mickey O to beat it was that I had a better connection than they had. Let's face it. Of course Whitey liked the way I handled myself and thought he could trust me. And he wasn't wrong. But it was connections I was bringing to the table, and that would be the source of my control. So until I could do better, I had to work with my Tony Montana.

The organization would fund the trips. I'd take a hundred grand or so usually, though sometimes double that. Before heading out, I'd put twenties together until I had a thousand, wrap it in rubber bands. Then individual stacks of thousands and block 'em in stacks of ten and wrap them and then wrap them again in stacks of ten and you got one hundred grand U.S. And so on. And then put it all in a gym bag.

I'd tell Tom to drive carefully but not too slowly. Slow's as bad as fast. "Drive about seventy, seventy-five, and look out for speeding cars coming up on you—usually they're the troopers. Troopers are always goin' eighty, ninety.

We have money going down, and we'll have product coming back." I say to him, "Dress neat, casual, like a professor or a guy who just walked off the golf course. I'll be like your son, kind of collegiate. 'Hey, son.' 'Yes, Dad.' "

One time I saw Weeks pull up to the liquor store in his wife's car. There was a baby seat in the back. I thought, who would ever suspect what this guy's involved in, with that baby seat in the back? I told Cahill to go buy a baby seat and get some Pampers as well, like a fuckin' grand-dad. We put these in the backseat.

"Should I get a bottle, too?" he asked.

I appreciated his enthusiasm for the chore, but I said, "No, we don't need no baby bottles, Tommy."

"I was always partial to the breast anyway," he says after a few beats. Funny guy.

Of course we got stopped, both coming and going. But it was never me who got stopped, although I did plenty of the driving. Cahill used to complain, "How the fuck do you do it? You can speed and get away with it. But I do it and I get fuckin' pulled over."

We went over it beforehand. Delaware and the Carolinas are the toughest spots. Cops all over looking for something to do. If we get stopped, I told him, "Stay loose and relax. If some cop is overly suspicious or has some bug up his ass attitude-wise, be extra careful. Wear your ma-rine ring," I told him. "Can't hurt down near Camp Lejeune. Can't hurt anywhere. If they ask us to get out of the car, we can't just sit there. You hit the gas and get ahead and let me jump out. I'll run with the fucking money and bury it—and the gun. If they tell you to turn off the car, don't take the keys out of the ignition. If he tells you to take the keys out of the ignition, he's gonna ask you to get out of the car. Step on it."

"Suppose it's on the way back?" asks Cahill.

"I run with the coke if it's light. I'm not running with fuckin' fifteen kilos, though, but we run anyway. We leave it. Let them prove we knew about it."

"But they need a warrant to search the car," he says. "Why run?"

"If they want to search the car, they arrest us. They don't need no reason. So you fuckin' step on it."

One evening we're on a tight schedule, and we're in the Carolinas, on our way back. Fourteen kilos in the trunk. We'd been down there too long— several days while Tony fuckin' Montana scrambled around to fill my order. I'd have to do something about him. So we were in a hurry. I don't want to keep my customers waiting. They can go elsewhere. Or my partners. They're up there in Boston scratching their asses, waiting for shit. So I spell Cahill on the drive. I want to move.

In a more leisurely scenario, we wouldn't drive at night. You are fucking conspicuous at night, more likely to run into rookie cops on the overnight shift, who are a little too eager to get some action. Better in the day, with all the working folks, moms and truck drivers. But tonight we're balling it up through the old Confederacy in the dead of night. We're driving my BMW, 3 series, four-door. We have the baby paraphernalia in the back. I'd just turned over the driving to him. We'd stopped for gas and a snack, and now I was gonna snooze. We hadn't been back on the road for more than a couple of miles, and we hear the *whoop-whoop* and the burst of the cherrytop. *Holy shit.*

"Just relax," I tell Cahill. "Relax, slow down, pull over. Don't do anything. Say hello. Say, 'What's the problem?' Say, 'Hey, son.' And I'll get the registration."

"Son?"

"Yeah, Dad?" I act all groggy.

"Can you get the registration out of the glove compartment for me?" Now Cahill starts to get chatty with the trooper.

"That's my son," he clarifies to the trooper, whose flashlight is beaming around the car.

I hand him the registration.

"Thanks, son," he says.

Then, of all things, he says to the trooper, "Mind if I get out of the car, Officer, and stretch?"

I wonder what the hell Cahill is doing. I told him to relax, not try for an Academy Award.

"Stay in," I say to him. "Dad . . ."

The trooper says, "No, I don't mind. Stretch 'em."

"Thanks, Officer."

Cahill's into it now.

"My wife had to fly home with the baby," he says. "The baby got sick. So we flew her home instead of drive."

Now I see what he's up to. He's trying to beat the ticket.

The coke's in the back, there's a gun in the bag at my feet. I don't want to shoot a trooper. I try to relax, let it play out.

Then I see the officer has a marine ring on. I can see it backlit by the flashlight.

Next thing you know, they're talking about boot camp.

I decide to sit this one out.

I hear the trooper talking in a rounding-it-up fashion, and I hear a sheet of paper tear. "Frankly," he says, "I wouldn't do this to you, knowing that you're a marine and you're on your way home to your wife and everything. But my supervisor was the one who clocked you, so I have to go forward with the ticket."

When Cahill gets back in the car and we head off, all I can say is, "Dad, grow up."

We had a good laugh. And I have to say, whatever he did, it worked. Fifteen hours later we were in Boston, cutting the coke.

We did this trip about once a month. That's when I started enduring more heat, because now I was one of the players and they knew who the players were, the big players, and they knew the connection was to

Whitey. All of a sudden, here's a new guy on the block. The agents, the police. I knew that they were all looking at us at that time, because of the information that was being fed back to us. Whitey had his connections in law enforcement, that's all we knew. We had no idea of the extent of it. Only he and Flemmi had the FBI connection in John Connolly, but it's not like we didn't all benefit from it, because we did.

I started making about fifteen thousand dollars to twenty thousand dollars a week. That's a lot of money every month for a guy who's only about twenty-one years of age, who quit school in tenth grade. But to keep it going, I knew I had to move past Montana. And since he had friends that he used when his supplier couldn't fill my order, I started paying attention to them. Eventually I met this one guy, Jesús Nodarse, and he was so unlike Tony Montana and such a pleasure to be around, I thought, This is my guy. In many ways he was your typical Cuban—kind of curly hair, dark, with dark eyes, a medium build. Not fat, not skinny. Just like Montana, except that where Montana was a wild man, Nodarse was a gentleman. He lived with his wife. He was easygoing, a nice trait in a drug dealer. One time I'm at this house as Montana tries to play catch-up on a big order by going to Nodarse. I tell Nodarse, "You know, I'd love to get away from this fuckin' guy." He nodded, didn't say anything but left the door open.

Next time I'm down there, I remember the route to his house from Montana's. Me and Cahill go and pay him a visit.

"I'd like to do business with you strictly. This other guy's a little too fuckin' crazy, so to speak. A little too nuts. Unpredictable. Fuckin' too much, drawing heat."

"What's the problem with Jerry?" he says.

I tell him I hate the Tony Montana stuff.

"I know," he says. "Not good for the long term, *no?*"

I say, "For the long-term fuckin' jail sentence, *sí!*"

Nodarse says, "Absolutely. But suppose he finds out, eh? What then?"

"How's he going to find out, unless you tell him?" I say.

"Hmm." He thinks about it for a few seconds. "Yes, absolutely. Business."

That's when we started doing business with each other on a regular basis, me and Jesús Nodarse. It was such a pleasure to go to his house and relax and not have a fuckin' scene going on. It was a funny joint, very modest. No pool parties and coked-up strangers coming through. In fact, the noisiest element was the roosters he kept in his backyard. Jesús was into cockfighting. I suppose it was a step back to be woken by roosters at dawn rather than Tony Montana's daughter, but the trade-off was worth it. It was a good connection. And it worked for a long time. Till our luck ran out and I no longer felt so good about Jesús Nodarse.

It was summertime, and me and Cahill were down there to make a pickup at Nodarse's. He didn't have it, which wasn't all that unusual. It happened from time to time that we had to wait on a portion of our order. This time I had changed things up. Cahill and I drove to Orlando and then rented a car there. I had bought a house there, with Tommy Connors. Paid eighty thousand dollars cash for it, a nice place on the St. Johns River, where Tommy could fish for his bass and I could crash on occasion. Of course I thought I'd vacation a little there but never did. It was a workstation for me. We left the Town Car back at the house and drove into Miami. We show up, and Jesús says, "We're going to go to a friend's house. My source is dry."

"Okay," I say. As we pull out of his driveway in the Lincoln, a pickup truck pulls up in front of us and stops. I looked in the rearview mirror, and another car has pulled right up behind me, right in the middle of a residential neighborhood, in broad daylight, blocked in on a side street. It's me, Cahill, and Nodarse in the car. "What the fuck's going on here, Jesús?" And then blue lights come on in the vehicle in back. And then guys jump out with guns pointed at us—shotguns, pump shotguns—and one of them says, "Don't fuckin' move, and get out of the car."

"It's the fuckin' law," I say. So I get out of the car. There's no place to run, not with four shotguns on us. Worse comes to worst, I'm out the money. Otherwise we're clean. The gun's a problem, but the laws are lenient on guns in Florida.

But these guys are aggressive. "Get the fuck out of the car, now!"

These guys are Spanish. Can that be right? Something seems wrong here. They search the car, quickly, silently.

Cahill and I have a shotgun trained on us as we stand on some Cuban lady's lawn watching three guys pore over our little rented Nissan.

My bag's in the car. We stand there in the Miami midmorning. It's already hot and getting hotter. I can feel the sweat running down my chest, but I have to remain cool and think.

Cahill comes up with, "What the fuck's going on? You can't be doing—"

"Shut your fuckin' mouth," says the gaucho behind us before I can say it. I hear him cock the pump action. "I'll fucking blow you away," he says for emphasis.

I look at Cahill. My eyes say, *Cool it!*

My wheels are turning now. I realize that we're not being arrested, we're being fuckin' robbed. I look at Jesús, standing next to me. *Jesús fucking Nodarse, you set me up, you cocksucker.*

I don't say any of that. But that's my line of thinking.

How did these fucking cowboys know we were coming down here at this time with all this money—two hundred grand? Usually I'd keep half in the hotel and half on me and carry it off in two transactions. That way it might keep someone from doing something like this. But I'd been with Jesus for so long, so many times, I got fuckin' careless. But then I made my resolve. *Stay cool, this ain't the law. They just want the money, fair enough. But somebody is gonna pay. What we don't want is to be sitting on this Cuban lady's lawn with holes in us.*

They finish with their search. They return to their vehicles. The guy with the gun on us makes us sit down on the lawn and then walks to our car and gets behind the wheel. All three drive off.

Tynan Community School Gymnasium in South Boston, South Boston Boxing
Show. I was seven. I won the fight by decision. It was 1972.

"Little Red" Shea
In a "Special Bout" of the evening at 106 pounds, "Little Red" Shea representing Connolly's Gym met and defeated Ramon Morales of Haverhill. After catching just about every combination "Little Red" threw, Morales was unable to answer the bell for round two. "Little Red" truly avenged his previous loss of two weeks ago - he traded in "our confidence" for Wisdom, Knowledge of the pursuit of Victory. Congratulations to "Little Red" and Tommy Connors, Trainer and Manager of this splendid young prospect.

"Little Red" Shea of South Boston - 106 lb. finalist.
On December 3rd, tonight at 8:00 p.m., at Freeport Hall, Little "Red" Shea will be fighting for the 106 pound New England Championship.

My first headlines, to be followed years later by my arrest. *Left:* I was fifteen years old and 106 pounds at the time. It was 1980. I won this bout by a knockout in the first round in a local amateur tournament. *Above:* This bout was held at Freeport Hall in Dorchester, Massachusetts It was the New England Amateur Championship Tournament. I was sixteen years old and won.

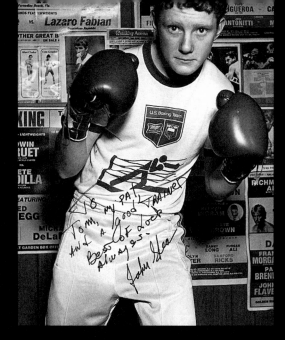

My professional promo photograph taken in Connolly's Gym, South Boston. I was eighteen.

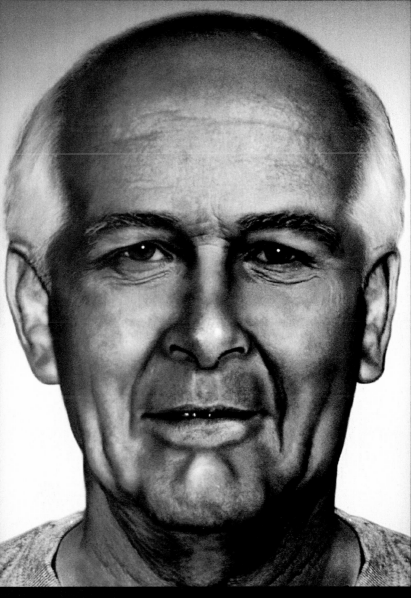

Legendary Irish mob king James "Whitey" Bulger has been on the FBI's Ten Most Wanted List since 1999. Here is a digitally enhanced photograph that suggests what the South Boston mafioso would look like today. A $1 million reward is still being offered for information leading to his arrest. I was considered his protégé and served more than ten years of hard time—refusing to rat—while my former "mentor" remains on the run. *Jessica Rinaldi/Reuters/Corbis*

FBI TEN MOST WANTED FUGITIVE

RACKETEERING INFLUENCED AND CORRUPT ORGANIZATIONS (RICO) - MURDER (18 COUNTS), CONSPIRACY TO COMMIT MURDER, CONSPIRACY TO COMMIT EXTORTION, NARCOTICS DISTRIBUTION, CONSPIRACY TO COMMIT MONEY LAUNDERING; EXTORTION; MONEY LAUNDERING

JAMES J. BULGER

Photograph taken in 1994   Photograph taken in 1994   Photograph retouched in 2000

Aliases: Thomas F. Baxter, Mark Shapeton, Jimmy Bulger, James Joseph Bulger, James J. Bulger, Jr., James Joseph Bulger, Jr., Tom Harris, Tom Marshall, "Whitey"

DESCRIPTION

Date of Birth:	September 3, 1929	**Hair:**	White/Silver
Place of Birth:	Boston, Massachusetts	**Eyes:**	Blue
Height:	5' 7" to 5' 9"	**Complexion:**	Light
Weight:	150 to 160 pounds	**Sex:**	Male
Build:	Medium	**Race:**	White
Occupation:	Unknown	**Nationality:**	American
Scars and Marks:	None known		

Remarks: Bulger is an avid reader with an interest in history. He is known to frequent libraries and historic sites. Bulger is currently on the heart medication Atenolol (50 mg) and maintains his physical fitness by walking on beaches and in parks with his female companion, Catherine Elizabeth Greig. Bulger and Greig love animals and may frequent animal shelters. Bulger has been known to alter his appearance through the use of disguises. He has traveled extensively throughout the United States, Europe, Canada, and Mexico.

CAUTION

JAMES J. BULGER IS BEING SOUGHT FOR HIS ROLE IN NUMEROUS MURDERS COMMITTED FROM THE EARLY 1970s THROUGH THE MID-1980s IN CONNECTION WITH HIS LEADERSHIP OF AN ORGANIZED CRIME GROUP THAT ALLEGEDLY CONTROLLED EXTORTION, DRUG DEALS, AND OTHER ILLEGAL ACTIVITIES IN THE BOSTON, MASSACHUSETTS, AREA. HE HAS A VIOLENT TEMPER AND IS KNOWN TO CARRY A KNIFE AT ALL TIMES.

CONSIDERED ARMED AND EXTREMELY DANGEROUS

IF YOU HAVE ANY INFORMATION CONCERNING THIS PERSON, PLEASE CONTACT YOUR LOCAL FBI OFFICE OR THE NEAREST U.S. EMBASSY OR CONSULATE.

REWARD

The FBI is offering a $1,000,000 reward for information leading directly to the arrest of James J. Bulger.

www.fbi.gov

August 1999
Poster Revised November 2000

Still on the loose and still on the lam along with Osama Bin Laden. James "Whitey" Bulger's current Most Wanted poster. *Courtesy of www.fbi.gov*

Billy Bulger, brother of Whitey, worked the other side of the street as the politically powerful president of the Massachusetts State Senate from 1978 to 1996, all during his infamous sibling's reign as arguably the most notorious Irish American mob boss of the twentieth century. Billy Bulger still lives in Boston, while the whereabouts of his gangster brother remain unknown to this day.
Rick Friedman/Corbis

Me and acclaimed East Coast mob lawyer Tony Cardinale at a party at Tony's house in Duxbury, Massachusetts, celebrating my release from federal prison and Tony's birthday. It was August of 2002.

Me and my top confidant, Fran Hurley. Taken at my apartment in Boston, New Year's Day, 2006.

Me and Mark Wahlberg on the set of *Departed* on location in New York, July 2005. Wahlberg has optioned the movie rights to *Rat Bastards* and wrote the introduction for this book.

The Cuban lady says, "Get off my fuckin' lawn," and goes into her house. We're a block and a half from Nodarse's house. We walk back. My mind's fuckin' rolling. Cahill's just goin', "Aww, you know . . ."

I say, "Tom, just shut the fuck up for a minute and let me think. With you, your babbling on doesn't help."

I was enraged, but I had to control it. There's a time and place for everything, but now wasn't the time or the place.

We walk pretty much in silence to Nodarse's. We get inside, where it is cool and dark.

"Jesús, my friend. Let's just review what the fuck happened here."

I get a lot of Spanish-accented bullshit from him. But it's still *boolsheet*.

"No, Jesús. What happened is this: You don't have the product. We go to a friend of yours. We get fuckin' hijacked right outside your door, and four fuckin' Cubans drive away with my money, my gun, and my car. That's what happened. And I want to know what you are gonna do about it."

Nodarse is a fucking nervous wreck. His wife comes in. "Sit down, *por favor*," she says to all of us.

I'm not sitting down, I am standing and shouting. I'm fucking ready to kill someone, truthfully.

We're standing in his living room. It is still early morning. I can hear roosters fucking around out back. If I had my gun, I'd go shoot the motherfucker's roosters, just to make a point. He's lucky his wife isn't better-looking. I'm that hot.

"I don't know," says Jesús, "maybe my friend—the guy I thought was my friend. I told him you were coming at this time. Maybe it was him, and they waited."

"Interesting," I said. It's plausible. But I don't know if I believe it.

"How about this, Jesús? How about you told him about me, how I was carrying all the cash this time, how you've been waiting for this fucking mistake! And you set the whole motherfucking thing up! How about that?"

Cahill is fucking mad now. I don't need this. Cahill's mad, and he wants to do something. I don't need him doin' something. "Tom, sit down," I say. "We need to fuckin' think out what happened here and why it went this way first." Then I tell Jesús to leave us alone.

Jesús and his wife leave the room. I can hear them arguing in the kitchen. She is trying to be soothing, but Jesús is too scared and nervous to be soothed. There is shit crashin' in there.

I say to Tom, "This guy definitely has something to do with it, one way or another. Whether he did it intentionally or unintentionally. And guess what? Someone's going to pay. Jesús is all we got. We ain't even got wheels. We ain't got two hundred G's, we got no gun. We ain't got shit."

I think, All we got is Jesús.

I call him in.

"I swear to God I didn't set you up, John. I swear."

"Are you fuckin' sure? I think you fuckin' did."

I look at him for a long time. I look at him with these cold eyes. I tell him I'll kill him—kill him and his fuckin' friend, too.

He swore up and down more bullshit. He said, "I swear to God, John, I didn't do it. I swear I would never do that to you. We've done too much business together. Why would I do that? I didn't have the supply, and I was reaching out to people. Yes, yes"—he said it like *Jas, Jas*—"I did tell them, 'My people are coming down here Saturday ten o'clock.' They said, 'Will they have the money?' 'Yes,' I said, 'my people will have the money.' I said that, John. I am sorry. *Lo siento.* Please!"

I realize that this might be true. I've been fucked, but this guy's been fucked, too. But without Jesús I don't recoup nothing, no chance. And if I whack him—I'd have to do something—all I've got is a dead body on my hands. And a witness. Two dead bodies. No. Jesús is going to collect it. He's gonna make it right.

I decided right there this was the last time I was dealing with Jesús. And leaned into him. I leaned into him hard. I told him we're going to go and we're going to go to his friend's house and I'm going to kill his friend and he's comin' with me.

I said, "Jesús, you know I don't give a fuck. Now, give me a weapon. I believe I need that Uzi I've seen here."

And so we took a ride by that guy's house—where we were heading to do the transaction before we got fucking waylaid—and there were a lot of people around there—cars and people. Not a good time. Numbers. So we left. And I thought about it.

Jesús drove us around. We got on a highway, and he drove so slow I thought we'd roll to a stop.

I told him now that he had made this fuckin' mistake, he needed to correct it. Otherwise he was going to be corrected. And I let him know that I wasn't alone. I let him know that I was with Whitey and that our arms reached very far. And he was scared. He was definitely scared.

"Let me take care of it," he said. He didn't sound confident.

We went back to his place. Tom and I went out back and tossed corn at the roosters, who didn't give a shit. Jesús made phone calls, lots of phone calls. And so he went out and came back and made some more phone calls and came back again. His wife made us lunch, which we didn't want. But she insisted, and Tom and I picked at it, to be nice. I realized that Jesús had nothing to do with it.

"You have any children?" I asked her.

"No," she said nervously.

"Good," I said, laughing, and Cahill laughed, too. We were twisting it in.

In the end Jesús scrounged up four kilos. I came for fifteen kilos, I had the money for fifteen kilos, and I got four.

"I bought this," said Jesús. "But you can take it and cut it and sell it. Just pay me back when you can."

"Sure," I say to him.

I know he ain't getting nothing. And he knows: These four, cut and on the street—admittedly heavily stepped on—will get me back what I lost. It ain't no business to do—all that work to sell four just to make your money back—but that's the best I could get out of it. It wasn't a total loss. I took the deal.

Jesús was relieved. He and his wife drove me and Cahill all the way back to Orlando. He said he was sorry. He wished me luck.

That's the last business drug deal I ever did with Jesús Nodarse, though I did call him from Boston to tell him he gave me garbage, complete garbage. That he was a fuckin' punk and that I better never see his fuckin' face again. I *would* see his face again, years later, in a different setting. And we'd play a game of poker.

19

COMMITMENT

I gave Penelope a diamond engagement ring, but I never asked her to marry me. Not because I didn't love her, not because we didn't get along or weren't perfect for each other, not because of her mother, who was great, or my family, who didn't really get involved or matter. But because I knew I couldn't give her what she wanted.

Her girlfriends were getting engaged and getting married, and I saw what she wanted. I wanted to give it to her, to give her everything she ever wanted. We were at my apartment in South Boston, near Thomas Park. We were lying in bed after making love. I was holding her against me, and I told her I had a surprise for her. I told her to close her eyes, and I put a ring box in her hand. She opened her eyes and saw the box. She opened it and broke out in a smile of complete joy. A three-carat diamond ring.

She had tears running down her face. She looked at me and said, "Oh, my God, what is this?"

I said, "You know what this is for."

"What?" she said.

"You know what it's for."

"What?" she said again.

It became our little joke. She was ecstatic, hugging me, kissing me.

At that moment, despite all that happiness, I had a feeling of sadness come over me. I knew that I could never marry this girl and continue to live the life I was living. I knew I wanted to, but reality has a way of overcoming dreams.

What did Penelope want? She wanted what almost every young woman wants—true love, a nice life, a good husband, caring, respectable, strong, protective; and she wanted children, children she would raise with that husband, with me. Kids who looked like us. They'd have been a wonderful mix, me with my red hair and Irish looks, Penelope dark and Italian. Beautiful kids. But we never went there, we never talked about kids' names or places to live or schools we'd send them to or how I'd teach our son to throw a baseball or our daughter to drive a car one day. None of that. I couldn't give her any of that.

I could, of course, but I wouldn't. Although I loved Penelope more than any person I have ever known, I had already made my choice, and I loved something even more: being a gangster.

But it wasn't just some romantic notion—being a gangster. It was more of a calculation than that. I loved everything about it. The money, the excitement, the power—it was at times as powerful a high as any drug could ever provide.

Later I would learn it firsthand, but I already knew it—that to have children is to make the potential for pain more than one can bear. In prison I witnessed no suffering like that of a man who saw his kids on a visit and then saw them leave. Little crying faces, little kids holding their mother's hand walking out of the visiting room. Some of these guys were devastated. Grown men, tough fuckin' guys, fighting back tears, smiling and waving good-bye but dying inside. You can't help but cry for the innocent. And what's more innocent than kids?

I say I knew this already, but how? From Whitey, who had no kids, who had no wives, who had nothing but the cold focus of a real top-level fuckin' mobster. This guy was the ultimate in seriousness. Everything he did was calculated to advance his cause and not compromise it. He would go to any lengths—any lengths, as it turned out—to do that. Having a wife, having a kid, no way.

Sure, everything might be fine if the law didn't get you. But if the law got you, they knew how to work it—the wife-and-kids angle. They work on your guilt, they work on your sense of being a man, they do everything they can to make you turn, talk, flip, inform. They can take something as beautiful as loyalty to family and use it to make you into a rat.

I knew. I knew from growing up on the streets, from how I was taught, that when you get into the ring, you don't quit, and when you get into a life of crime, you don't rat, ever. It doesn't matter what's at stake or what the reward. They can make the stakes the highest—your dignity or your life. And you have the choice, you can choose. It is up to you. Do you want to have your life—and your wife and kids and fresh air—or do you want to have your self-respect? Go ahead. Take your time. Sit in that cell and give it a think.

And I always knew what my choice would be. I would not choose life, I would not choose Penelope, I would not choose our kids. I had already chosen. In a way I was already spoken for. That doesn't mean I didn't do everything I could to protect Penelope. It means I refused to marry her because of my chosen life. In my mind to bring a wife and kids into this life was unfair and selfish. Dragging them through the turmoil of the life is just something I wouldn't do. I never wanted to have my wife and kids visiting with me in jail. Sitting in that visiting room with hundreds of other families, wondering if Daddy will ever be coming home. Shedding tears every time the visit ended.

Whitey was right about the way he lived. He never married because he did not want a wife or children, which would have made him vulnerable. In Whitey's life everyone was temporary and expendable. Nothing to tie him down. When he needed to go, he took off.

That's extreme, I know. But it's the choice I made and the life I led. Mistake or not.

20

INNER CIRCLE

Whitey wanted it all, and that was his downfall in the end. Of course I thought I wanted to be Whitey. I wanted to be the boss, and I knew I was learning from the best. He could read people like a brilliant psychologist. He'd gotten to the top by understanding who to befriend, who to betray. You make a mistake there and you're dead. But he survived. He ruled. He survived the federal penitentiary system, and he worked his way up, gang to gang, till he was the king.

He knew how to chose the people to do his work. He tabbed Weeks because he could serve as muscle and he could follow orders. Whitey entrusted him with the dirtiest work. He chose Flemmi because he knew that Flemmi was ruthless and was protected—Flemmi had his own FBI handler. He chose Kevin O'Neil because he needed legit businesses run by a legitimate guy. He chose me because he knew I was loyal and ballsy and could not be intimidated. He chose his women because they were blond, his cars because they were nondescript, his turf because it was home. But because he wanted it all, he went too far. He wanted to take the Mafia out, so he partnered with Connolly and the FBI to do it. He was willing to cooperate in order to have it all. He was willing to violate the code of the street, of Southie, in order to get what he wanted—the

ultimate protection for himself. Whitey would do no more time. He was
a rat in the end, and rats are greedy. And now the rat has been running
for over a decade.

I'm not saying Whitey didn't try to protect us some. He told me to be
careful on the phone, to be careful about the cars I was in, the places I
went, how I dressed, what I drove, how I acted. But as a guy who was
playing both sides, and playing them well, he had to act like he was on
my side. It was in his interest.

I remember Whitey going down at night to Castle Island all by himself to meet someone. There were rumors that John Connolly was his guy
and that he would get good FBI information from Connolly. There were
definitely rumors. Did I know that firsthand? No. Did I think that
Whitey might be getting information that no one else had? Of course.
He always knew things that no one else knew. He knew that the state police were trying to bug the Lancaster Street garage, which prompted his
takeover of the liquor store. He knew when his car was bugged. He saw
angles that no one else could see, like the time he became a "partner" in
a winning lottery ticket that happened to be sold at his variety store.
Whitey could get a piece of *your* pie if he wanted it.

I'd meet with him down at Castle Island. We'd walk around the fort
and talk business, out of reach, he said, of the parabolic mikes the cops
had set up somewhere I never knew. There were always guys taking pictures, but pictures couldn't indict you. Tapes could.

There are guys, when I think back on it, that Whitey told me to be
careful around. Guys in our own crew. He didn't say they were rats, but
he seemed to sense those who could turn. John, he said, be very careful.
And I fuckin' was too young to realize it. *Be careful when someone tries to
drag you into something,* he said. *Never do anything that someone could hold
over your head for the rest of your life.*

I'm saying to myself, What's he mean by that? I figured it out: Don't murder someone in front of a witness. Anyone who ever says I murdered someone doesn't know what he's talking about. I never did anything like that. I take care of my own business, my own self, by myself, just like Whitey said. Whitey was telling me a good truth—he was giving me such vital information, great information, but look at him. He didn't follow his own advice. He took out people, plenty of people, with Flemmi and others. He had Weeks move bodies with him. He thought he had it all, thought he was covered. But he wasn't. John Connolly wasn't God. Whitey's mistake was killing other people with other people. He fucked himself.

Let's get this straight. Whitey was like a godfather. He didn't get involved in the day-to-day; he didn't want to be. He didn't want to be seen with me or most of the crew. He saw the two Kevins as needed but was seldom seen with Flemmi and only occasionally with me. I was hot, of course, handling lots of cash and product. After a while I managed my own financing and gave appropriately, through various avenues. Whitey knew I was an earner, a big earner, but I was handling narcotics, and the FBI couldn't call all the shots when it came to narcotics trafficking. There was a little thing called the DEA. Whitey couldn't control everything.

My daily routine: Penelope would call me at around ten from work and get me up. We'd talk, maybe arrange to have dinner later. *I'm just waking up, baby. How are you?* and all that. *Good,* she'd say. *You just waking up now?* I'd say, *Yeah, yeah, yeah, baby. Workin' hard.*

Then I'd read the paper—the *Boston Herald,* hardly ever the *Globe.* The *Globe* is just too much of fuckin' pull this paper out, pull that section out. I'd rather just go through the rag, so to speak. Read it front to back—sports first, then look for people I knew on the front page. I liked it when I knew no one. And then I'd do my training. I'd definitely train every fucking day. There wasn't a day I didn't train. For my health, yes, and because I needed to stay on top of my game because of the life I lived and the life I was involved in. I needed it because I knew that a challenge could come at any time, and you had to be ready. Some guy'd be high on drugs or drinking too much and try to take you out. Or they'd think I was too small, small enough to push around, and they'd push their fuckin' luck. Or maybe somebody'd be short of the cash or try to fuck me over or give me some kind of shit or another. I had to be primed, ready.

I'd work out in the morning, do my six or so miles, play racquetball, shower. I'd have my protein drink. Take my amino acids. Vitamins E, C. I'd take lunch at K Street Deli or at Joseph's Deli, or I'd eat in my car, down at the beach—Castle Beach or down to Castle Island—Pleasure Bay. The Lagoon. Meanwhile I'd call my fuckin' guys, like Jackie Mackie and Walter Bagley. *What's up? How ya doing? Anybody call in? Anybody call you?* If I didn't get a call, they would get a call for a delivery or something like that—or to pick up money. *Did you do this? Did you do that?* I'd check in with them. I might talk to Penelope again, see how her day was going, and then I'd check in with Weeks at Triple O's or into the variety store when Whitey was around in late afternoon. I'd drive by, see if their cars were there first. If yes, then I'd stop and I'd go in, either the liquor store or the rotary store. Whatever store they were in at the time.

In the store is where you might see any kind of Whitey, you never knew. He could be the most charming, funny, smart person you've ever met. He could be gentle, playing with his dog, say, or even talking tenderly about one of his women, Theresa or Catherine or the little blonde he had on the side-side. He could tease you like the greatest coach you ever had; he could teach you a lesson with the gentlest reminder. He could tell you things without humiliating you or surprise you with a nice story about some old-timer he took care of who needed a break and was somehow funny enough to deserve it. Or he could be like a thunderhead, he could be like some Old Testament Judgment Day bolt thrower. Whitey could enter a room and the temperature would drop; I swear, the lights would dim. It would grow dark. His moods were as violent as the worst crashing, thrashing weather—and all done with words, that was the amazing thing. Talk about the power of words. If there was a guy in there who made a mistake—and I'd seen a few—he could make the guy shit his pants. Literally. No joke. As he did with the guy holding out on him for something or other—collecting a debt, I believe, that Whitey had covered for the guy. Whitey reams him a new asshole, verbally.

I'll kill you, you motherfucker. I'll fucking pluck your eyes out, how's that? Whitey would be in the guy's face, spitting all over him, his breath hot on him and bad, and you better not flinch, because Whitey had a reputation. He was a very serious fuckin' guy, so everyone knew this wasn't all talk. Everyone knew that people had disappeared.

Of course it's now well documented, how Whitey and Flemmi had meetings with their main FBI guy Connolly and another fed, John Morris. Connolly and Morris were so in love with Whitey and his power that the two of them were played by Whitey, rather than the other way around. People are attracted to royalty, and Whitey was king. Let's face it, these guys were gumshoes. Whitey had one of them, Morris, by the balls, simply because Morris needed some scratch to fly his mistress somewhere. For a thousand bucks, Whitey put this guy in his pocket. As for Connolly, who knows? He was a Southie kid, but pretty rotten. The number of other law-enforcement guys whose efforts he sabotaged is enormous. Since so many other organizations had to keep the FBI informed of their investigations, their wiretaps, their lookouts, their undercover stings, Whitey had the perfect ally.

With Whitey having to play both sides, he helped out, he spread his knowledge a little. I'd noticed myself being tagged by a little red four-door Toyota—not an easy car to miss once you are looking for it. A red flag, all right. So I asked Whitey. He got back to me. He knew.

So I see the guy tagging me again, about four in the morning, just after I dropped Penelope off. But I pulled under a streetlight and stopped. This guy gets out of the car. He has someone else with him.

"Hey, what's up? How are you doing?" I say to him.

"What are you doing?"

"Nothing," I say, "and what's it to you?"

And I knew. I knew that this guy was a Boston detective named Beers. More important, I knew, thanks to Whitey, that he was working in conjunction with the Drug Enforcement Agency, more feds in the bed . . .

Beers just figured he'd been fingered as a Boston cop, doing his job, undercover. No big deal. So he tried to act frank with me and casual.

"Oh, we were just over in Roxbury tonight," he says. "Routine shit."

He made himself seem harmless, fuckin' feckless, but I knew different. The DEA was not to be fucked with. Meanwhile he was investigating. He was fuckin' trying to put me in jail. He was trying to see what the fuck was going on. And he was pointing me out to his partner, probably DEA, that's what he was doing. He was showing the guy in the passenger's seat, showing him who I was and what I looked like and everything. *There's Red Shea now.*

Later I'm standing with George Hogan on the street corner in front of the deli, and I see the red Toyota again. I stop his car. He looks a little flustered. I wave George Hogan over. "This is Kenneth Beers right here, that's B-E-E-R-S. Kenny Budweiser. And he's the new man out of D.A. Flanagan's office, and he's helping the DEA."

How do you like that, motherfucker?

Another time I'm with George's son Michael Hogan, and there's fuckin' Beers following me in some other vehicle—he's ditched the red Toyota, such a clever guy. So I do a little evasion, up this street, down this street, through this alley, turn my lights off. Then I see Beers going by, and I pull up behind him and start following him, and I turn my lights on and follow him here and there and sit behind him at red lights, and eventually he can't shake me and decides to pack it in: He drives to the police station and gets out and goes in. He's pissed.

After a while this shit gets to you. It's like gum on your shoe—hey, hence the fuckin' nickname—these guys poppin' up all over. I lost it once, seeing Beers and the partner, who Whitey tagged as a DEA agent named Carr, down by the D Street Deli. There they were, parked down the street under some trees, among the other cars, doing what, I don't know. So I see them and walk over there and jump on the hood of their car. I was standing on top of their car, and I was in a rage, yelling at the two of them to get the fuck out of their car, I was holdin' my balls and tellin' them they had no fuckin' balls themselves. "Get the fuck out now if you're any type of men!" I screamed, and the whole neighborhood could hear. "Neither one of you could hold my fuckin' jockstrap!"

I remember it clear as day.

Beers got out of the car and called me a moron. I remember that, too. He put his hands to his side. He wanted no trouble. He didn't want to arrest me. This wasn't what they were watchin' me for. They needed me on something large, not this.

"What did you call me, you motherfucker?"

"A moron," clarified Beers. "Want me to spell it?"

"Fuck you, you cocksucker!" I jumped down off his hood.

Beers got back in his car. They drove off. I gave the quarter panel a kick as it went by.

Believe me, I've thought about what Beers said—moron—more than once. A Boston detective working with the DEA, I just wonder what he knew about Whitey and the FBI. I wonder if he knew what I didn't know: that I was working for King Rat.

Things were heating up, no doubt about it. It was clear I was under in-vestigation. It got so I was being followed all the time, and it wasn't just

Carr and Beers. One license plate I tagged Whitey said was the Suffolk County D.A. working with the DEA.

Whitey never told me I was a target specifically. I didn't know how extensive the investigation really was, but Gerard O'Neill and Dick Lehr, a reporter at the *Globe,* and Kevin Cullen, another reporter there, were publishing stories suggesting things weren't right at the FBI. They were also all over Whitey's brother Billy, who was trying to win reelection against a squeaky-clean veterinarian—which gave Billy a great line: "I know Boston's going to the dogs, but it's not time to call in the vet." Anyway, I just kept doing my thing.

One afternoon I got a call. I was told that they were raiding the liquor store and the Rotary Variety. I drove by, and sure enough there were federal agents all over the place conducting a raid. So I decided to get off the streets. I went and worked out for a while. It helped me to pump some iron, get the heart rate up, sweat and sweat and clear my head. I took a long shower and then headed back to my apartment. I had decided to get out one of my other cars, a Pontiac Parisienne, an older model, perfectly nondescript. I thought I might leave town for a bit—go to New York or Atlantic City. I put some clothes in the car, opened the hood—it needed oil. Out of the corner of my eye, I saw a minivan speed past. I knew something was up.

I looked again and I spotted Detective Beers in a car with four other guys. He came over.

"Red, how ya doin'?"

The other guys got out of the car. They were gonna raid my place, too. I said, "Good," and then I turned and took off on foot.

In front of me, I saw a wall of agents. Beers and the gang of four came up behind me. They surrounded me, and then they grabbed me. I was put up against a car with my hands held behind my back.

Beers told them, "Take it easy and let him go. Red," he said, "we want to search your house. Will you let us in?"

"Go get a fuckin' warrant," I said.

"I got a fuckin' warrant," said Beers. "I was just being polite."

"Go fuck yourself," I suggested to him, "you piece of shit."

Beers approached me. I told him to get back. I was like a wild animal. "Who wants to get it first?" I said.

One agent, out of the twenty or so surrounding me, came at me from the back. I kicked him in the gut, and he backed off. They all seemed apprehensive. I could tell they all thought Beers had made a mistake not cuffing me. My hands were free. My hands were dangerous.

Then they all rushed me in a gang tackle, and I was under a pile, and when the pile moved off, I was in cuffs.

They took me to my apartment. I was living in Thomas Park then, in a beautiful bilevel apartment, with a master bedroom and bath and another bedroom that I used as a workroom on one level, and then up twenty-five steps or so to another level with another bath with a washer/dryer, and then a wide-open space with château ceilings. The living room there opened onto a deck through sliding glass doors. Off of that was my kitchen. At night, with the shades open and the lights off, I had a panoramic view of Boston.

They sat me down, in cuffs, on the Soloflex machine in my workout room and proceeded to tear the place apart. They had a black agent watch me. He started talking to me about boxing. He was from Virginia, and he was friendly with the fighter Pernell Whitaker, former junior welterweight champion of the world. It was a little surreal, my two lives—boxing and crime—playing out here in my living room while the feds destroyed the place. Then there was a knock on the door.

"Get out! Get out of here! The DEA is in here!" I yell by way of warning.

The door was opened by one man who held it open for a second man, wearing a long cashmere coat and a fedora. It was obvious he was in charge. I said to myself, This guy must be pretty big and this must be serious. This was Eliot fuckin' Ness.

Actually, the guy was among the top brass at the DEA in New England. He walked straight at me. I was sitting, cuffed. "How you doing, son?"

"Not too good right now," I said. "I think my left wrist is broken, thanks to these guys. Could you uncuff the one hand and just cuff me to something with the other?"

He didn't say a word. He walked past me and looked out the window. He lit a cigarette. He smoked it halfway down and then stamped it out on my carpet. He came over and reached behind me and squeezed down hard, closing the cuff on my sore wrist even tighter.

"I don't want to see you weaseling out, son." And then he and his fuckin' hat left the room.

Beers said, "Well, Red, you pissed him off. Now we have to arrest you. We were just going to search the place."

"Arrest me? For what?" I said.

"Assault and battery of a federal officer," said Beers.

"You mean for kicking that asshole?"

I got taken to the federal building downtown and was then transferred to the police station, where I spent a fucked-up night. A guy I knew named Bobby Toumey was working the shift. Bobby was cordial to me; he knew me from Southie. He let me keep my shoes. There was a black kid in another cell, and he started bitching because I had my shit and he didn't have his. So I'm listening to him complain and cry, and I go up to the bars to him, calmly but seriously, "Why don't you mind your own fuckin' business? I don't need to have this shit taken away from me. At least somebody got lucky, and it wasn't you, so big fuckin' deal. Mind your own shit, pal."

He got fresh with his mouth, and I freaked out and started really yelling at him. Bobby came back and says, "What's the matter?" I tell him, "Just pop open that cell and let me get at that fuckin' crybaby, I want to snap his fuckin' neck."

Bobby says, "Relax."

I say, "I'm not relaxing when this guy wants to take my shit away from me. I'm lucky enough to have it."

Bobby just says, "Cool it."

I listen to this fuckin' nigger ramble on for an hour, and finally he grows quiet. I try to get some sleep in the cell, which is all metal: metal bars, metal walls, metal bench. In the middle of the night, they bring another nigger in, and he must be fucked up on some drug, 'cause he's raving mad. They put him in the cell next to me, and he's banging on everything. The cell is shaking, the bench is vibrating. I just try to ignore the guy and get to sleep, but this guy is flippin' out. But toward morning he passes out, and I get a little sleep before I get taken to federal court, where Tony Cardinale is waiting for me. He tells me the situation—that it's assault and battery right now but that they also found a few pounds of marijuana, a .357 snub-nose, and ammunition, but no charges on that yet. I get released on twenty-five thousand dollars' bond.

"It was a general search and seizure," he tells me. "You were the only one arrested. But this won't stick."

I did get away for a few days. Penelope and I went to New York City. We stayed at the Plaza Hotel. We had dinner with her asshole brother-in-law and Penelope's sister at Tavern on the Green, where this jerk decided to make fun of the place and the waiter, and when I tell him I'll take care of it, he makes fun of me, like I'm delusional about my power. When the women are off powdering their noses, I offer to tear his head off and stick it up his ass, which shuts him up, but the evening was ruined. Still, Penelope and I had a good relaxing time walking around New York, spending some money, enjoying the midtown nightlife—great restaurants, theater people coming and going, ball games blaring in crowded bars, people from all over the world, beautiful women sashaying down every sidewalk looking available. All the while, though, I'm thinking about my future.

I've got plenty of money, several cars, three properties in the Boston area, a house in Florida, and hundred of thousands in the bank and in suitcases all over. I'm wealthy, I'm in good health, in great shape, with a beautiful woman I love. I'm only twenty-four years old.

Penelope and I are walking through Central Park. She talks about what she'd like to do with her life. She often does. She thinks about going back to school and becoming a teacher or making children's clothes or opening a restaurant. I can read between the lines. She asks me what I want to do. "John, isn't there something you wish you'd done? When you're old and gray, what will you regret not having done? Anything?"

I kind of brushed it off and kept the focus on her happiness, but by the time we got back to Boston, I had decided to talk to Whitey.

We were having our walk out by the Point. We had business to discuss. I was now getting all my product flown right into Boston, a great price, good supply, things were great on that front. We had a few personnel issues, as usual, but that's it. We had the turf.

"Things are good," I say to him.

"That's when you have to be the most careful," he says.

I say, "I know, I can feel it. I can feel the heat. And I've been thinking—"

"Careful there," he says, and laughs.

"I mean it, Jim. Things are good, but there is something I think I need to do. And I can do it now. I've got enough, I've got mine."

"What the fuck's that?" he says. He seems to think I'm joking, or maybe he's hoping I am.

"I want to go back to boxing. I'm in great shape. I know more now than I ever knew. I can afford my own training. I can own myself for once."

We walk on for a bit. The wind is whipping hard off the bay, and you kind of have to talk in between the gusts. Finally I hear him say, "John, you know, boxing's for niggers."

"C'mon," I say. "Cooney, Quarry, Marciano."

"It's for niggers today, John. And how long'll it last? And everyone will know your face, if you're lucky. You want everyone to know your face, John?"

I thought about it.

"For niggers, John."

And I thought, Something's not right here. *Something's not right.* But I didn't know what.

21

GOING DOWN

Tony Cardinale took pictures of me. He took pictures of me at home, amid all the wreckage of the raid by Beers and the DEA. He took close-ups of my swollen hand and of my face, with some of the nicks and knocks. I looked like I'd been in a fight. Nice.

Since I knew that my phone was probably bugged, I decided to use it to my advantage. People would call, and I'd say, "Yeah, they busted the place. They're charging me with assault and battery, but they worked *me* over, not the other way around. I surrendered. They ganged up on me. It was an army out there."

I told more than one person on the phone that I had witnesses as to what the real assault and battery was. The lady next door, I said, and my neighbor out back saw it all, how they surrounded me, how I stood there defenseless, unarmed, and was gang-tackled by a swarm of federal agents. I said my lawyer had pictures of how they wrecked my place and nearly busted my wrist. I did no assaulting and no battering. If I had, they would have certainly known it.

I made all this up—about the witnesses coming forth—but the charges were dropped. Sometimes you get to the truth in crooked ways.

Still, I'd gotten the bad press. Or some kind of press. I suppose all press is bad when you're a gangster. But people were reading that

"Whitey Bulger's protégé John 'Red' Shea was arrested for assaulting a federal officer," eventually followed by "Charges against Whitey Bulger's protégé John 'Red' Shea were dropped. . . ." That was nice, I have to admit, to have that status—*Whitey's protégé*—out there in the public arena. Because that's what I was. And though I knew this wasn't the end of it—it was more like the start of something, actually—it was at least going to give me a chance to prove to Whitey that I was his guy, that he could count on me, that his faith in me was well placed.

I slowed down a little. I started showing up at my job a little more often. I worked construction for the Boston Housing Authority, a spot that Penelope's stepfather helped me get. I was still doing some hitting and running, but I slowed the business way down. I knew they were coming, I can say in retrospect. I knew something was coming. To be truthful, I almost welcomed it. I don't know why, other than to say that it seemed to be the direction all of this was always going in, and now the suspense was soon to be real intense and exciting and then finally over. A lot of mysteries would be solved—who knew what, who was talking to whom, who would talk, who would step up, how the lawyers would maneuver, how the feds and the cops would fuck up or show their true colors or both. But things got eerily quiet. I could swear the level of activity, or surveillance, of ball bustings, had wound down. This wasn't a great sign. Calm before the storm.

I decided to lie even lower for a while. I went back to Marina Bay, where I used to have a place, and I stayed on a boat in the harbor for two or three days, to wait things out. I guess I was confused. I guess that's what happens when you start to realize that something else is beginning to take over events.

Nothing happened. I listened to the radio and had a kid run the newspapers out to me. Nothing. So I went back into Southie, went back to Thomas Park, to feel things out. There was a beehive of activity, and I have to say I welcomed it. Let's get it on.

It was a cat-and-mouse game to me. I'd be tailed by agents when I was leaving my apartment. I'd be followed to the D Street Deli. So I walked places, to make it a little harder for them to tail me unseen. A slow-moving cruiser is easy to spot, or a fed having to walk through Southie on foot, pretending he's sightseeing. So I walked to the deli and then walked into the D Street projects. Then I'd cut through a building, then double back again. I'd sprint down an alley or through traffic across Columbia Road as if suddenly I was taking a jog—or on the run. I wanted to mix them up, make them earn their fucking money. I wanted to humiliate them as to who they were: people paid to follow a guy like me wherever I decided to go. I went into the public toilet down at the Point and stayed there long enough to make the agent come in, and I walked right past him as he entered. "Don't forget to wipe your ass," I said.

August 8, 1990, was hot. August is always hot in Boston. It was particularly hot that year. I busied myself with a few errands. I worked out. I went down to see Paul Moore and Kevin Weeks at the deli. I dressed for the weather, in a pair of shorts and a polo shirt. It would have been a nice night for a ball game, but the Sox were out of town, playing late on the coast. Too bad. We had just crawled into first place. I knew, because I had spent the last night on the boat rocking in the harbor listening to Castiglione and boys well past midnight.

It was late afternoon when I saw Detective Duwan drive by slowly as I was walking along Columbia Road. About a block and a half ahead, he pulls over. I knew this was it, so I turned and ran. I ran a couple of blocks, to George Hogan's house. Michael was there on the porch.

"Mike, watch this. Any minute an agent is gonna come around that corner."

If I'd kept running, they never would have caught me. But I didn't want to run.

Michael tells me the feds have just hit the deli. His father's down there. And here comes Duwan. So I run, for the hell of it, for the love of the chase, not to get away but to be a wise-ass, to make 'em work. I run past Duwan, who's headed in the opposite direction. He turns around, heading the wrong way up a one-way street. He catches up to me, jumps out of his car, and points his gun at me. He's shaking.

"I'm a citizen, you fuck, put that gun down."

He walks over to me, his gun still trained on me, his hand quivering. He holds out a pair of cuffs and tells me to cuff myself.

"I'm not cuffing myself. Are you crazy? I have to do all your work for you?"

Duwan is by himself. The rest of the troops are already down at the deli, picking up Paul and George Hogan. He gets on his handheld radio. He's standing there, a jangling mess—gun waggling, cuffs dangling, radio crackling.

"I got Red Shea! I got Red Shea!" he yells. "Get down here. I need backup!"

So I'm talking to him like I'm the fucking boss. "Take it easy, Duwan. I don't want you to hurt yourself, or me. That gun could go off, you know. They're dangerous. You ever shoot one? Don't try it now. Don't drop your phone, Officer. Now, why don't you just put that gun away?"

Three minutes pass, and here come reinforcements. Twenty-five cars come roaring up, agents jumping out. They wrap me up, acting like they just captured a whole battalion. Carr and Beers pull up in a Bronco. Carr gets the cuffs on me, and they pile me in the back. He gives me a punch in the side with his fist. I fart at him.

"My mother can hit harder than that, you fuckin' pussy."

"Did you fart at me?" He goes to hit me again, but I move my feet in such a way as to make that maybe not worth the price.

I'm down at the local police station, in a cell. "Is that you, Red?" I hear from the cell next to me.

It's Paul Moore. Then I hear Tommy Connors come in. "Hey, Tommy. What do we got here? A fuckin' party, right?"

But they are quiet. They seem subdued, scared. Then I hear them whispering, like they don't want me to hear. I decide to take control of this situation immediately.

"Strong as a rock!" I bellow out. "Remember that. Strong as a rock, boys."

Then we go our separate ways.

I get taken to the Kennedy Building. Two cops I know—John Daley and Tony Quinn—have the paddy-wagon detail. There are agents in cars in front and back as we make it to the federal building.

Daley and Quinn have nothing to do with the investigation. They are sympathetic.

"We're really sorry, John. This is tough. Anything we can get you?"

"Yeah," I say. "Make sure someone calls Tony Cardinale and tells him where I am."

At the Kennedy Building, I get put in a room the size of a closet. You'd think it would be warmer—and it would be if they didn't have the A/C going full blast. It was very cold.

Two DEA guys come in to talk to me.

"Where's my lawyer?"

"John, we're just here to answer your questions."

"Okay: Where's my lawyer?"

"John, he'll be here. Cardinale, right? Don't worry."

"Do you have any questions, John?"

Silence.

"John," one of them says. "So you know Jesús, eh?"

I think, *Who the hell are they talking about? What's this about? Jesús who?*

"Yeah," I say—now putting two and two together—"I know DeJesús. He's something. Very tough. A real pro."

The two dickheads get very interested, very animated. They pull up chairs.

"So you know Jesús, eh? How?"

I say, "You know him, don't you? Esteban DeJesús. Tough guy. A real pro. He'd take your head off."

"*De* Jesús?" one of them asks.

The other knows what I'm doing. He knows I'm talking about the lightweight fighter who beat Roberto Duran.

"He's playing games with us." Then they left.

Then they came back.

"Where's my lawyer?"

"John, why don't you play on our team?"

"Your team?" I say. "Yeah. I'd love to."

"That's good, John, that's good."

"Tell me, fellas, what team is it? Baseball, football, basketball? I like sports."

"He thinks this is a fuckin' game."

Later I'm handed to three other guys.

"Where's my lawyer?"

"Do you know Whitey Bulger?"

"Whitey who?"

"Shea, why don't you just cooperate with us? You're a young guy. You're not married. No kids. We can put you anywhere. We can resettle you. Tell us what we want."

These guys were trying to play it like they were trying to help me. It disgusted me to even have this topic brought up. It was a fucking insult to my manhood.

I told them in no uncertain terms. *"Forget about it!"* I screamed so everyone could hear. *"I'm no fuckin' rat!"*

"Red, you're a young guy, we can help you if you work with us. If not, by the time you get out you'll be Gray Shea. Forty years, that's a long time, Red. It's a life bit. That's what you're looking at. You are a bright guy. Be smart."

Now I'm playing hardball.

I got up out of my chair still handcuffed.

I moved toward the agent and leaned in only a few inches from his face. I looked right in his eyes. He was clearly startled. In a slow, delib-

erate voice I told him, "I am no fuckin' rat. You got that. There is nothing worse than life, is there? So go fuck yourself.

"The fuckin' games are over. It is finished. You got it. Put me back in
my cell."

That brought the interrogation to an abrupt end.

This was it. It was what I always knew might come. I walked into this
life realizing that I might someday face doing time, maybe having to
spend the rest of my life in prison. I was facing what had loomed out
there as a threat, or a promise, all along, since I made my first trip with
big money to Florida. I didn't think of Penelope at all. I had already
thought it through. I didn't think of my mother or my sisters. I thought
only of my main responsibility, to live by the code I agreed to live by
when I came into this life. I walked in a man, and I'll walk out a man. I
would rather die than become a rat. Even though I loved life, and I loved
Penelope, I could never live without my self-respect. I would show
Whitey he was right. He could count on me.

22

FRONT-PAGE NEWS

They had rounded up fifty-one of us in what the papers called "a sweeping blow to the criminal organization of reputed underworld figure James J. (Whitey) Bulger." The charges ranged from distributing cocaine up to conspiring to operate a criminal narcotics enterprise.

I was at the top of the list of all fifty-one: "John (Red) Shea, 24, of Charlestown." Followed by the likes of Jackie Mack, 42, Walter Bagley, 38, Tom Cahill, 42, George Hogan, 44, Tommy Connors, 44, Billy McCarthy, 26, Paul Moore, 40, Jackie Cherry, 39, Kevin (Andre the Giant) MacDonald, 33, Eddie Mackenzie, 22, Louie Sasso, 40. And fuckin'-A: "Jesús Nodarse, 50, Miami." Sorry, Jesús.

No Whitey, no Flemmi, no Kevin Weeks or Kevin O'Neil.

The paper said, "Shea, Mackie, Moore and Cherry are charged with operating a continuing criminal enterprise through their narcotics business, an offense which carries a 20 to life sentence." Hello, RICO—the federal racketeering act that has been used to clobber organized crime for about two decades. A nice touch, RICO, throwing all kinds of activity that a guy used to able to pursue within local jurisdictions, with perhaps friendly, connected judges and cops, into the federal arena, where friends were harder to come by and the sentencing got fucking medieval and the prisons ain't likely to be near home. Of course RICO has been used mostly to make people rat.

The arraignment is on Friday, August 10. They take us down to the U.S. District Court in Old Post Office Square—me and Jackie Mackie go together. Detective Frank Duwan is escorting us with some federal marshals. He decides to break our balls.

When we're in the hallway between the holding cells and the courtroom, he starts on Jackie.

"I see Millie is out there. Millie's out there in the courtroom."

"She is?" says Jackie. Millie's his girlfriend. "No, she can't be. She shouldn't be here."

"Yea, Millie's out there."

"Hey, Red. Penelope's out there, too. What's she gonna think, eh?"

Now, I know Penelope's not out there. We talked about it—after the assault and battery, I knew stuff was likely to be coming down. I told her to steer clear. I knew this fuck was fucking with us.

I jumped all over this guy. Here we are in shackles—hands, waist, feet—and he's gonna be cute.

"I'll bite your fucking nose off, you motherfucking prick, you cocksucker! You coward cocksucker! You are some fuckin' man! I'm in shackles, we're in the gutter, and you're laying the boot on us! You're some man!"

I moved at him. I could still shuffle, and I could still fuckin' bite.

"Open the door," I said. The doors were locked at both ends. I kept screaming at him. I was ballistic, I was out of my mind. I kept it up in the elevator, and I think Detective Duwan wished he had some other duty right then.

I'm livid. My eyes are burning. He can't get far enough away from me in the elevator. The marshals don't want no part of it, no part of me. And I didn't care if they did. I didn't give a fuck now.

Then I see Tony in the courtroom. "Don't talk to this fuckin' prick," I tell him as he gets nice with Duwan. Of course it's his job. But I was out of my mind. Court security comes over, and I cool down a bit. I sit in a chair. We wait for the magistrate to come in.

I hear a *pssst* behind me. It's fuckin' Kenny Beers, the prick.

"Hey, John, how ya doin'?"

"Oh, I'm real good, Beers." I say sarcastically. "And how are you?"

"It's all a game, eh, John? All just a little game, eh? Forty years, John. Yeah, it's just a game."

Then I turn on him.

"Beers, c'mere, I want to tell you something." I make like I need to whisper something in confidence. His eyes brighten. He scoots closer on the bench he's on.

"Beers, it's about your mother. I fucked her hard there a week ago. But she wasn't too good."

Then the magistrate came in. Her name was Bowler, and she looked like Doris Day. In fact, my helpful mother and sisters, seated in the courtroom, could be heard making that very same observation, which I can't imagine improved the situation. You had to be careful what you said to the judge. The rest of 'em? Fuck 'em.

The indictments were read. We pled not guilty. No bail at this point. We were going to be transported to the closest federal prison.

We took the three-hour trip by bus to Danbury, a federal prison in the middle-of-nowhere Connecticut. A huge joint that was its own encampment, like some pioneer village, protected by walls and barbed wire and surrounded by open fields like a no-man's-land.

The trip sucked—shackled up and with a bar running the length of the bus that went through your chains. You are fucked in a bus wreck, let me tell you. You'd burn in those chains.

They put us in the hole for twenty-four hours. This they did as a matter of security, as they'd make some kind of check to be sure that once you were let out into the population, you wouldn't kill or be killed. Some cop would review paperwork to see if any of your lifelong enemies might be sitting there waiting for you with a shiv. Or vice versa. The hole was a room with very little light and no space—a basin, a toilet, a bench on the wall. Air for about a half hour. A day of that was enough.

I turned twenty-five years old in that hole, on the second day. I made all the guys in there with me—Paul Moore, Eddie Mackenzie, Tom Cahill, Louis Sasso, Walter Bagley—sing "Happy Birthday" to me. I was young, younger than all these guys, but I wasn't going to let my spirits lag, nor theirs. Everybody was feeling blue. They were down. I'd already started to sense their fear; I'd heard Eddie Mac starting to make his excuses—"I would never rat out my friends, John. I got an ace up my sleeve," et cetera—so I decided to make them sing me "Happy Birthday."

"C'mon, you guys," I said. "Keep your fuckin' chins up. Let's go. You better do it."

But they dragged. "Nah, John, not now." So I told 'em, "Every one of you is going to sing me 'Happy Birthday,' or you're gonna have a problem with me when we get out of this fuckin' hole."

An orderly who was mopping the floor overheard what was going on. He asked a guard if he could bring us in a little something for the celebration I was trying to mount. He must've gotten the okay, since he brought in a bag of popcorn. I started the chorus, "Happy birthday to you, happy birthday to me," and slowly every one of them guys joined in, and we passed the bag down through the bars, each grabbing a few kernels, the bag going back and forth till it was empty. *Someone* had to loosen these guys up. There was a lot ahead of us. We had to stick together. We all had a good laugh.

Whitey had given me some pointers about the realities of prison. *The first few weeks are the toughest. Don't be the first or the last in line for anything. Watch who they put in your cell. Show everyone you are not to be fucked with. Demand respect; return it in kind. Don't be tricked into talking. They'll work on you every which way—stories about everyone else talking; stories about your girlfriend crying; stories about how somebody's gonna fuck you up the ass and make you suck dick.*

I was on my guard, as usual. I was going to be disciplined, strong,

silent, and vicious if I had to be. What did I have to lose? I was in fuckin'
Danbury facing serious time.

On my first day in general population, I met a good guy named Carmen Tortora. Turns out he was in there with Raymond Patriarca Jr., the
son of the onetime king of the New England Mafia. Carmen and Raymond had been indicted together. The Patriarca group knew we were part
of the Boston crowd and part of Whitey's crew, so they took good care of
us right away. When you first get to prison, you need some things immediately, small things—flip-flops, shampoo, toothpaste. You arrive with
nothing, and it takes a while to figure out what's what. It takes a while to
get any access to any money. But the Italians were very accommodating in
that respect. They come by with a big grocery bag full of soap, shower
shoes, toothbrushes, fuckin' floss, combs, little shit that makes all the difference. They had bought it from the commissary with their own money
to give to us—out of respect. And it was very appreciated, believe me.

On that first day, Carmen says to us—I was in the common room
with Paul Moore, Tom Cahill, and Eddie Mackenzie, my cellmate,
unfortunately—"Hey, you guys, you know?" And he showed us a newspaper. "See this?" he says

It was a Monday paper—must have been August 13. The headline
says WHITEY BULGER A STOOL PIGEON, and there was a picture of a bird
on the stool. It was the good old *Boston Herald* saying that the reason
Whitey wasn't included in the indictments was that he was giving information. He was an informant.

Clever, I figured. Whitey was right. These motherfuckers were clever.
They float some bullshit to the *Herald* just as we hit the joint, just as
they're putting the squeeze on us—on me!—to fess up about Whitey.
And now Whitey's a rat?

This was a test right here.

Three or four of us were the guys that mattered as far as getting Whitey was
concerned. There were three or four of us who could finger Whitey pretty

good. Me, Paul Moore, Andre the Giant, Tom Cahill. But mostly me. Still, this was no time for anyone to roll. There would never be a time for anyone to roll.

I had to handle this situation. I had to watch and be in charge. I had to take care of these guys. So they couldn't get to Whitey. They sure weren't going to get him this way, through us guys.

I was looking at anywhere from twenty years, a minimum of twenty years, to life. So what?

I was sitting on a table, and all these guys—my guys—were looking at the paper that Tortora had brought in. I just sat back and watched 'em. I observed everything. I observed everything to see what their actions would be. *Who are my enemies here? Who do I really have to be concerned about?* They didn't realize what I was doing. None of them. But I'll tell you one thing, the Italians—they watched. Patriarca, Tortora, them others, they were watching. I didn't run up and go, *Oh, oh . . . What's this about Whitey?* They knew I was a different breed. I wasn't showing anything. I guess that comes from the good training I got from Whitey, from my boxing background, where you never show a weakness, never tip your punches. So I sat back, listening and watching, just trying to absorb everything that I could at that time. Listening and watching.

Later that night I heard the whispers. The whispers that came from Paul Moore and his cellmate, big Andre. At that point all I could tell is they didn't want me nowhere near them, because they didn't want me hearing anything. A little later, they called my name. I don't say anything, like I'm not there. Then I can hear them. "You know, if Whitey's doin' this, we've gotta do it before him." Moore says this. Pole Cat. Running and spraying.

But I don't run out on them like I'm crazy. I'm gonna act like a leader. I have to remind these motherfuckers what the code is, how they should behave. I have to remind them what a man is.

I understood: These guys were nervous. It had all come down. There had been just enough rumors about Whitey that they could believe it was true. It was convenient to believe it was true, if you wanted to tell the feds everything and get the fuck out of this mess. Paul, I know, had never been in prison. He was shook up. It was my job to keep him from getting too rattled, so rattled he'd talk. He could hurt not only Whitey but me.

We get to go outside every hour on the hour—for about ten minutes. When that door opens up, I say to Paul Moore, "We're gonna go for a walk, me and you. I wanna talk to you."

He says, "Okay."

"Let me just begin by saying one thing: Be a man."

Here I am tellin' an older man who I looked up to as a young guy— one of the toughest guys in South Boston with his hands in the street— here I am telling him how to be.

"I just turned twenty-five years old fuckin' today," I tell him. "You're fuckin' forty, and I have to tell you how to act, how to be a man? Shut up!" I have to tell him as he begins to run his mouth.

"Let me ask you a question. Before you entered into this life of crime, did you know that this could happen and what was involved? Or were you living in some fuckin' fairy tale? Listen to me: Before you crossed that threshold into this life, you knew what could happen. You knew you could get arrested. If you couldn't handle it, if you haven't thought about this moment, you had no right to get into this life. You had no right to work with me, with Whitey, with anybody.

"But, Paul," I added, "I know you. You're a man. Continue to be."

I told him, "That front page. It's a ploy by the FBI or the DEA and the prosecution, because everything's happening right now. Whitey told me, the first forty-eight hours are the worst. So everything's happening right now, and they've got the pressure comin' on you—boom, boom, boom—and they're hittin' you with everything, hoping that you would act the way that you're acting now. I don't believe it. It's a ploy. So keep your mouth shut.

"And one other thing. And this, Paul, is more important. It doesn't matter if it's bullshit or not. Two wrongs don't make a right. You knew before you crossed that threshold what could happen. Even if Whitey is ratting, you don't rat. You continue to be a man."

It seemed to work.

As for Whitey and why he wasn't indicted, I looked at it this way: The pressure was on, the heat was heavy, and he had to feed them. He had to give them somebody. They swept everybody. But if Whitey was right, if he had surrounded himself with the right guys who had also picked the right guys, he'd be okay. And we'd be okay. We'd do our time and live to fight another day. That was the worst of it. So what? We chose this life. Them's the breaks.

Penelope was devastated. "How could you have done all this?" she'd say, sitting across from me in those screechy plastic chairs in the visitors' room. She was past crying at this point. She wasn't mad, she was in shock. "How could you have done all these things they say? You were with me all the time."

It broke my heart. I said to her, "Not all the time, baby. Not all the time."

Penelope was on my visitors' list—along with my lawyer, my mother, my sister Paula, and Deirdre, my pal the bartender from Triple O's. Deirdre was my connection to Whitey and Kevin Weeks.

Deirdre would come regularly, every two weeks. She'd bring a bag of quarters for the vending machines in the room. A candy bar actually tasted good. And she deposited money in my commissary account, from Whitey, five hundred bucks at a time.

I never asked any questions about what was in the papers, about Whitey being an informant, because I didn't believe it. Deirdre must've have told them I asked nothing, because Kevin called me to explain.

He said, "When they can't get you, they try to attack your reputation. They can't get him, so they're doing this."

"Kevin," I said, "that's just what I figured. And I told Paul and the rest of the guys it's a fuckin' lie."

After a while Penelope improved her outlook. I tried to keep things positive. I told her Cardinale was working on getting me out on bail. But her spirits started to sink as the others started to leave: Paul Moore, out; Tom Cahill, out; Andre the Giant, out; Eddie Mack, out (and talking); Walter Bagley, out. Me, still sitting.

"It's a good possibility, baby. Tony's working on it."

Deirdre would pass along to me Whitey's and Kevin's regards, their encouragement. They were taking care of things. Eventually, when our first shot at bail was denied, Whitey sent word that maybe I should try another lawyer. But I still had faith in Tony.

To be truthful, Danbury wasn't bad. Although I had no prison experience to compare it to, I began to realize that you could, in the right joint, be surrounded by bright, honorable tough guys—interesting guys with charisma and smarts. It could be entertaining, informative. Everybody had a story, and a good one. And these are the guys that would respect you. That kind of thing ain't so easy to find on the outside.

One of the nicest surprises was running into Jesús. I mean, it wasn't nice—not nice for him, all the way up here from Miami on account of my phone being tapped. I was sorry about that. But what the fuck?

"Hey, Jesús, man, how are you?"

He was not good, I found out. Jesús had lost everything, he had nothing.

"I got a public defender," he tells me.

I liked this guy. He tried to make right by me. He and his wife had driven us all the way back to Orlando. I don't know if he had to do that. And I was so pissed off, who would want to do that? I appreciated it.

I say, "Well, Jesús, there's a lot of wisdom in this house. You need to ask something, ask me, I'll find out."

I see him in the yard one day, he's looking very bad. He's losing weight. He doesn't want to talk to me. I see him hiding behind someone so I can't see him, just to be alone. I make my way around.

"What's up? Tell me what's wrong, Jesús."

"She wants me to, you know, work with them."

"Who does? Your wife?"

"No, man. My lady lawyer."

"That fucking bitch lawyer of yours?"

"Jas," he says.

"That ain't right, Jesús. That's fucking wrong. She's a lawyer, provided by the government, like you have a right to. And she's telling you to cooperate? With the government? That ain't right!"

"I know, but she says it's my best shot. She doesn't want to hear nothing else."

"Jesús, listen to me. You tell her you want someone else. I know. You don't have to accept your publicly appointed attorney."

"I don't know," says Jesús.

"You fucking think about it, Jesús."

A few days pass, I see Jesús again. He's still ducking me, this time in the mess hall.

"Jesús, man, what the fuck? C'mere."

I can see he is still thinking about it. "You change lawyers?"

He shrugs.

I take him over to my table. I sit him down.

"Let me tell you something"—and this is where I play a little poker with Jesús Nodarse. "So you flip, Jesús. What do you got? You got what? They want someone up here. Why the fuck you think you are here in fucking New England? They don't want you, but they just shaking you to see what falls out. But, Jesús, suppose I flip, eh? Suppose someone a lot fuckin' closer to who it is they want flips—and there are a lot of them in here, besides me—then where will *you* be? They'll drop you, motherfucker, like a hot rock. They won't need you. And you'll be a fuckin' rat for nothing. You want that? 'Jesús the Rat.' Nice!"

I shove today's sandwich at him—grilled cheese.

"For rats," I say.

Jesús got a new lawyer and held his tongue. I'd bluffed him.

The problems in the joint were with the screws, of course. You'd run into mostly assholes, guys who hated their jobs, hated you, and were bored out of their minds. Fucking with you was entertainment. But many of these guys could be handled. You could make it clear that you were not to be fucked with, and there weren't too many hard-assed enough to ignore that. They were doing time, too. And some of them were decent. All they wanted was a little respect. You wonder how much respect they got out in the real world: *Hey, handsome, you're lookin' good. What do you do for a living? Me? Well, yeah, I'm a fuckin' prison guard, professionally.*

Eventually I got fucked. And it got me shipped out of Danbury. One of the guards inside got wind of who I was—part of the Irish mob. He thought he could see that the Italians were taking care of me. *Who is this kid with all this respect from Patriarca? This guy shows up, and he's treated like this?* So he starts doing a little research, and he contacts a reporter out of Providence. Or—who knows?—maybe the reporter contacted him, I don't really know or give a fuck. This reporter, from the *Providence Journal,* sends me a letter one day talking about this boxer by the name of David Galvin, who was a top amateur boxer and who actually fought once for the bantamweight championship of the world and lost by a point. This reporter sends me a letter about David. He says, "Give me a call about David. David says hi." So I figured, wow. Let me give this guy a call, because even though I'm inside, it's been a long time, David's a good guy, I know David and respect him a lot. The reporter knows I'm a fighter, that I was a good fighter.

So we talk on the phone. We talk a little about how I knew David. "Yeah, David Galvin, a good guy. I roomed with him in Montreal when

we were both on in the nationals." We talk about my career. And then he
says, "Well, what about you and Patriarca?"

"Me and Patriarca?"

"Do you know him? Isn't he in Danbury with you? He's another Providence guy."

I say, "Yeah. I know him. What of it?"

He says, "Listen, I gotta go."

Click.

The guy writes an article about me and Raymond—that I'm Raymond Patriarca's bodyguard inside. As soon as that article comes out
about John "Red" Shea, part of the Boston Irish mob, protecting Raymond, things got fucked. I didn't like it. I don't like people watching me,
thinking they know something, especially when they don't know shit.
I've got enough problems with some fuckers thinking I got some special
deal with Raymond or what-have-you. And Raymond certainly didn't
need me to be his bodyguard. He had plenty of people around him. Of
course if Raymond had a problem, or any of those guys had a problem
with some outsiders or whatever inside, if someone outside the circle
made a challenge, don't think I'm not gonna be there. I'm gonna be
there. Absolutely. In a heartbeat.

Yeah, me and Raymond talked. I enjoyed talking to Raymond. I introduced him to Tony Cardinale. Tony had come down and brought a
bunch of us out. That wasn't such a good scene. Here's this Irish kid
among these Italians, and, you know, it's like, *What's he all about?* In retrospect, that made too big a scene. Just a few days later, the assistant warden comes walkin' by with a couple of his fag guards for protection. He
says, "You. Come here. I want to talk to you."

I look at the guy like, you know, *First of all, is that the way you address
people? I haven't been sentenced. For all you know I could fuckin' walk outta here
tomorrow. But because I've been arrested, indicted, whatever, I'm a bad guy already, huh? That's the way you look at me already? Well, fine.* I just think that,
I don't say it. Instead I give him a smug look back and say, "Who, me?"

He says, "Yeah, you."

Everyone else has scattered, so of course it's me.

Now the warden speaks. "I know who you are," he says.

"Oh, yeah? Who am I?"

"You're the Irish go-between between the Irish and the Italians here."

I say to him, "Hey, listen, I don't know what you're talkin' about, first of all. I ain't a go-between for nothin'. I got my own case I'm worryin' about and fightin' right now. Gimme a break. I don't need more problems."

"I got my eye on you," he says, like a prick.

"That's good. You do that. Keep an eye on me."

I'm thinking, here's this fucking assistant warden, trying to interrogate me out here. I am looking at forty years, life, and everything else, and he thinks he's gonna scare me by saying something like that to me? I don't think so, buddy.

I think to myself, If you knew what I was thinkin' right now, you'd be scared. You'd be intimidated. I'm thinking of what Tommy Connors used to say: *My goal is to put my hand through someone's head.* I often pictured it in my mind. I always wanted to put my fist through someone's head. Straight through the face, right through. It's not possible at all, it's like a cartoon. Nevertheless, the assistant warden's face was in very bad shape in my mind.

I decided to walk away. Vicious is not stupid.

Shortly after that, I ran into the head warden himself, who is originally from Winter Hill—from Somerville. His name was Sullivan.

"How are you doin', Red?" First time I ever had words with the man. But he knew who I was.

I said, "Pretty good, Warden. Except for this bullshit that's happenin' here. People are writing stories that aren't true."

He said, "Well, it's the press, and you can't fight the press."

I said, "Yeah, I know. That don't make it right."

The next morning I got woken up about four-thirty. "Pack your shit." I said, "I'm not going to court today. I don't have a court date today." "Pack it."

So I packed my shit. I went to R&D, receiving and dispatch area. And here are the U.S. marshals coming. *What's going on? Where am I going?*

One of the marshals says, "They want you moved outta here."

I said, "Really. Can you tell me why?"

"They just wanted you moved."

Actually, it was a good thing to move. The bad press wasn't a good thing. Later on I appreciated what the warden had done.

They sent me to Plymouth County Correctional Facility, the old Plymouth County, with old-time jail cells, cockroaches all over the fucking place, up and down the walls like moving curtains. But each cell had its own black-and-white TV. And I was closer to home by a good hour and a half.

23

THE BRACELET

Tony was a top mob criminal lawyer. One of his first big cases was defending Jerry Angiulo, the head Mafia guy in Boston's North End. Angiulo's place of operation on Prince Street had been bugged by the feds, and we now know that Whitey and Stevie Flemmi were in on it. They knew that the place was bugged, thanks to John Connolly, who was determined to make his bones by taking down the Italians in his fair city—which fit the agenda of Whitey and Company to a tee. Problem was, the tapes incriminated not only Angiulo but Whitey and Stevie, too. Angiulo could be heard complaining about never getting back the quarter of a million dollars he had lent to Whitey back in the day, but he also said that Whitey and Stevie were killers. Connolly had to do some fancy footwork to squash this bad news about his favorite boys. Angiulo had told his consigliere, Larry Zannino, that those fucking guys owed him two hundred fifty grand. Zannino, who Whitey once told me was the only real man in the North End crew, wasn't afraid of Whitey. He told Angiulo just to go after the Irish fucks with a machine gun. But Whitey always said Angiulo didn't have the balls.

When there wasn't much progress in my bail situation, Whitey was quick to recommend I look somewhere else. He got word to me that maybe I should consider another attorney. Looking out for me, no doubt. Looking out for himself, of course. Whitey said, "Fuckin' Tony Cardinale. What's he ever got for anybody? He got Angiulo forty-five years and Fat Tony Salerno life." Harsh. But his point was, You want to be on the street? You want bail? Do something.

I didn't like hearing this, because I liked Tony. He was my guy, not Whitey's. I told Whitey I was going to give Tony a chance. I kept it in the back of my mind, though. If things did not go well, I would have to consider making a change.

We had been fighting for bail for close to five months. With the heavy "continuing criminal enterprise" charge of twenty years to life and my record of traveling, they were afraid of flight. I was young, without family. They figured I didn't give a fuck. A life on the run, why not? A lot of guys had disappeared, for whatever reasons. But they didn't know me. I never ran, never will. I just wanted to get as much freedom as I could until things calmed down and we could work out a plea. As Tony did explain to me, "John, they are gonna drag this shit out. They want you to get crazy. They want to break you, so get ready for the long haul. I'll take care of it."

But we lost. The magistrate denied bail. Tony presented our case this way: I had a girlfriend, a mother, a sister, nieces. I had a job waiting for me. Tony, with the help of Deirdre, Penelope, and a few others from the gang, rounded up seventy-five signatures from the neighborhood attesting to what a good guy I was. The prosecution team was not to be outdone by these maneuvers. In order to prove what a risk I would be to run, they decided to demonstrate what a risk I was to the public, especially the rats. They played tapes of phone conversations—one in particular that came to define not only me, Red Shea, but to define how real gangsters think about rats. It was a conversation I had with Penelope from before I went in. She wanted me to give her some information about a guy cheating on his wife. I went ballistic. I told her, *"I am no fuckin' rat. I would never do that to someone, and I would never want anyone to do that to me. Never ask me something like that again."* I told her exactly what I'd do with a rat—it involved a baseball bat to the head and the use of a chain saw on the fuckin' digits—feet first, then hands. The prosecution used it to their full advantage. They had speakers in the courtroom and they played it nice and loud for everyone to hear. The message was loud and clear, too: This guy is a maniac. Way too dangerous to be on the streets. Every time I looked up at the female magistrate, she was wincing.

"I would tie him to a chair and take a baseball bat across his head with my best swing and then take a chain saw and start cutting his toes off and then work my way up."

It was fuckin' ugly.

Tony jumped up as soon as it was played and objected—it was an illegal tape, because they had no right to admit into evidence a conversation that had nothing to do with criminal activity and which was with my girlfriend. He requested a recess to review the tape. We went into a room and listened to it. The magistrate agreed with Tony about the tape, but the damage was done. The government had made their point. John Shea is a danger and should not be released. Tony attempted to argue to the magistrate, "Mr. Shea was just boasting, Your Honor." But she wasn't buying it.

My bail request was denied.

At the end of the hearing, attorney Richie Egbert showed up to say hello to Tony. He introduced himself to me. This was no coincidence— it was Whitey behind the scenes calling all the shots. *It's time to get a new lawyer, John, and here's the guy.*

Tony appealed the denial to a Judge Keeton, the judge assigned to preside over my case. Again I was denied bail. It played out the same way as in front of the magistrate. After the government was through, I looked like I was a fuckin' serial killer.

After that I changed lawyers. To be fair to Tony, at this time he was in the pretrial stages of his work on the John Gotti case. Gotti and his consigliere, Frankie Locascio, were on the docket in Brooklyn, thanks to tapes and the turning of Sammy "The Bull" Gravano, so Tony had a lot on his plate.

Whitey talked to me—more or less through Weeks and Deirdre—about Richie Egbert, because Egbert was friends with Stevie Flemmi. He'd helped Stevie out with some stuff. Richie, like Tony, is top shelf in Boston as far as the criminal attorneys go. So I went with Richie. Tony took it well. He was not only my attorney, he was my friend. So it was a hard thing for me to say, "Tony, this isn't working. You're all wrapped up in the Gotti case. I like you and all, but my life is in jeopardy here. I gotta do this."

Money wasn't a problem. I was paying out of what I still had cashwise hidden around. I was taking care of my bills to Cardinale and would do the same with Egbert. Basically you give them a big chunk to start—ten, twenty thousand—and then keep hittin' it.

Richie told me that he thought Tony did a great job and the judge should have given me bail. Whereas Cardinale was working on bail on the basis of me being a good guy, no threat to run, good young fellow who will always show up in court to accept whatever happens—which the judge found a little hard to believe—Egbert took a different tack, seeing this one hadn't worked. He took the offensive; he came out fighting. He didn't try to pretend that I was such a nice person, beloved by all (or at least seventy-five people), that I'd never leave the Commonwealth. No, what he worked was my defense. Actually, I'd have to say we went on the offensive with our defense—like Bobby Orr or Ray Bourque. Egbert took the due-process route. He decided that if there were all these hours of tape—something like fourteen hundred hours of it—then he would need to listen to it to build my defense. Which means I would have to listen to it and take notes and confer with him and listen with him. Can't do that in no loud fucking crazy joint two hours outside of Boston, all those miles from his office. No way.

But Richie worked it slow. I wanted to be out, back home, of course, just like everyone else. I wanted to be with Penelope, touch her, hold her, and just talk to her outside of a prison visiting room. I wanted to run and run. I wanted to fucking gut a heavy bag till I was drenched with sweat, and I wanted a warm shower and then a cold beer and the Red Sox up on the TV at Triple O's or someplace nice and quiet. I wanted to cruise around Southie in my Lincoln at night with no worries and the A/C on and me all dressed in black, going to work. But I had to be strong. And patient. I was in a big fucking jam, but first things first: Let's get bail.

Richie decided that we would go back in front of the judge who'd denied the request for bail. We wanted to let him know, without disrespecting him and going above him to the First Circuit. We wanted to say, *Hey, listen, what was said then was this—and it's true—John is not a dangerous guy. He's gonna do the right thing. He's gonna face the music, believe me. But, Your Honor, there's even more to it. And we're coming back, and we want to present our case again, and then maybe you can understand what we need to mount a proper defense. This young man deserves due process. Like every defendant, he has a right to examine all the evidence in the presence of his attorney.*

I heard from a guard that another correctional facility was opening in Middleton and that I was going to be moved there—newer, cleaner. Quieter? I had a hearing the next day and realized the feds were going to move me to Middleton and argue that this facility was all set up and they could provide an area for me to listen to the tapes. Right away I called Richie. He immediately contacted Middleton and got some very helpful information on the facility. He knew that Middleton was not set up at this point for me to listen to the tapes. I needed a quiet place to listen to the tapes, and the head marshal had to admit that they could not guarantee that I would have a place to listen to the tapes and be able to assist in my defense.

In making that plea, Richie was counting on the strength of argument showing not only that Plymouth was inappropriate but so was Middleton, unless the judge was going to go on record as admitting that one facility was better suited to giving a still-innocent man (till proven guilty) a bigger shot at due process.

So the judge agreed, and it was a great fuckin' move. We never wanted to go to the First Circuit, which Richie knew was hard-ass as hell. You go to the guy who made the decision in the first place, tell him we have a new argument, and see if he will reconsider, rather than going elsewhere with an argument he hasn't heard. Very smart. This was the kind of thinking Whitey knew Egbert could bring to the table.

At first all we got was an agreement that I could listen to the tapes in Middleton, in my cell. But Richie made the case that I had to listen with him—or his assistant. He brought my friend Fran Hurley on as a special assistant to handle this aspect. He asked the judge, "Can you guarantee that my client can be available when my assistant is? Can you guarantee this?"

The government claimed I'd be able to be in my own cell, listen to the tape recorder myself, and this and that, and it's Egbert's problem getting me lawyer help. But Richie was ready for them. He knew all about the new facility. Noise, schedules, capacity. The government called the head U.S. Marshal as a witness to say that I could be housed in Middleton and I would have a secure and quiet place to listen to the tapes.

Richie argued, "The TV's too loud, the inmates are too loud. The place itself is too loud. We have tried, John can't hear a thing. He needs total quiet." He offered the judge a chance to listen to the tapes himself to see how hard it is to decipher what the fuck is going on, who is saying what and about what.

"Your Honor, you can't ask my client to depend on the transcriptions of the prosecution in the admittance of these tapes."

The prosecution was blaming me for everything. They were laying it on thick; that was their strategy. They felt they had their man. To take Whitey down. They wanted me—they wanted to throw the big full book at the youngest guy who had his whole life to live, who was at the center of the DEA's case on drug trafficking, which was the heart of the continuing criminal-enterprise charge. They thought, If we can scare this young kid with life in prison, he'll flip. And he'll give us Whitey. They were dead wrong!

Of course, law enforcement had been after Whitey for a long time, but they couldn't lay a glove on him. Whitey's guys in the FBI, Connolly and Morris, were making sure of that. That's why the Suffolk County District Attorney's Office Organized Crime Unit and the DEA had made a secret partnership with the DEA to prosecute. That's why it was the DEA head guy, Paul Brown, who led the roundup of all fifty-one of us. The FBI was out of the loop. That's not to say that Whitey didn't get tipped to the indictments coming down. He also knew that the DEA was trying to get him through me.

Richie kept pressing the issue about the problem with the tapes. Of course what he was angling for was bail. The prosecution brought a Boston police detective to the stand, a guy who was on the Joint Organized Crime Unit of the D.A. and the DEA. He got on the stand to say what an explosive temper I had and referred to my chain-saw quote, which Richie didn't appreciate, and Richie said to me, "Don't worry, John. I don't know what's going to happen. I really don't. But I can tell you one thing: I'm gonna defend you, and I'm going to rattle their cages." That's all I could ask for, Richie.

And he fucking did. He tore this guy a new asshole. *So the DEA is afraid of Mr. Shea? So the DEA has to make baseless charges, unrelated to the case, about what a violent guy he is, like Mr. Shea is going to out and terrorize the community therefore he surrenders the right to defend himself? And the court is going to deny due process to this young man because this detective is shaking in his boots? What kind of law enforcement do we have, when they get on the stand here and claim they can't protect the public from a guy who is trying only to mount a case in his own defense against very serious charges that could take his life away from him?*

I remember those words. And for me, that's all I needed. Whether Egbert won or lost, it didn't matter to me, just as long as he fought against 'em. He gave his best, you know. I mean, I would have been disappointed that day, don't get me wrong, but I would not be disappointed in Richie, because he was giving it his all. He was standing up for me, for my rights. He was aggressive. He was like a pit bull. He rattled their cages on the witness stand, and this guy got beet fuckin' red when Richie questioned him. He made him look like a fool. I walked out of that courtroom like a champ. Richie fought the government toe-to-toe. He went to war that day, fighting for my life. I smiled all the way back to Middleton.

But I figured it was a lost cause, just like the previous time. And then the judge turned to the prosecution team and, with a little sweep of his chin, said, "Was this worth it?"

I was shocked. I couldn't help but stare at the detective, who looked like he just went fifteen rounds with Marvin Hagler. The judge granted bail—and a bracelet. It took two days because of the paperwork. Three-quarters of a million bail and an ankle bracelet. Richie said, "Don't get your hopes up just yet. They have the right to appeal also."

I said, "Back to the judge?"

He said, "No. To the First Circuit."

The money was put up right away. Automatically for me, from Whitey. And they did appeal. They went and appealed in the First Circuit, like Richie said. So he argued my case again in the First Circuit. But they kicked it back to the judge, because the First Circuit said that they needed more reasoning from the judge for why he was releasing me on bail. So Richie realized that we had an ally of sorts in this judge, who had heard enough whining from the prosecution about Mr. Shea. Being as intelligent as he is, and as aggressive as he is, Richie went right after it and did the research himself, and he submitted it to the judge, so that with the judge being asked to give his reasoning, Richie was making sure we hadn't just burdened this guy with more than he wanted to do. I mean, judges like to play golf, too. Richie did the work for him, citing all the relevant case law. When the judge gave his reasoning to the First Circuit, he used everything that Richie had researched. The First Circuit went along with the judge and denied the appeal. I finally got bail, the last one of fifty-one.

All this took a year. A year of court hearings and appeals and appeals of appeals, fighting tooth and fuckin' nail, long rides from Danbury first, then from Plymouth, to Boston, shackled from ankles to fuckin' waist to wrist. Two or three hours, depending, there and back. While Richie argued our case, I still had to do the best I could with the tapes in the joint, which was a joke, and then in the federal building, in one of the rooms that people would go into to see their lawyers. From Plymouth I went every day, woken up four-thirty, quarter of five in the morning and taken out, sittin' in the fuckin' back of a van, no windows, on a wooden bench. My ass fuckin' killing me the whole way, in bumper-to-bumper traffic. Shackled. Always shackled. Fourteen-hour days, easy. I didn't get home—back to my cell—till about seven-thirty at night. Long days.

Up in the federal building, I'd go into the room and I'd listen to tapes. They'd bring me lunch and stuff like that while I was in there. But I'd have to knock on the glass of the door, tell them to let me out. Then there were cells, holding cells with bars up there. One day, when I'm going into a cell to take a piss, I see this fuckin' guy named Klein, who I'd known very slightly—by sight—from Danbury. Just another inmate. I didn't chum around with the guy, knew him just enough to say "How are you doin'?" or whatever. That was the extent of it, in passing. And the place is full that day, with a lot of people up there for court. And of course, being cocky as I was and stuff, and still at this point wishing we had the bail so I didn't have to ask the marshal to take a piss, I pushed a lot. I pushed my way around a lot. I knew how far I could go, too. I could see it was in my interest not to take too much of a liking to this situation, where after all I was busy trying to avoid a life sentence, but without going too far. And I wanted to make them realize that maybe one of the last things they really wanted in their day—be it U.S. Marshals, court officer, public defenders, prosecuting attorney, or the general public—John Shea in a red jumpsuit. Not when I could be on bail and out of their hair for the time being. So I pushed.

Two FBI guys bring this guy Klein up from downstairs. Klein, I've heard through the grapevine, was in the process of giving up numerous amounts of people in a marijuana case. No wonder the FBI had two guys on him. He was doing all their fucking work. Save himself, this piece of shit, rat fuck? They had just taken him out of the court after testifying downstairs, and they were putting him up here on the top floor in a holding cell.

And I come out. My hands are not cuffed, and I'm in this, like, neutral area. I mean, I can't get out of the place, but they are used to me every day, and I give no one any trouble, and I'm not about to make a run for it in a federal courthouse in a red jumpsuit. I have a federal marshal with me, a good guy from Boston, an Irish guy, from the neighborhood. He's not looking to break my balls, he's just doing his job and letting me take a piss. And as I go into the cell to take a piss, they are just putting Klein in the cell next to me. Klein says to me, "Hey, how are you doing?"

I look at him. I go, "What?"

That was just the start of it.

"Don't you ever say fuckin' hello to me, you fuckin' rat, fuckin' punk! You get that, you motherfucker? I'll fuckin' tear your fuckin' head off!"

The marshal is fumbling around, he doesn't know what to do.

Mind you, I'm uncuffed. The two FBI guys are standing there, with a look of *whoa* on their faces. "John," says the marshal. "Red, relax. Please, take it easy. Relax. Relax."

I say, "Don't fuckin' tell me to fuckin' relax. No rat says hello to me. You got that? No rats speak to me."

They asked me to calm down. I stood over near a window. Klein disappeared from sight, deeper into the holding pen. I liked the marshal, he was a decent guy. So I let it go at that. I made my point.

"I gotta take a piss," I say. I laugh to myself in the bathroom. I wipe the sweat off my forehead. It felt good!

When I come out, the two FBI agents look at me and say, "Hey, how are you doin' today?"

I turn to them. I say, "I'm doin' fuckin' good today." And I go back into my room and listen to my tapes.

That evening we're being taken back to Plymouth. It's the county people who are coming to take us back. We get shackled again, from our ankles. The chain runs from a link connecting the ankles up around the waist, and then our hands are shackled to a chain around our waists. And then they run a chain down through all of us so we're all connected in a chain gang. How fuckin' nice.

You walk out in single file, in line together. The guys from the county don't know what's happened earlier in the day. But all the other inmates going back knew what happened. Who do they try to link me up next to but this motherfucker Klein.

"What are you, fuckin' crazy?" I say to the county guy. "What are you doing? What the fuck are you doing?"

The county guys know who I am. I say, "You're not sticking that rat motherfucker next to me. Get this rat motherfucker away from me, or else we are going to have a big fuckin' problem. You stick him down the other fuckin' end of the line."

They respected that, the county guys. None of the other inmates said a word. Not one of them chimed in and said anything to that rat fuck. I verbally tortured that motherfucker. The next hour was brutal for inmate Klein, a.k.a. fuckin' rat, who heard nothing but that all the way to Plymouth County Correctional Facility. Even the cops joined in.

Klein complained to the cops that the radio was too loud. The cop told him to shut up, he was a fuckin' rat.

It was beautiful.

I got out of jail, finally. The bail bondsman was paid. Deirdre brought the money, which she got from Kevin Weeks, and brought some clothes for me, which she got from my mother's place. Ma was living in Charlestown in a small apartment, and that's where I went to live at first. But it was too small. I'm sleepin' on the couch. Or my mother's sleepin' on the couch and I'm sleepin' in the bedroom. It's just too small. But this is just temporary. Our larger plan is for me to live with Frannie at his town house, but he hasn't quite finished turning his garage into a bedroom for me. Meanwhile I have this bracelet on my ankle, two antennas on it. I am allowed a range of 150 feet from the transmitter, which is a box that goes into the home phone. If you're out of range, a signal tells them that you are. You get so many seconds to get back in. If not, it sends another signal, and then the phone rings. If you don't pick up, that's when they call the probation people and then the next step is the U.S. Marshals.

After a few weeks, Richie arranged for the monitoring equipment to be transferred to Fran's place, seeing that he was my co-counsel at that time. He'd worked a little bit with Egbert in the past, but basically Fran was there for me. It's the way I wanted it. He was for me, my second opinion. Richie's a good guy, and he's trustworthy, but I needed my guy. I moved in with Fran. The whole garage was converted into a bedroom. It was in Southie, but on a quiet side street. Just the sound of the kids in the neighborhood playing. When I lay down at night there, I could feel the knots in me slowly loosen in the dark.

I ran. I played golf and racquetball, everything with my attorneys, otherwise I couldn't do any of it. The only time I was allowed to leave the house was to meet with lawyers, go to mass, or get medical care. I had to call in when I left and call in when I came back home. So I played golf with Fran, racquetball with Cardinale, and I ran with Egbert. Or some combination thereof. Basically I was all over town, out and about. The

government got a little annoyed, telling Egbert that we should stop rub-
bing it in their faces, especially the racquetball in Southie at the Boston
Athletic Club, where some of the agents worked out. I was gonna get my
workouts, no matter what. I'd jog to my lawyer's office and back—
meeting with my lawyer, all right.

During this time I was totally clean. I'm not stupid. I had some contact with Whitey. He saw me at Egbert's office one day, along with Kevin.
They were smart in that regard. They couldn't bug my lawyer's office:
attorney-client privilege. They couldn't bug Fran's place either. Same
thing. Most of the time I got messages from Whitey delivered by Kevin.

Whitey gave me advice that day. He said, "When you go away, look out.
The prison system's changing. You might have problems in there. There
might be some rioting goin' on." He said, "Might be some lockdowns."

I asked him why.

"Because of all this mandatory sentencing for everything in the federal system," he said. "Especially since they went after the crack niggers.
It's a hundred to one, crack cocaine over the powder, you know. A gram
of crack'll get you what a hundred grams of powder will get. These places
are crawling with niggers looking at twenty years, looking at life. They
are pissed off, and whatta they got to lose? You'll have to watch your
step."

I felt like Whitey was guiding me into this abyss. *Don't be at the front
of any line, and don't be at the back. Be in the middle. If there's a food strike
where no one goes to the chow hall and you're in your cell, and the guards
come by and ask you to step out and eat, even if it ain't your fuckin' beef, you
stay. They ask you why, you tell them you have to live with these people.*

I listened. It was good advice, but I already knew what I needed to
do. It was in my blood.

*You don't want to break no picket line and you don't want be singled out,
like you're a rat.*

Then he tried to soften the blow a little. "John, it's not as bad as it
sounds."

I just listened.

"Yeah," he says. He's sitting in a nice big leather chair in Richie's office. He straightens his cuffs. "Yea, they have salad bars in the prisons now. You go and fill yourself up on salads."

I just stared at him. "I look forward to that, Jim."

He gave me one other bit of advice. "When they put a rat into your cell—and they will—you just tell them you don't want to live with a rat and you request a change. Tell them that he's gotta get out or you get out. Tell 'em, 'Put me in a lockdown, then. I ain't staying with no rat.' "

Most of this I just listened to and nodded out of respect. I didn't need to be schooled at this point. I couldn't give a shit about a fuckin' salad bar. Whitey was playing his usual role, playing the chameleon role to a tee. Looking out for number one, himself.

Whitey was counting on that: people keeping their mouths shut. He put the fear of God in people. He killed snitches, he killed girlfriends of Flemmi's, he made some people like Mickey O run for their lives. But there are a few people out there who didn't need to be scared shitless into keeping quiet. Whitey might have thought Jerry Angiulo was weak, but that guy's in his eighties and still doing time—did he ever say anything about Whitey? There's Larry Zannino—and Whitey was right about him. He died in prison with all his secrets. He was a man. They were both men. They entered this life knowing what it was about, and no forty-five-year bit, no life bit, is going to make them dishonor themselves, make them a traitor to the life. Zannino would be turning in his grave seeing what's going on today, people facing a lot less trouble flipping to save their asses, blaming their parents or the neighborhood or using Whitey and Stevie as an excuse. Kevin Weeks complains, "They left me holding the bag." Paul Moore figured Whitey gave me up, why not? That's not what I say. Two wrongs don't make a right. And Larry Zannino would puke knowing that there are guys on the street today who made a deal and people who now accept them, forgive, understand. Guys accepting them because they didn't rat on them. Afraid of the secrets they may tell about them. Fuck 'em. Tell them the way it is: You're a fuckin' rat. That's never been the way. It should never be the way. Whitey the rat or no Whitey the rat, you have to know the code and live it, whether someone else can or cannot. You take your cue from a fuckin' rat? Fuck you.

I can live with the bracelet, I can live with the time. I could live with getting life, as long as I can live with myself.

24

THE SENTENCE

There was talk that I'd get twenty to life. They had me charged with an 848—running a continuing criminal enterprise. They thought they had me by the balls. So they made a lot of overtures to me to flip, right from the get-go. They wanted Whitey, bad. One thing I knew was what I had been told by Patriarca and those guys in the can in Danbury: no grand jury appearances. I told Richie, "I'm not pleading guilty to anything if I don't have this. Get that clause saying I can't be called, because you know they're gonna run more investigations and more grand juries. And if they can bring me in there and I plead the Fifth—because I will, I'm not telling them anything—even if they grant me some immunity and I still don't say anything, they can give me eighteen months or the life of the grand jury—tacked right onto the end of my sentence. They can continue to do it up to fifty-two months. No way." That's one thing I knew and insisted on.

Richie had his work cut out for him. The supervisor of the Organized Crime Drug Enforcement Task Force was a U.S. Attorney named Jonathan Shields. His boss had been a guy named Wayne Budd, U.S. Attorney for the whole District of Massachusetts, but he had just been kicked up to Washington, to the attorney general's office, by the Clinton administration, which had just come in. A guy named John Pappalardo, who was the first assistant under Budd, took his place as acting U.S. Attorney. We'd have to deal with these guys.

Fortunately, we had a fair and reasonable assistant United States Attorney assigned to handle my case, George Vien. He was a guy we could talk to. Richie had a meeting with Vien. "Suppose we plead the guy guilty," he said, "to a lesser charge. We can't accept this 848. My client's too young. This is twenty to life. Don't bury the kid. He'll still do a good amount of time. He's got no record, he's young. We'll plead to a lesser charge. Save everyone a lot of headaches."

Vien says, "I've got no problem with it. It's not me, it's my boss."

Jonathan Shields.

Richie went to see Shields. Shields told him no deal for John Shea, none, zip, nothing.

So Richie decided to play his ace. He would go above Shields to Pappalardo, who was a friend of his, a graduate of Suffolk University Law School—like Cardinale. If you're a lawyer in Egbert's business, you have to play your cards carefully. You don't ask a friend for a favor unless you have to.

"I should go to Pappalardo," Richie tells me.

"Do it," I say.

But there's one problem. This guy's in line to replace Wayne Budd. "This shit gets political, John. Pappalardo might not want to be seen being soft on you."

But then we got a break. Pappalardo was passed over by Bill Clinton for the head job, and he was ready for the private sector. So Richie made our case to Pappalardo.

Richie told Pappalardo, "This kid isn't gonna talk. If you think hitting him with the 848 and the twenty to life is going to get him to cooperate, you're mistaken." Then he threw on the desk a picture of me at six years old, sitting on a stool in the corner of a ring in the Baby Golden Gloves tournament. "This is the kid you want to give life to? Because that's what you're doing. He'll rot in there and give up nobody."

Pappalardo picked up the photo. "That's Red Shea, eh? Little Red Shea . . ."

They gave it to us. We pleaded guilty to distribution, trafficking, and a managerial charge, but not the 848. At first they wanted fifteen years, but Richie worked on them, and we ended up with eleven years, four months, including time served. I'd be out in the twenty-first century, around 2002. I'd be thirty-seven years old. Bring it on.

And no grand juries.

Now, one might have thought all my fuckin' goin' off the handle—against Klein in the courthouse or to Penelope on the tape or wherever or whenever—was the raving of a crazy man. But one thing I can tell you is that when it came time for Richie Egbert to tell them no grand juries, you're getting nothing from this kid, they believed him. They knew it was the truth, no bluff.

A few weeks before I had to report to federal prison I met Whitey one night in the Old Colony projects.

"John," he says, "you know I went away at the same age just about the same day in March. Quite a coincidence, huh?"

"Yea, Whitey. That's something, I guess."

"I'll be here when you get out. You'll be taken care of as soon as you're out. I'll set you up in a business right away. You'll have no worries. Kevin will make sure your mother is okay, and if she needs something, she'll have it."

Whitey wished me luck and shook my hand. He whispered in my ear, "You're one guy I always knew I never have to worry about. You're just like me."

Penelope knew that it was coming to a head. The big day was coming. We tried not to think about it or talk about it too much, because what's gonna happen is gonna happen, so why dwell on it? But the time came.

I was able to get the bracelet off for the weekend prior to the sentencing. Richie did a great job getting them to agree to a self-surrender.

By me self-surrendering, it would actually bring my points down. They credit you for that, so it was a good deal all around.

That last weekend we went to our favorite Italian restaurant, David's. Our last dinner together, the very last. Needless to say, Penelope was inconsolable through the whole meal. She couldn't eat a thing. She just cried and cried. It was painful to see her like that. It was devastating, really, seeing someone crying like that, someone who had nothing to do with anything, an innocent, her only crime just being someone that was in love with me. I tried to console her. *Well, you know, baby, it's a long time but it isn't a long time. . . . Life is long,* et cetera.

I was trying to be the optimist, trying to be strong for her.

"You never cry," she said. "You never say anything. You never complain or say anything. Maybe it's time to start complaining, John."

She thought I was getting too much time for a guy who's never been in prison. "This is your first time," she said. "What are they doing?" She couldn't believe it. She couldn't accept it.

I ate my venison chops that night. This was gonna be my last good meal for a long time.

Then we went back to my house, and she really started weeping. Wailing. And then she got mad. "Why did you do this? How could you do this?"

It was the most excruciating night that I have ever experienced. And I've seen it all and been through it all. I could walk up and hit someone with a baseball bat across the fuckin' face and watch it smash, deservedly so. I could stab someone, deservedly so. But to see the woman you love, who's a citizen and has no connection to anything like that life, who just loves you and wants you and wants to have a family with you and children and everything else—to see that just taken away from her, ripped away from her and to watch the pain that she's experiencing come out of her, especially when I love her so much, it was very hard. She cried the whole night. I don't even know if she had any more liquid in her body, she cried so much. She just wept and wept and wept like a baby as I was holding her. All night.

Finally it kind of calmed down toward the morning, though she was still crying on and off. And I started getting up out of bed, and she pulled me back down because she wanted to be with me one last time. Of course she cried through that, too. She left the house crying, and I did what I had to do. Got dressed, packed a few things. I already had a plane ticket ready for me, one way to Detroit. I would serve my time in the Federal Correctional Institution in Milan, Michigan.

I paid for my own flight—five hundred dollars straight out to Detroit. I was going to have company on the flight and for my last night as a free man—Billy Mahoney's brother Vinny, who worked for an airline, said he'd come along, no problem, and he'd drive me to the prison. Billy and I had a few drinks at the bar, but Vinny never showed. He did call and said he'd catch a later flight, but that never happened. It was starting to snow, and I got out just before they started canceling flights. I called my mother before boarding, but she was crying so hard. I called my sister Paula. We said good-byes.

It was a weird feeling, being free for just a few more hours and being thirty thousand feet in the air. Everyone else on the plane was going to jobs or family or some kind of recreation. I was going to prison. Everyone treated me like everyone else. I guess we had all earned the respect of being at the very least a customer. I paid my way, so I got the same. *Is there anything I can get you, sir? How is everything, sir?* I looked out the window and watched all of Boston wheel into view for a second, too quick for me to spot Southie before we swung out over the ocean. I had another drink on the flight, stayed away from the food, and stared straight ahead.

I took a taxi over to the hotel and then checked in. Or tried to. The room was under Vinny Mahoney's name, because he had the credit card. I didn't have a credit card. So I said, "My friend's not here yet. He's stuck in Boston. I got in before him. I'm supposed to stay in his room. My name is John Shea. I got a license, and I can pay cash."

They told me to talk to the manager. Just what I need: no room at the inn. I'm ready for the bullshit. I don't tell the manager that I start my prison sentence tomorrow at Milan, but I will if necessary.

"Is there a problem?" I say to the man with the manager pin on his burgundy Crowne Plaza sport coat.

"No problem, sir. Cash in full will be sufficient."

I go upstairs to my room. I chill out. I order a steak from room service. It sucks. I talk to Penelope on the phone, my mother, Fran. Everyone is sad, no one knows what to say. I try to keep it upbeat. *The room's nice! A great steak! Cold beers in an ice bucket. Great to have a steak and a few beers before I go in, you know?* But there's no breaking the gloom. I go to bed. I don't feel like checking out Detroit in the least. I stay in. I sleep well.

Vinny was going to rent a car to drive me to the prison in the morning. I'll have to get there on my own. I don't even know where Milan is. I hail a taxi out in front of the hotel.

"Where are you going?" the cabbie says to me, a black guy.

"Going to Milan, Michigan. Federal prison."

"Yeah?" he says. "That's a long way, man, about fifty miles."

"Don't worry about it," I tell him. "Take your time."

We shoot the shit a little on the way. I don't see any of Detroit, really, just highway and highway traffic.

"Man, going all the way out there, I can wait for you, man," the cabbie says. "Be there when you're through with your visit or whatever."

He's looking through his rearview mirror at me.

I say, "You'll be waiting a long time for me, my friend."

He gives me another look in the mirror.

"About eleven years," I say.

He turns around. "Get the fuck outta here, man. You're goin' there to do your time?"

"That's right," I say.

He starts to pull the cab over. "Hey, man, You want me to turn this motherfuckin' cab right around, right now? You just tell me. I'll turn this fuckin' thing around *right now*. I'm dead serious, man. I'll turn this motherfucker around and get you the fuck outta here."

He's a funny guy. I appreciated it, but I have to decline his offer.

"I got an obligation to meet my friend," I tell him.

"You got balls, man," he says.

I give the guy a forty-dollar tip at the prison gates. "Thank a lot. Good luck," I say to him.

"No, man, good luck to you," he says.

25

FCI MILAN

When I walked through the doors at Milan Federal Correctional Institution, I was told to sit and wait. Just like in the movies, I heard the door clang behind me. In fact, the sound of many clanging doors, not just the one behind me. It's the constant music of prison, doors shutting.

A few minutes later, a couple of guards escorted me to R&D— receiving and dispatch. I told them who I was, of course, and they checked the paperwork. They sat me in a cell where I had to undress. Off came my Armani coat, Armani dress pants, Armani briefs, Calvin Klein shirt, Bally shoes. I put them all in my Louis Vuitton bag and put it in a box. They said they'd send it home.

In return I got a V-neck khaki shirt and pants with an elastic waistband, boxer shorts and a pair of blue deck shoes. Everything used, everything stiff from harsh laundering. I was given a bedroll, a pillow, a sheet, and a thin wool blanket. I was told I would be housed in B-2 unit, second floor.

The few chains I had on—the one that Penelope had given me, a nice little gold chain with the medallion on it of St. Jude, a St. Christopher's medal from Frannie's sister, and another religious medal from Penelope's mother—they let me keep. I would wear these throughout my time.

*   *   *

Milan was built in 1933, the same year as Danbury. It was a brick structure, two floors dormitory style. There were about 130 inmates on each side of my unit, with a TV room in the middle. There was a guard station, a counselor's office, a case manager's office, and a unit manager's office.

As they walked me to B-2, I noticed that this was a very dark facility, much darker than Danbury. It was about 80 percent black.

My unit was old and dirty. The guys in it, I would come to find out, were mostly gang members from Detroit and Chicago.

Two men to a cubicle.

My first roommate was an older black guy who was completely fucked up. Right away I could tell he was a drunk, and he was a sleazy fuck. We are in a six-by-eight cubicle, and his first order of business is to tell me what's his.

"This is mine," he says, gesturing to nothing in particular.

I tell him I don't need to have him tell me anything. I know my bunk, my locker.

I showed him my edge right away. The next morning I check my stuff to make sure this fucker doesn't try to hide any of his shit on me. I let him know I'm hip to that fuckin' trick. I keep checkin' my stuff every day.

Around the third day, the lieutenant on duty decides to bust my balls. He calls five of us in for a Breathalyzer test, four black guys and me. The lieutenant, who is black, administers the test to these four black guys one after the other and dismisses them. Then it's just me. He gives me the breath test, like suddenly I'm a big fuckin' annoyance, like I'm the one motherfucker just ruining his day.

I don't say anything. Then he tells me to get the fuck out of there.

I felt like smashing his skull right there, but I think better of it. I turn to him and say coolly, "I'm not new at this, and why don't you calm down?" And I left.

*   *   *

Milan was a complete madhouse—smoking, drugs, drinking, gambling, fighting, rampant homosexuality. A fucking free-for-all. No one had any respect for this place—not inmates, not guards, not brass—no one gave a flying fuck about the place. As far as I was concerned, it was a sea of vermin.

Eventually I met a few decent guys. I got a job in the laundry, where I met two guys from Dearborn, a father and a son doing thirty and forty years, respectively. Drug operation. The father was white, and the son looked half Latino. I met a one-armed older guy named Moe. Moe got off on the wrong foot with me, handing me orders. He was in charge of handing out boots and clothing. He told me to bring some shit somewhere, and I stopped him right there. I told him no one talks to me that way. He didn't like it. When I told a guy back in the unit about Moe, he told me Moe was a serious dude, one of the head Muslims in the joint. I said I didn't give a fuck. But after that, Moe was cool with me. We had no trouble. He knew where I stood. Vice versa.

Eventually I ran into some Italians from Rhode Island and New York. A little bit of Danbury. I'd socialize with them some, take a walk and talk in the yard, see a few of them in the gym. Then who the fuck shows up but my old pal Raymond Patriarca. As soon as he came in, I returned the favor his guys had shown me in Danbury. I hooked him up with all new clothes, underwear, and cotton blankets, and a new pillow. None of that used and scratchy shit. Little things like that make doing time a bit easier. Raymond and I played cards, ate together. It was good to see him again. He was a good man.

One friend I had early on was a guy named Joe Scalamo, from Worcester. Joe was a jovial, energetic guy with a lot of money. He was always talking and laughing. He loved to play cards and gamble. Everybody liked hanging out with Joe. We used to eat together a lot, and Joe took a real liking to me. He even offered to put two grand into my prison account, but Patriarca gave me a word to the wise. He'd heard from another guy that Joe was a rat. His son was accused of being involved in some crime that involved Howie Winter from the Winter Hill Gang, and Joe had given up some people to save his son. I had someone from Boston check this story, and it turned out to be true. I then exposed this piece of shit Joe to the rest of my circle. A rat has to be treated accordingly. I had told a lot of people about Joe Scalamo—Joe this, Joe that. I'd introduced him to a lot of people. My reputation was on the line. I had to make it right.

So I put a distance between me and Joe, but one guy I told, this half-Jewish, half-Italian guy, kept playing cards with him. He ended up losing money to Joe and then decided he wasn't paying him. "I don't pay rats," he says. What a fuckin' scumbag. But that's what happens when you're a rat. In my mind the other cocksucker is just as bad. He plays cards with a rat, takes his money, but now calls him a rat when he loses. Dancing with a rat. Two fuckin' rats, they deserved each other.

I decided to confront Joe about what I'd heard. And he did a very unratlike thing: He admitted it and told me the truth. I could see he was struggling with what he had done. He said he didn't hurt anyone, just some Colombians. He said he did it to save his son. I told him I had compassion for him, I really did, but, "Joe," I said, "a rat's a rat."

Joe was old, and he was conflicted. He had done time before and had a well-deserved reputation for being a stand-up guy. But the love of his son made him sacrifice his reputation, his honor. This was a prime example of the feds using something as beautiful as loyalty and love for your son to turn you into a rat. If he wasn't so conflicted, I'd have handled it differently. I told him I was sorry, but I couldn't hang around such a guy. He started to weep. Every time after that, when we passed in the unit or wherever, he hung his head. At least he had a clue. . . .

Another thing in Milan that sickened me was men lying down with other men. One night I woke up around three in the morning by an unbelievably loud slurping sound. I learned to sleep very lightly in prison, as if with one eye open. I started looking around from my bunk. I did not see anyone moving and could not detect where the sound was coming from. The sound stopped. Then all of a sudden, I saw a black guy coming out of another black guy's cubicle. It was obvious what was going on with these two fags. The guy leaving was a gay black guy who did laundry in the unit, ironing clothes for anyone, and they would pay him with commissary. The other guy was not an outed fag. He was one of countless men in prison that would lie down with another man to satisfy their sexual urges. Like fuckin' animals.

The fag situation in Milan was out of control, and it sickened me to have to be around it. You're trying to sleep or take a fucking shower, and you're exposed to it. I had just come back from a five-mile run and was going to take a shower and go to bed. I walked into the shower room of my unit, which is a communal area, wide open, with ten showers. As I turned the corner into the shower room, I saw this massive black guy sodomizing a small Hispanic. The black guy had this Hispanic up in the air with his feet dangling, and he was literally fucking the shit out of him. I immediately turned around and walked back to my cubicle, utterly disgusted. I realize this happens in jail, but I didn't want to be around it or condone it. That old adage "What happens in jail stays in jail" is total bullshit in this situation. I don't care if I was in jail for ten years or a hundred fucking years—no man should ever enter another man in my world.

But to me, just as there are no part-time rats, there are no part-time fags. You're either a fag or not. Just like rats, there's no gray area.

I don't say it's easy being a man in prison. Whitey told me the first year would be the toughest, and though I had done a year or more already, in Danbury and Plymouth and Middleton, it never seemed that Penelope was far away. I had hope, as we worked on getting bail, which of course we actually got. And then, out on bail, I saw her a lot, for almost two years. But now, when the Milan doors slammed behind me, I knew I was looking at another ten years or better without Penelope, without any woman.

That was the roughest time. Physical cravings are one thing. You can do yourself and do without and use your mind over matter, but it's the heartache that gets you, the loneliness of the night and the bunk and the need to escape. I always had a Walkman, and at night I could drown out the sounds of the population with some nice R&B radio music, songs of love and romance to get me to sleep. Thoughts of Penelope and the good times, down to every detail, rethinking everything we did, everything we said, and every inch of her body, I never found boring. They always got me through to the morning.

Needless to say, I hated Milan. Fran Hurley was working on a way to get me transferred out of there, somewhere closer to home. It had to be done before I killed someone in there. Rats you find everywhere, fags, too. That's prison life. No picnic. But this place was scumbag after scumbag after a while, the screws included, and it was just an organizational break-down all around—blackouts, bad food, no heat, fucked-up scheduling, hostile counselors. It was a fuckin' shithole.

Penelope gave me a big hand in getting a transfer. Working out of Mayor Flynn's office, she was able to contact the Southie congressman Joe Moakley—who was not only a buddy of Whitey's brother Billy Bulger but a guy who played football with my Uncle Larry—to make an appeal on my mother's behalf. Given her age and some poor health, it was a hardship to have her only son doing his time halfway across the country.

Moakley came through, placing a personal call to the Bureau of Prisons. This resulted in my counselor at Milan summoning me to his little office. I sat there. He sat there looking at me. He had a little wispy half-chewed mustache, a little green behind the ears, and I don't mean Irish.

"I got a request for a transfer here," he says, kind of sour. "Some congressman. You got high friends, eh?"

"I'm a long way from home," I say to him. "I'd like to see my mother once in a while."

"Your *mother*," he says, "is making my life miserable. All this paper-work I gotta do for this."

This guy's desk is a mess, stacked with shit, not much of it looking official, all of it looking old and coffee-stained.

I'm paying attention now.

"What did you say about my mother?" I ask him. I stand up.

I guess he didn't mean it, he was just bitching about doing his fuckin' job. So he started to verbally backpedal immediately.

"Should I relay that to the congressman, that you're having a paper-work headache? That my *mother* is giving you a fuckin' headache?"

"No, no, Shea, sit down."

"Listen," I say to him. "I ain't asking for no breaks for myself, you understand. What's my mother done wrong, eh? Should she have to come all the way out to fuckin' Detroit, Michigan, or wherever the fuck this is to see me when I could be a lot closer? It's still jail, isn't it? But it will make a world of difference to her, and to my girlfriend and my sis-ters. I'm sorry you have to do your job, pal, but gimme a break."

This guy ball-sucked me after that, for as long as I stayed at Milan. He processed all the paperwork and in a couple of weeks came by my cell to give me the good news: The transfer to the Eastern Region was ap-proved. Probably Fort Dix in New Jersey.

Still, I had a few weeks before the date of my transfer. Nothing comes easy.

A black gangbanger kid from Chicago came into my unit. He was a lit-tle bigger than me, a little taller, about 190 pounds, strong and cut. I could see in the first few hours we were gonna have a problem. He had a chip on his shoulder from the minute he walked in. I can understand having an attitude—a don't-fuck-with-me air—but this guy had more than that. He was looking for trouble where there wasn't any. He looked at the wrong guy. This was headed for war.

I could see he was trying to impress his newfound buddies in the unit. He had to be a man among these older black guys. Why not pick on this easy mark, this lily-white redhead who looks like a teenager? This went on for more than a week, as I bided my time till I was out of there. Or tried to . . .

Then it came to a head. I was talking to the young black kid who lived in the cubicle next to me—decent guy. We were just bullshitting about sports when the Chicago kid walks by and stops in his little strut. He asks the kid I'm talking to, "You bein' pressed upon?" The kid looked up and said, "No, man, it's cool." But I stood up.

"You got a fuckin' problem?" I asked.

The Chicago kid said, "Do you?"

I looked him straight in the eyes. "Yes, I got a problem. You. Let's go!"

In that second I said "Let's go," I could see surprise in his eyes. He had underestimated me. Something Whitey had always taught me never to let happen—never be caught by surprise and always be ready to act.

In that split second, I blasted him with both hands blazing. Right hand, double left hook. I could see he didn't know how to handle what was happening. I backed off and let him scuffle a few punches up. But each time he punched, I moved to the side and weaved and nailed him with a counterpunch. I punished him inside, to the body, hook to the liver, straight right hand to the heart. I could have knocked him out with a shot right on the button, but I wanted to make him suffer, feel the pain.

He could see that trying to box with me was a joke, so he started to grab and wrestle. Gee, another mistake. I used his momentum and body weight to flip him over and smash him headfirst onto the cement floor. Then his eyes rolled back and he was out. I leaned over and gave him a few more shots to the ribs for good measure.

I backed up and surveyed the damage. His face was a bloody mess. His eyes were swelling shut. He was starting to moan and curl up in a ball. Saliva and blood drizzled from his mouth into a little puddle by his cheek. His head looked crooked on his neck. I'd fucked him up good. A couple of his new buddies helped him back to his cubicle before any guards came around.

The night passed. Chow was tense. The word had spread. The Chicago kid didn't show, not surprisingly. Later, after lockdown, though, I got a visit from ten black guys. They surrounded the front entrance of my cubicle. One of them stepped forward as the spokesman.

"You gave that boy a beatin' today. You called him out a name. You called him a nigger."

I stood up and went to the edge of my cell. I said, "I am insulted that you would come to me and accuse me of that. Ask this kid here." I nodded toward the cubicle next to mine. "He saw the whole thing. Or ask my bunkmate or anyone else that was around. They will tell you what happened. It was nothing like he told you."

I knew that these guys were worried about me. That's why they came in a group of ten. It was a mind game. They thought they'd try to intimidate me, maybe appeal to my good sense. As if being outnumbered meant anything to me. But I had been taught by the master. You never show fear. I knew how to play it. Defiant. Confident. Ready to go. They went away.

Still later, that night, two of the guys came back. I figured, Whatta they got, the run of this fuckin' place, roaming around doing this fuckin' business? But I let them speak.

"There's no problem," one of them said. "We checked the story. He had it coming."

I saw one-armed Moe the next day in the laundry. The Chicago kid had made an appeal to the Muslims, all right. Moe had stood up for me. He was second in command and had a lot of respect. He said they told the Chicago kid, "You called for it, you got it, now go on your way."

The very next morning a correction officer woke me up. I figured, Shit, I'm going to the fuckin' hole. He said, "Get your shit together, Shea. You're being transferred."

I actually enjoyed eighteen hours in shackles on a bus headed to Fort Dix, New Jersey.

26

FORT DIX HELLO

Prison is prison no matter where you are, because of what you don't have there: freedom. But within prisons there can be a world of difference. Fort Dix was different, and as things go, I was lucky to do most of my sentence there—nearly nine years.

Fort Dix didn't look like a prison, and it wasn't designed as such. It had recently been converted from an army barracks. I thought I was back in the projects in Southie for a minute when we pulled into Dix. Three-story brick buildings connected to each other. It looked like the Old Colony projects.

There were trees and grounds surrounding the place. There were no bars on the windows. It was a far cry from Milan, with its controlled moves. No more doors opening every hour and ten minutes to get where you're going. In Dix you could move around freely, very freely.

It was on the East Coast. I just felt different, better, closer to home.

I went through the usual R&D—and the shower and the paperwork and the medical check. My unit was in a building that was nearly empty still, as the conversion to the Bureau of Prisons was still under way. The unit wasn't broken into cubicles, so there were rooms. Dix had ten-, eight-, six- and two-man rooms. I was one of the first guys in my unit, but in the luck of the draw I got screwed. No two-man room for me. I got assigned to an eight-man room.

There were about sixty of us in the unit; there would eventually be more than three hundred. The first thing I noticed were the beds—four-inch-thick mattresses that had been used by the soldiers, rather than the inch-and-half scraps you had to hold together with prison-issue canvas belts at Milan to keep them together. They had shower stalls, not community showers, so it looked like I would be spared any homo shit. The compound itself was enormous. I was soon able to gauge that one and a half times around the entire compound was a mile.

The population was different from Milan's, also, about two-thirds Hispanic, maybe a quarter black, the rest white and whatevers. And these proportions pretty much held as the entire population grew. New inmates were coming in every day. There was a huge, nearly regulation-size soccer field and a softball field. There was a gym with a full basketball court, a small racquetball court, and a separate weight room packed with Nautilus equipment and free weights. Outside, there was a weight pavilion. The prison also had an education department, a chapel, and a work program, called Unicor, where the money was decent if you felt like working your ass off for the government. I vowed I'd never work for the government, help them run the prison. Fuck that!

For the first few days, I chummed around with just the guys I'd arrived with from Milan. But then one day, walking out near the gym, I heard a Boston accent. It was a few guys from Boston. One of them was John Christian, who the papers had nicknamed "the yuppie bank robber." Big, tall handsome guy, Harvard educated, who'd been a bit of a sensation back home. I introduced myself—"John Shea, Boston. South Boston, actually"—and he was pleasant enough, but cautious. The next day he comes to me. "Are you Red Shea? You're not Red Shea, are you?"

"I am," I say.

He apologized. He said he was told I was coming and to look out for me. "It didn't click," he said. "I'm sorry." I reminded him that we'd met years ago at McDonough's Gym, where he was doing some boxing with a trainer I knew. I was just a kid at the time, but he said he remembered me. No doubt he knew my name from the news from Boston and the af-filiation with Whitey Bulger. John showed me around the prison. He helped me get a job in recreation and introduced me to some solid guys. Although I had a long way to go, Fort Dix was certainly going to make it just a little bit easier.

The following day I was sitting on my bunk and I heard someone yelling up to the window, "Red Shea! Red Shea!"

I looked out the window and saw this thin, about five-foot-eight-inch gentleman with a crew cut and graying hair looking up at me. "My name is David Boisner," he said. "We share the same attorney, Richie Egbert. I want to thank you for all you did for me, trying to help me out."

I had never met him before, but I knew he was a stand-up guy, and I had tried to help him after one of the guys rounded up when I was in-dicted, Eddie Mackenzie, set Boisner up for a fall in order to lighten his own load.

Since Boisner was Richie's client, Richie asked me about the situation. I told him everything I knew about Mackenzie's bad character and lying, con-artist ways. Boisner had never been in trouble before, and that piece of shit Eddie had used him to get himself out of doing time in our case. Eddie's big excuse line is he didn't rat out his friends, but ratting out any-one, even a Martian, still makes you a rat.

Eddie even contacted me to try and work out a deal with David to alter his testimony and minimize David's role for a certain amount of money. Obviously he was either trying a con, as usual, hoping to give the government someone else, or he was sent by the government to try and sting me and Richie. He was met with a short answer: No! Poor Boisner had just been an interpreter in a drug deal and got ten years for his trou-ble. Thanks to scumbag Eddie Mac.

I was starting to get into a routine and find my niche at Dix. I had a job working in the recreation department handing out equipment. I actually

gave a boxing aerobics class. I was not supposed to teach anyone anything, and they frowned on kicking, but a lot of punching and moving
the arms around was a good workout, and the guys liked it. And it was a
good workout for me; I fucking killed myself in there. A decent CO from
Boston named Ed Tuite got us some mitts—boxing mitts that you hold
up and let the other guy work his punches. Jab, jab, right hand, left hook.
We weren't supposed to have them, because it allowed you to sharpen
your game, and they eventually took them away, but they were fun while
they lasted. It was a good way to get some aggression out.

As the joint filled up, though, this little incarceration vacation started
to turn. It began innocently enough—this Jamaican kid was on a
moving-lockers detail, and when he brought a locker into my room, he
had decided he was just going to kick the fucker in. *Bang, bang, bang,
bang!* He edges it across the floor, right in from of me, with kicks.

"Why you doin' that?" I ask him.

No answer.

"Do you have a fucking problem?" I say.

"No, *mon,* do you?"

"Yes, I do. You're kicking these lockers in my room. It's disrespectful."

He gave me some Jamaican Rasta jive, called me something like a
"fucking bummer clot."

"A fuckin' what?" I said. "I'm going to ask you again: Do. You. Have.
A. Problem?"

"Do you?" he says.

I am up and at him in a flash. Jamaica takes off running like a rabbit.
A counselor steps out in front of me. "Whoa, whoa, take it easy, Shea.
What's the problem?"

"No problem," I tell him. I turned to him nonchalantly. "I was just
fucking around."

I headed back to my room. The counselor followed me. "Is everything
okay?" he asked.

"Absolutely."

"You don't look like everything is okay. You look like your Irish temper is showing. Are you sure?"

"Absolutely."

He went on his way.

Later that evening there was a fire alarm. We were all told to evacuate the building. We milled around in the yard. The lights were on, but there were pockets of dark. We were out there a long time as they checked the entire facility. It was a little uneasy. Guys were edgy. Were there searches going on? Then they ordered us to file back in.

That's when I spotted the Jamaican kid. He had a friend with him.

I barked at both of them, "I ought to kill the both of you." Neither of them said anything. They just scurried away.

I was back in my room—the swell of new cons had moved me into a big cell with ten guys. Only Frank Fragente was there, an Italian from New York. I was by the window, doing my elaborate hookup to get the Red Sox game on my Walkman, which involved a wire as an antennae taped to a water pipe coming through, for better reception. That's when the door swung open and six big Jamaicans walked in.

They say, "Red *mon*, Boxer *mon*, do you have a problem with this guy?" They parted a bit to show my little Jamaican buddy.

I stepped up and into the middle of the room. Frank was behind me.

"*Ya, mon,* I have fucking problem!" I mocked them, I shouted at them in their own fuckin' accent.

They seemed surprised. They came with six guys, with another ten on the tier. They expected to intimidate me, but it wasn't working. The biggest Jamaican was doing all the talking. "What did this guy do to you, *mon?*"

I told him very serious. "He was kicking lockers and slamming doors."

"Like this?" said the Jamaican big dude, and he grabbed a locker door and slammed it hard. *Whang!*

"No," I said, "more like this," and I grabbed the same door and slammed it even harder.

You could hear the echo running down the hall. His next question was, "Do you want to go with him, then, eh?"

I knew I had two metal pipes atop my locker and a game plan for what I was going to do. "Yeah," I said. "Let's go." I started to walk toward the group and toward the Jamaican kid in particular. I was positioning myself in front of my locker.

Frank Fragente hadn't said a word or gotten up. I knew I was on my own. The pipes were in reach as I approached the group.

I was about to make a move for the pipes and smash their skulls in.

Then I hear a voice coming through the hall outside, trying to get in. "Look out, watch out, move out of the way!"

It's another of my roommates, coming back in after the fire alarm. Big John Jeziak from Pennsylvania. He stands right next to me. Shoulder to shoulder.

Nobody says anything. John continues to stand next to me. There is a long silence. It's a standoff. Six plus ten Jamaicans against me and John Jeziak. Not the best odds, but win or lose, some of them are going to end up with their heads bashed in.

Then I hear from out in the hallway, Spanish-accented English. "Do you have a problem?" one guy says. Then I hear another voice, same accent, repeat the question. "Do you have a fuckin' *problema*?" Then again, in a kind of singsong. Then it's quiet again. The big Jamaican guy is fidgeting. He jerks his head to instruct someone to check it out.

Then we all hear in a low, clear voice, Spanish accent again, "You are not alone." Serious. And I know that voice. It was Freddie Leone, the head Dominican, whom I'd only met in passing.

The tide was turning.

The Jamaican leader, like a good general, decided it was time to retreat. He and his little fuckin' posse headed out of the room backward. He decided to save some face and threaten me: "If you bother him again, we'll get you."

Just as he got the words out of his mouth, I hit him with a left-hook slap to the face—*Whap!*—and his head spun around.

He kept moving backward. He was stunned. Everyone seemed to be stunned by it.

I gave him a verbal fuckin' slap, too. "You come here with all these guys! I should be disrespected, but you know what? I feel the opposite—I feel respected. All of these guys for one guy. Now you're here, man, let's do it. Come and get it now."

He just continued backing up. He'd made his decision. They were outnumbered, odds no longer in their favor. They left.

Frank Fragente said to me after, "I was hoping you were as good as they said you were, John." I turned toward him and just looked at him. I didn't say a word. He looked like he'd seen a ghost.

This was not over. It was an important moment, a challenge, a power struggle, in a facility just starting to figure itself out. That evening I got hold of John Christian, and we rounded up all the white guys and met in the gym. I talked to Freddie Leone. Now, Freddie and the Dominicans—sounds like a band—had had their problems with the Jamaicans, and it didn't start in Dix, just like no racial conflict really has its roots in prison. It was a street thing, a turf thing. Drug trade, wars, territory. It just carries on in prison, when you have the principals in there taking their hit for what went on in the streets. But in prison alliances are made out of necessity. Just like the Italians and the Irish, the Dominicans teamed with the Colombians behind bars. And Freddie Leone brought over a hundred Dominicans and Colombians into the gym as well. We all joined together. I had called for it.

Fort Dix was wide open at the time. It hadn't established yet the kind of inner policing that most federal joints had, so there was a lot of stuff around. I had a knife and a pipe. The Dominicans showed up with two guitar cases, but they weren't for playing music. They were full of weapons—pipes, knives, chains.

The head Jamaican was working out in the weight room, right off the gym. His name was Rock—massive guy, dreadlocked, chest like a fuckin' mountain slope. I went in, with John Christian. John stood right next to me. I told him what had happened. I told him if they had a problem, let's settle it right now. You have an army, I have an army. Let's do it right now. He had no idea what awaited him outside the weight room.

He walked out into the gym to see a small army massed there. He was taken aback.

I tell him, "You go talk to them right now and tell them we're waiting for them. If I have to, I'll go to them."

He walked around us and down to his tier. We waited. If he didn't come back, we'd have gone in. This kind of challenge required an answer. No answer was an answer.

But then he was back. He had his hair in a rasta bag, like he was some kind of king. But I knew what was coming.

"They want no problem with you, *mon*. They won't even come out."

I said to him, "If any of them so much as looks at me the wrong way or says a fuckin' word to me around the compound, they are going to have a serious fucking problem."

We had no trouble there on out from the Jamaicans.

Every time I saw this Jamaican rabbit, I would look right in his eyes. He always put his head down and scurried away.

27

TEACHING DOMINIC

A kid named Dominic Scabetta came into our room as a new roommate. He was from Bayonne, New Jersey. He was a boxer at one time, fought professionally. I think he was in for robbery. Six foot two, curly brown hair, blue eyes. He seemed like a pretty good guy in the beginning. He was polite and respectful. He got along and went along. But eventually I started figuring him out.

There was another Italian guy, Vinny Black, from New York, who would often drop by the room. We had a room full of mostly white guys, so it was a popular spot. Vinny was a little crazy guy, a little nuts. He'd come in and join the bullshit, play cards, listen to a ball game. He was all right. One night I'm laying in my bunk, which happened to be close to the wall, and I hear Vinny talking, obviously to some black guy. Vinny's trying to collect a debt from a card game.

"Hey, listen," Vinny says in a lecturing tone, "I won at cards. When I lose at cards, I pay you. When you lose at cards, you pay me. *Capisce?*"

There's a silence. Then I hear some feet scuffle, like into position. And I hear the black guy say, "Oh, yeah? Then why don't you come and get it like Tyson?"

More silence. Then Vinny says, "Oh, that ain't right, you know."

Then silence, and then I hear the black guy laugh, and then I hear his steps walking away. I can hear the strut.

The next day Vinny comes into the room to see everybody. I take him aside. "Vinny, I heard what happened last night. I was listening. That guy told you to come get it like Tyson, right?"

"Yeah," he says. Then, real sheepish: "That's what I get for gambling."

I say to him, "No, Vinny, that ain't how it goes. You know, I would have backed you up on that."

"Ah, John," he says.

"No, Vinny. Vinny. Listen to me. You need to stand up for yourself, no matter what—win or lose. You understand, Vinny? You could have come and got me. I would have gone it there with you. I'd back you up."

"Red, I don't want any trouble."

"Don't you ever call me Red. You're not my fuckin' friend," I tell him harshly.

"Yeah, I am sorry, John. I'm looking to go home early, John, you know? John, I can't fuck it up."

I just look at him. I look at him real hard.

"Listen to yourself," I say. "It's fuckin' white guys like you, Vinny, who make white guys look weak in prison. You want to be one of those guys?"

"I don't want trouble," he says.

"Do me a favor, Vinny Black. If you don't want to do anything about it, then don't come into this room anymore. Don't talk to me. No cards here. Don't say hi to me no more. Don't do any of that. And furthermore, I'm going to let everybody else know, too, the people that hang around me. Win or lose, Vinny, you gotta stand up and be a man. And if you can't do that, then don't come around me, because I don't hang around with people who aren't men."

This is where Dominic Scabetta comes into the picture.

"Yeah, Johnny's right," says Dominic, right on my coattails.

A few months later, Dominic Scabetta is the one getting ready to go home, but he's having a problem with a new guy in the room, a black guy who'd just been with us a few days. I'm in the commissary, and a Colombian in there says, "Hey, what happened to your buddy?"

"What do you mean?" I say. And he gives me the two fingers, wiggling, like somebody running.

"Who?" I say.

"Your friend Dominic, running like a rabbit from the black guy."

So the Colombian guy tells me the story.

Dominic has a run-in with this black kid. Dominic plays the boxer card: *Hey, listen, I'm a professional fuckin' fighter. I'll take you apart like no tomorrow.*

The black kid thinks about it, leaves, and then comes back with a metal mop wringer. It is the quickest weapon he could put his hands on. You can pick it up by a handle. It can be a nasty little weapon if you know what you're doing

He grabs hold of this mop wringer, and he says to Dominic, "All right, motherfucker. You're the boxer. You got your weapons, I got mine. I guess we're even."

He swings the mop wringer.

Dominic jumps back. "Hey, hey, take it easy, put it away!"

"You're the fuckin' tough guy. Remember? You're going to take me apart, right? Let's go."

He starts going after Dominic with it. Dominic runs out of the room and down the tier. He runs and hides out in the gym.

The Colombian gives me the little wiggling fingers again and laughs. "Your Dominic."

Of course Dominic knew I was going to find out, and he knew he was going to hear it from me.

I confronted him in the room. I tried to keep it between him and me.

"Dominic, you know better. You know better. You gotta do something. You gotta get that motherfucker. You gotta do it. You've gotta take care of your business."

He says, "Johnny, I'm sorry. I couldn't do it. The guy had a weapon."

"All right," I said. "Listen, I'll go in and I'll shake him down. I'll go take that fuckin' weapon off of him."

We make a point of hanging around the room trying to catch the guy alone in there.

When he comes in, I say to Dominic, "You do what you got to do. I'm not fightin' your battle, you have to."

But Dominic is all nervous. "I don't know if I can do it, John."

"Dominic, you fought professionally before. What the fuck are you talkin' about? In a fair fight, you'll fuckin' crush him."

"Johnny, I can't. I want to go home. I want to go home right away, at my time."

All of a sudden, he looks at me and says, "I can't do it, Johnny. I really can't. I know what you're going to say, and you're right. You're a hundred percent right."

I look at him. "And you had the balls to tell Vinny Black what to do? To tell him to do what you don't have the balls to do yourself?"

"John, I wish I could be like you."

He fuckin' hugs me. It's pathetic.

I twist out of his hug.

"John, I know what you're going to do. You have all the right in the world to do it. You're not going to talk to me anymore. I just want to thank you for being my friend."

I walked away from him, disgusted.

Dominic was right. He got the same treatment that Vinny Black got. But in his case it was even worse, since he should have learned from what happened to Vinny. And he still ran. He had a real hard time on the compound after that. Every time he walked past our table, he was called a pussy or a punk. He was tortured.

After a while I decided that something needed to be done. It was time for Dominic to check into protective custody.

I went into his room. I had an Irish guy, a former wrestler, watch the door.

As soon as I stepped into his room, he knew something was up.

"Dominic, it's time for you to go," I said. "People want you off this compound. I have to do it because you were my friend."

"Johnny, I knew this day was coming. Please straighten it out for me, talk to them."

I smashed my forehead into his face and followed with a left hook right on the chin. Just enough to jar him and let him no there was no more talking.

"Give me time to pack my shit," he sputtered, "and I'll check myself in."

"I'll wait while you pack."

Dominic spent about a week in protective custody. He sent word back to see if it was okay to come out. I sent a message back, just one word: "No!"

Dominic was finally transferred to the other side of Fort Dix, the west side. He stayed there till his release. If he'd stayed put, his fate was sealed. He had a choice to be a man. He flunked.

28

DOING TIME RIGHT

I looked at prison as a place to learn things. It was another place to learn how to survive. As always, I wanted to get the best I could out of what I was doing—whether in the ring, on the streets, or in prison. They are all kind of connected. In the ring you have to protect yourself. In the street you protect what's yours. In the joint it's more basic. You have to protect your humanity. In a caged environment like prison, everyone has the potential to become an animal. Your job is to not let that happen, even though the whole deck is stacked against you. Against that, you have to hold on to what you are. And you have to learn.

So you haven't had a woman in a long time. What do you do? Some figure, well, homosexuality will be the way to go, and that it's okay because it's in prison and not outside. No, that is not okay. Not going to go to the other side, how do you endure it? Very easily. You take care of yourself.

There was plenty of pornography in Dix, for a while. But they severely cut it back, pretty much eliminated it, which forced you to use your imagination, regardless of which side you were on. You had to picture it in your own mind. Fortunately, I had such strong memories of Penelope I could make her materialize almost instantly, late at night, closing my eyes, and using my mind to get myself somewhere else. It was better than looking at some slut in a cheap magazine, when you think about it.

Speaking of other bodily things, the doctoring could be pretty top-notch in the federal system, if you had a big problem. You could get to a place like the Mayo Clinic in Rochester, Minnesota, though a lot of guys ended up in Springfield, Missouri. But the medical care in Dix, as in Milan and Danbury, sucked. Half these fuckin' doctors they get have been fired from regular hospitals. They're rejects. I can't say all the doctors are like that, but a majority, in my experience and from what I've heard. And it was as much the attitude of these so-called professionals as their actual skills that were the problem.

Once I was in the hole when I had a dentist appointment. No way I could get to the fuckin' dentist, because I was in segregation for some altercation. When I get out, I put in what's known as a call-out to the medical department, saying I missed an appointment but needed to get my teeth checked. Eventually they responded, and I was put on the call-out sheet, which is where they enter appointments of prisoners on a computer, so guards who stop you when you're moving about can check to see if it's legitimate.

So I went down to the dentist's office. I sit in the chair, and the dentist woman, a blonde, comes in, doesn't look at me but at my paperwork. I'm sitting there with my mouth open.

"Oh, you missed an appointment 'red,'" she says. "You missed one. Yeah, you missed an appointment."

I say, "Yeah, I know I missed an appointment."

"Oh, then you've gotta get out of my chair. You gotta get up. Let's go."

"I couldn't be here because I was in the segregation, in the hole," I explain to her.

"I'm not taking care of you," she says.

"But I couldn't fuckin' walk down here for my appointment. I put in a call-out. I'm on the list, ain't I?"

"I don't care," she says. "That's your problem. I'm not taking you. You missed an appointment."

What could I do? She had protection in there. All the civilians have these radios with a beeper on it. If they push that button—it's what they call deuces—if she pushes the deuces, the whole fuckin' prison comes runnin', full of guards, to that location. She's not alone in there. Plenty of people watching out for a blond dentist buttoned up in a nice white cotton coat.

I never went back to the dentist my whole time in prison. I even toughed it out with a bad wisdom tooth till I got home.

Of course this is part of prison. This is part of what they take from you. There are things that you have to cope with. This bitch is supposed to be a humanitarian. She's not. Maybe she hates her job. Maybe she was supposed to have some fancy practice, and she just wasn't good enough. She has a lousy career, but she has power over me. Well, I hope it made her feel good.

The priests, I'm sorry to say, were no better. In Milan I saw a fuckin' priest, wearing his collar, holdin' a fuckin' shotgun while prisoners were coming off the bus. Is that his fuckin' job to do that? He's a priest, and he's holding a fuckin' shotgun! A man of the cloth! I couldn't believe it. I made up my mind that I would never go to church in prison, but after I got to Dix, I was thinking about giving it another chance. When you're raised a Catholic, there's a certain tradition to confession and communion. Everyone's a sinner, and a church or a chapel is a good place to think.

In Fort Dix we had Father Pete. He was a Filipino. A lot of Filipinos are Catholics, which I didn't realize. When March 17 came around, I wished him a happy St. Patrick's Day.

"Happy St. Patrick's Day, Father," I say to him when we passed in the hallway.

He gives me an ornery look. He stops. "In my country we don't celebrate St. Patrick's Day," he says with a real edge to him. And he starts to move on, like he's scored one.

"Just a fuckin' minute, Father." He stops.

"In my country," I say to him, "—and this is *my* country—we do celebrate it. And so does the cardinal in New York, Cardinal O'Connor."

And then I stole a line from Billy Bulger. "Father," I said to him, "I want you to know I respect the cloth, but I don't have to respect the man."

And I moved on.

We got a little revenge on Father Pete the Filipino. A priest came into the population. He was charged with aiding and abetting some type of an armored-car robbery in upstate New York, and the IRA was involved. My kind of priest! Father Patrick Maloney, a small Irish guy in his sixties, with a twinkle to him, to say the least.

Father Pat helped kids in the New York City. Somehow he had let some people stay somewhere, some Irish guys who ended up in the robbery, and he took a fall. But as soon as he entered prison, I could tell he was a good guy. I said to him, when I heard he was a priest, "You can't judge 'em all, Father!"

I was good to him, helped him out, and showed him around the place. Introduced him to guys. Everyone liked Father Pat. And he was smart man, very well read, out of the Franciscan order.

Father Pat gathered that no one cared too much for Pete the Filipino. So he approached him and said, "I'm still ordained, and I'd like to give mass for the boys."

I loved that. Stick it right up his ass, Father Pat.

Pete the Filipino, the little fuck, asked him how he could trust that Father Pat was ordained.

"Check with the cardinal," said Father Pat. "Here's his number."

"I don't know about that. I'm gonna have to check this out."

Pete the Filipino. He was being a prick about it, because he's taught to be a fuckin' cop before a priest. When he fucked around long enough, Father Pat went back to him and said, "As a Roman Catholic priest, I wish to receive the Holy Communion every day. It's my right."

It wasn't long after that that Father Pat was shipped out, transferred to a small, low-security facility in Loretto, Pennsylvania. A few months later, a guy coming through said Father Pat says to say hello to a red-headed guy named Johnny Shea from Boston. Turns out Father Pat liked Loretto, which is in the middle of the countryside, and he was serving mass there on a daily basis himself. We all took to discussing child molesters when in Father Pete's earshot, just to get his goat.

Still, it pays to watch your step in prison. They can take privileges away from you—using the phone, going to commissary. And those things look pretty big from inside. Being able to buy a little something—a new pair of flip-flops, a better razor, a can of tuna—not to mention being able to call home, can bring a little sunshine to the dreary, dark day-after-day. You do something wrong, they'll give you a shot. It's called a shot; there's a 100 series shot, and then the lesser ones: 200, 300, and then really fuckin' small shit. Overall it made no sense. Having a knife was a 100 series shot, and stealing an onion was a 200. Lip to a CO could be a 300 shot, or could get you the hole, depending on the mood of the officer or the fuckin' day of the week. For some reason the warden had it in for guys stealin' onions. And you know why? Not for what an onion was worth. Because an onion tasted so fuckin' good to a prisoner. It was hard to beat a can of tuna, some bread, and a little chopped onion.

I used to have a stinger to make my pasta. What we called a stinger was a heating element from a hot water heater or a clothes dryer. It could be any kind of heating element. Whatever you could get your hands on. You could heat water with it.

I happened to have a fuckin' fantastic heating element. I would take a trash can and get a plastic bag. Clean, everything would have to be clean. I would fill the plastic bag with water and fit it into the trash can, so there was a belly of water suspended in there. Then I'd plug in my heating element and stick the end in the water—these two hot prongs. It would take a while, but gradually you'd see small bubbles, like balls of mercury, start to appear on the element. In a few minutes, it would be lined with them, like they were pearls. And then you'd watch, and the surface of the water would start to swell, and then the first gurgle would break, and eventually you'd have a clear bag of water at full boil. Then you remove the element and dump a box of pasta in there—the thin kind was best, the cappellini. It cooked in about three minutes.

They had microwaves in prison, but not many, and you didn't want to have a bunch of guys standing in line to boil water, it would take forever. But once I got the pasta cooked and in a bowl, I'd open up a can of Contadina spaghetti sauce or, my absolute favorite, baccalà, a salted Portuguese cod in red sauce. I'd pour that on the hot pasta and take that to the microwave and give it a shot. Man, that was a meal I'd still enjoy right now.

I had a hiding place for my stinger: up inside the hollow legs of my bunk. They had jammed the legs with pieces of wood just to stop this very thing, but guess what? You could take the wood out.

I took care of myself. I made sure I had my fucking heating element. I ate some very good meals with the guys, at Christmastime especially. The holidays in jail can be a lonely time. But you have to make the best of things, and that's exactly what we did. They kind of give you a little free rein around the holidays, so we were able to buy cakes and hot chocolate at the commissary. We'd make some tuna dip with the tuna and salad dressing and vegetable soup mix. And we'd get onions, real ones or dried, it didn't matter. We'd have a party in my room all weekend long. The Boston guys would come over, along with some other solid guys from New York, Jersey, or wherever—all white guys, to be honest—and we'd have a good dinner. Usually pasta—ziti or spaghetti or whatever we had—and the baccalà. It was delicious. A real feast in the company of good, solid guys. Guys like Al Skinner from Charlestown, Kevin Kershaw, and Mike Salonen.

One particular Christmas we had a guy at the dinner who was slightly unexpected. His name was Khalid. He was a black kid from Philly, a Muslim. Short, five foot six maybe, muscular, with the biggest biceps I've ever seen on a guy his size. I use to always see him lifting weights in the gym when I was working the heavy bag. One day I was tearing up the heavy bag, and I heard someone say, "That boy can hit that bag like no one I ever seen." I look across the room, and it was him. When I was done, I walked past him, and we spoke for the first time. We introduced ourselves. He said, "I'd like to learn how to hit that bag like that." So I made a deal with him. I would teach him to box and hit the bag if he would lift weights with me and show me a few things. And so we did.

After that, Khalid would come to my room to talk or just kick back and relax and read. He read his poems and songs. He was into rap and was always writing songs. He turned me on to rap, actually. I liked it because it spoke the truth about the streets, about snitches, about how to be a man. I liked the street truth that resonates in rap. Like me, Khalid had been ratted out by guys at the top. We had some other things in common, but that was the main thing that bound us together. We'd both been betrayed.

That one Christmas, Khalid was accepted at the dinner by all the guys because he was my friend. He was treated no different and respected no less. I was grateful for the way he was welcomed and embraced at the dinner. He was the first and only black guy to come to the Red Shea Christmas Dinner. It was the best party we had in the eight years I was in Dix. We were not black or white; we were men of honor.

But if there was a best time in prison, it was getting to enjoy the Red Sox games at night, listening to Joe Castiglione on the radio. I think it was WEEI, 850. At nighttime you get a broader band, and the games would come in really good. What was greatest about it is that for half the year it was something to look forward to most every night. You could count on it. Eight, nine, ten o'clock, there would be Joe Castiglione, the Boston accents, the local car-dealership ads, the Jimmy Fund drives. And the games themselves. What do they mean, really? Nothing. But that makes them all the more meaningful, especially when you're in prison. It's a game; you care. Someone wins, someone loses, every night. Then they're back the next night.

I had a steam pipe that ran through the floor, and it was wrapped with a protective cover made of tin. When I put my radio—my Walkman—up to it, it gave me a better reception. It acted as an antenna. As the evening went on, the better reception I got. So I'd hook that on there, and then I'd like sit there in the corner, because my bed was right next to it, and I'd sit behind my bed in the corner, real crouched, so to speak. And I'd just lean back and enjoy the game.

I knew Fenway, from TV of course, but I'd been to quite a few games. Never as a kid, but once I got into the business, I went a lot. I was even at an '86 World Series game, saw Bruce Hurst beat the Mets in Game 5. We had the lead, goddamn it, three games to two, heading back to New York. I know that a lot of people give Clemens shit for taking himself out of Game 6 with the lead against the Mets, but c'mon, fuckin' Bob Stanley in relief? When they depend on you in relief, when they call your name, you gotta show up. Roger had pitched good. He brought us as far as he could. Then Bob Stanley stinks it up. And fuckin' Bill Buckner . . .

But all that was forgotten during my time at Dix. My team was still the Red Sox, and they made my time just a little bit better. They were good for the spirit. I don't know about them letting Clemens go to Toronto, to be honest, but he was looking washed up, what can I say? They counted him out too early. Don't count out the tough guys. They'll come back to haunt you. They'll show up.

29

POPS (AND NIGEL BOWE)

I t was a strange thing: Word came down in '95 that Whitey had taken off as indictments landed on him and Flemmi. He just disappeared, as those who knew him knew he always could. He was world-savvy and smart. He'd be ready for a day like this. So law enforcement the world over was looking for Whitey Bulger, and right about that time a guy comes into our room who looks just like him.

First I should explain about the rooms at Dix. Early on, I had the luxury of a two-man cell for a bit, because the place was new and far under capacity, but I moved around a lot in subsequent years, into six-, eight-, ten- and even twelve-man rooms, due to the increasing population and my behavior. Of course there were occasional stops in the hole, when you're alone. With no one for any conversation, no TV, you spend the days reading and thinking. Thoughts drifting to home, to Penelope, to life after this place. After the hole you wouldn't be in a two-man room for a while, but if things went well and you kept your nose clean, you could get back to it.

When Frans van der Hoeven arrived at Dix, he was put in with me and ten other guys. As I said, I'd just gotten news that Whitey was "missing," but I knew he had taken off. And here was a guy who looked like the Dutch Whitey.

This guy came in like a good old fellow—thinning white hair combed straight back, trim build, very athletic-looking. He kept to himself, obviously intelligent, and he didn't say much. Although you always have to be careful with a new guy in the room, I immediately read van der Hoeven as a stand-up guy. He could prove me wrong, and I would be wary, but my first impression was that this guy wasn't trouble.

In fact, van der Hoeven was a professor. He was always reading a book. He'd taught in Holland and in the States. That's all he told us at first. We took to calling him Pops.

Pops was in for being on a ship that was stopped in international waters, headed for Canada with a boatload of hashish on it, coming from Holland. The American coast guard ended up stopping them, and the funny thing about it is that he basically was just taking the cross-Atlantic adventure. He didn't need money or anything like that. Pops, it turned out, was a world-class adventurer, who of course loved to take risks. This one bit him in the ass.

He said to us, "It was a fantastic trip. Gigantic swells, we took on water heavy twice. We had to replace the mainsail. But we were through the worst of it when we heard the siren."

It wasn't his boat, and he made it clear early on that he wasn't interested in talking about just what his role in the trip was, and I can't blame him. All he would say is that he had no judgment about guys who want to smoke hashish.

"That was their business," he said.

Pops had a very reserved aspect to him, disciplined, spare. He approached prison life as something like monastery life. Life of the mind sort of thing. He didn't shower much; he remained aloof. He wore only the standard prison garb they issued—he didn't trade up to track pants, good shoes. He wouldn't buy anything special in the commissary. I don't think he owned a comb. He'd run his fingers through his hair and leave it at that. He'd accept my secondhand sneakers, and that was about it for his luxuries.

About the only thing that could raise the temper of Pops was another guy who entered our room, a huge black Bahamian named Nigel Bowe. Nigel was a character—bigger than life. And Pops couldn't stand him.

Nigel, I'd have to say, didn't seem to love white people. And what made it all the stranger was to hear this guy—big, dark as an eggplant, with a proper English accent. He was schooled in England and was a big-time lawyer in the Bahamas. He knew a lot and talked smart, full of bluster. It wasn't all bullshit. But Pops, being a kind of sophisticated European, I think took exception to this big island dude who talked about Churchill and Stalin. Worse yet, Nigel didn't have a high opinion of German culture and apparently took Pops for a kraut. Nice mix.

But Nigel's biggest offense in the room, as far as all of us were concerned, was his farting. This big fucker would rip off shots that would make your eyes water, that would make you gag. You'd swear there was a pile of shit steaming in the middle of the room. But Pops, you couldn't stop him when Nigel cut one.

"You *Schweinehund*! Fucking *Schweinehund*! Go, leave! Go die somewhere, you *schwarze* pig!"

This would get Nigel going, all right. He'd start to rumble and move, like a volcano about to happen.

"Don't move, Nigel! You'll fuckin' fart again," I'd say.

What I meant was, *Don't touch Pops*. And Nigel knew I meant don't touch Pops. He'd be sorry.

I came to like Nigel Bowe once I heard his story. He'd been involved in some high-level shit, no doubt, but he was nailed by a big-time informant, Carlos Lehder, who worked for Pablo Escobar in the Cali coke cartel. Carlos had given Nigel up, and he didn't like it. And he didn't like rats, which was music to my fuckin' ears.

"Informants are like a pack of cigarettes," he told me. "When you smoke all the cigarettes, you crumple the pack up and you throw it in the garbage. That's what happens to informants. That's what they deserve."

I respected Nigel, despite his gastro problems. He was smart, and I learned a bit from him, but mostly I knew he respected me. He knew what I was standing up for and what it meant. He knew I could've taken down a few people and not be sitting there in a twelve-man cell smelling his fuckin' farts.

Pops was the one who taught me the most about history. Being European, he had personally lived through major world events. Although I had been doing some reading—Whitey had said, "Make the best of your time"—Pops gave me a different perspective than a book did.

He had been a teenager in Holland when the Nazis arrived. He saw the Jewish kids rounded up, and of course he lived to know what their fate was. He came from a town called Hilversum, and I think his family built boats—yachts and such. They survived the war and thrived after that. Pops became the adventurer in the family.

Pops wasn't big on small talk or bullshit, but he loved to talk about history and culture, particularly German culture. It's something he knew and loved. I tried to learn everything I could from anyone I met, and Pops had a lot to offer. I used to ask him to tell me a bedtime story. "Pops, tell me the one about Beethoven." He used to tell a story about Beethoven that would make you—and him—cry.

I'm wasn't sure at first what it meant to him, but he would tell me about how Beethoven, a great genius of course, was told to take some cold baths for something or another, and it lead to his deafness. His hearing went away gradually, which must have killed him, to have to slowly realize that what made his world—hearing music—was being taken away. He got very involved with Napoleon, who at the time was marching across Europe. Napoleon was a hero, said Pops, to the little guy and also to artists like Beethoven, who saw Napoleon as proof that anything could be accomplished. But the personal tragedy happened when Beethoven's brother died and made Beethoven the guardian of his son. Beethoven loved this kid, he wanted only the best for him, and he hated the kid's mother. But he had to fight her for him, for this kid, while his own health problems were making it so he couldn't even hear the music he had written. He got more isolated but wouldn't give up trying to win this kid in court. He used to take long walks thinking about his compositions, trying to imagine what they would sound like, trying to go back into the past, back to when he could hear. And he tried to think about the boy, and the man he would make of him, if he could just shake this fuckin' woman, who he thought was a whore.

He won the kid in the court, but then the kid grabbed a couple of pistols and took off for Beethoven's favorite walking path. He then shot himself in the head. He didn't finish the job but hurt himself pretty bad. He asked to be taken to his mother's place.

I don't know why this would have made *me* choke up, but it got to Pops, too. Something about it—maybe the love of a son or the lost world of hearing or what used to be before the wars in Europe. Maybe this connected to what Pops himself had seen as a kid in Holland. I couldn't tell.

It was a good story, and I liked hearing it, and Pops liked telling it. But when Pops told me more about how he ended up in Dix, it became a little clearer.

One night I said, "Pops, how was it you got nailed in international waters? You don't seem like a drug runner."

I remember the night, a long one with storming outside, wintertime, the darkest time in prison. When the place is cold, the only thing you look forward to—getting outside—isn't much fun. It's not like you can reach for your Irish sweater and your parka and your wool gloves and a half pint of whiskey. So he told me—and the rest of the guys listening—about his adventuring. It was as good as going to a movie or seeing one of those Discovery Channel documentaries.

This guy was more than an adventurer—he was what he called an expeditionist. Back in the sixties, he and four guys went on a four-month trek to Antarctica. Brutal cold, injuries, frostbite, fishing through the ice, making ice shelters. I believe he said some mountain there is named after him. He did long-distance road rallies across the African desert. He flew these ultralight planes across the Alps. He crossed the Atlantic in sailboats. He had money and investments and was far into computers just as they happened. He was telling us all about the World Wide Web there in Dix, and I had no fuckin' idea what he was talking about.

The deal with the drugs was that they were coming from Amsterdam bound for somewhere in Canada with a load of hashish. He was the adventurer, he decided to be more or less a hand on the boat, going along for—what else?—the adventure. And also to look after his nephew, who was in on the deal.

The coast guard spotted them, and as the boats and planes circled, he made the decision, right there in the North Atlantic, to set the boat on fire and scuttle the thing. He figured they would be rescued, and maybe without evidence. He got badly burned. He had to get skin grafts, and he spent a lot of time in the hospital before making it to Fort Dix. Although he was innocent of the drug deal, a couple of the principals in it laid it all on him and his nephew. Pops got eight years. Pops said his nephew got twenty.

Although he was a philosophical guy, with a great positive spirit, I think, like Beethoven, he felt deep love for his nephew and felt somehow responsible for what had happened to him.

Pops used to feed the cats that came in from the outside, from off the base. And he would feed them all the time tuna fish. When he left the prison, I took it over. The cats had come to expect it, and they were the most innocent thing in that joint. Of course you weren't supposed to feed the cats. The guards were always trying to round them up. They would try to cage them. These guys looked ridiculous trying to corner a cat in a prison yard. It was like when a cat runs on a baseball field. There's a lot of room, and cats are quick and smart. But eventually they'd be outnumbered and chased into a cage.

One time I saw an inmate doing it, helping out. I saw it from my room. I ran right down to the yard, and I kicked the cage shut, and I said to the inmate, "Hey, how do you like being locked up? Do you like being in a cage? Do you like it?"

He said, "No."

I said, "Neither do they."

He went on his way, and he told his boss from Safety, "Listen, I don't want to do that job no more."

Pops was a good friend to me after he got out. I told him everything—gave him updates on the guys, kept him informed about my situation. When Pops was out, I told him about word that Whitey was an inform-ant. He was very sympathetic and encouraging, telling me to hold on, that I was a stand-up guy and that's what I would take from this whole experience and that it would be the most valuable thing in the world. He was right.

He would send me checks, a hundred dollars for my prison account, from wherever he was—Monte Carlo, California, Italy, back home in Holland. He was adventurous as ever, back to his old tricks. He told me about a new ultralight plane he bought for thirty grand. He was headed for Africa, from Holland. He crossed the Italian Alps from France to Italy over Austria, but he had to stop on the isle of Crete off the coast of Greece. He couldn't go any farther due to some engine trouble. When he landed, he didn't have the proper paperwork, no doctor certificate, air-worthy certificate, insurance, proof of ownership—no flight plan. Some son of a bitch Greek airfield director confiscated his plane. He then had to steal his own aircraft back and fly it three hours over the Adriatic to Italy again. While flying over the Adriatic to Italy, he flew over a United

States Navy ship. The ship attempted to contact him, but there was no response. Pops made the papers and TV news when he landed in Italy. He was fortunate that he didn't get blown out of the sky. He headed back for Africa, got as far as Ethiopia, where he landed the plane among herds of zebras.

He wrote to me: "John, I'll try to slow down now. But Fort Dix made me restless."

His letters gave me courage. This guy kept up the fire. He wrote to me: "It's not easy being a stand-up guy, especially after you looked up to somebody that's doing the opposite."

But I knew I could do it, even if I had landed among rats.

30

FREDDIE AND *FÚTBOL*

My right-hand man when I was at Fort Dix was Freddie Leone. Ever since I heard his voice in the hall, his Spanish accent saying, "You are not alone," we were tight.

Freddie'd come out of nowhere, saw me facing all these Jamaicans and taking a stand. He stood behind me and brought his people with him. Freddie kind of had a hold on the Dominicans, and a lot of the Spanish, in Dix. So we became very good friends. If I had a problem, I knew that he was on my side. And vice versa.

Freddie was a handsome guy with a big smile, though his smile could just be a cover for anger or a plan for retribution. He was always Freddie, but you had to watch him to see what he was really thinking. He was a man of action.

I taught him how to hit the mitts. He was a strong, fit guy but didn't know the first thing about boxing. I'm sure he was tough as nails in the street, but I taught him about balance and footwork and the art of throwing combinations, how one punch, thrown right, transferred weight and power for the next. You start out shifting and stepping slowly, like dance steps, then you speed it up, add power, and it becomes second nature.

Freddie was in for drugs—his being Dominican, you could pretty much count on that in a federal joint. But he did his time as best he could, with his main goal being keeping his own integrity. And he did.

Freddie called me Colorado, meaning "Red" in Spanish, an obvious reference to my red hair. Not many redheads in the Dominican Republic.

Freddie got out before I did. I would call him once in a while when I was still in. "Hey, Colorado!" He was so happy to hear from me. "You know, when you come out, you come to the Dominican Republic," he'd say. "I have lots of girls for you. For you, Colorado. Lots and lots of girls for you."

He was running a club down there, and he had more girls than you can think of.

Freddie was pretty essential to my strength with the Spanish, especially, of course, the Dominicans. It made things a lot easier. I hung out with these guys as much as with the few white guys in the joint. But I earned my way with them on my own as well. They all liked to play soccer, so I thought, Why not? Let's mix it up with these guys.

Now, I never played soccer in my life but I had played plenty of hockey in Boston as a kid, and I saw it as essentially the same game. Maybe that tells you the level of hockey player I was, but so be it. I knew one thing: Aggressiveness counted for something in both sports.

I watched them play on the big soccer field at Dix. I said to Freddie, "You know, I want to play that game."

He said to me, "Colorado, but you can't use your hands." And he faked me a left-right combination. "What you gonna do?"

I said, "I know, Freddie, but I can kick some ass, can't I?" And then I faked him with my head. "See? No hands! Boom!"

Finally I ventured into it. I practiced a little, dribbling the ball around, bouncing it on my instep. Forget about it. These guys could fucking think with their feet. But I knew what I could do with them: run.

I got into it. I found my niche: defense. It wasn't easy getting past me, and I could scare guys off the ball with just pure fury. In one game an African taught me a lesson. I went full steam for the ball, but with my head down. Next thing I know, the ball is somewhere else and I feel like I've been sucker-punched from the side. The African had elbowed me right in the side of the jaw. I didn't know what happened exactly till I asked the guys on the sideline. "Elbow, Red."

The next time I contested the ball with this guy, he got an elbow to the ribs that doubled him over.

"You want to play that way, motherfucker?" he says to me.

"You started it," I said. "And I just finished it."

He never came near me again. After that I always ran with my head up. And that became my reputation. I was always running guys off the ball in our end, looking as much at them as at the ball.

I played on some so-so teams for a couple of years, winning, losing. I didn't always play as much as I wanted to. I wanted more. I could run for hours, and I wanted to be in there every minute. Freddie encouraged me to form my own team, so one year I did. I chose the guys—a mix of Mexicans, Colombians, Africans, and me, the only white guy.

Most of the people who watched were Hispanic. When I came on the field, they were always kind of razzing me. But I had their respect. I respected the game and the guys playing it. There were some excellent players there, guys who'd played all their lives. But I became good, real good, out of fierceness and speed. As in the rest of my life, I found what I was good at and perfected it. Whitey had said I was like a cheetah—the fastest thing on earth. And I knew that ball was everything, and when it was mine, it was mine.

I mischievously named my team the Shamrocks. The recreation department would give us shirts that we could only wear in the game. So we had all these Africans and Spanish guys running around with a shamrock on their shirt. Believe it or not, we won the league championship. And I have the pictures to prove it—my white face in a sea of different shades of dark.

It was a great day. Our prize was a few six-packs of Coke. I celebrated with Freddie and his Dominican guys, some of whom were on the team. It was like being a kid, a little nicked up, tired, happy, drinking a Coke. These guys, in the small world of Dix, became like a band of brothers. To them I don't think I was any longer a white guy, and they weren't spics or niggers to me. For the time being, we were Shamrocks, and we were the champs.

Prison had its moments.

31

LOLLIPOP

There were no conjugal visits allowed in federal prison. No way to even finagle one, for a night in a hotel with your wife or your girlfriend, like sometimes happens in state joints. There was nothing.

That's not to say there weren't a few women around—which is a fuckin' travesty. There should be no women around an all-male prison, period. I can't see any justification for it. The women shouldn't want to be there, and we shouldn't have to see them. It is, in my view, cruel and unusual punishment, not to mention potentially very, very dangerous for them.

Of course it could also be dangerous for the inmate. All you need to do is be caught touching a female in the joint, whether consensual or not, and your ass was cooked. Because even if it's consensual, what is she gonna claim if the two of you are caught? Rape.

My last few years in Dix I had this case manager named Miss Monroe, and she was hot—half white, half black. Miss Monroe had an ass on her that wouldn't quit, and she knew it. Everybody on our compound used to watch her when she walked in with her fuckin' nice slacks on, summer slacks molded to her body, just prancin' across the yard, swinging the door open, her ass hard and round, then down the hall she'd go.

We'd run toward the hall just to take a look at the shaking going on, her breasts loose in her shirt. Guys are in prison a long time, when they see a woman come in like that, they stop work or whatever—they stop breathing. They're lookin' at the shape of everything. What they can't see, they imagine, and what they imagine, they can't do.

Miss Monroe used to date white guys who worked there. This girl's body was more than hot.

I didn't often go out of my way to see her. Who needed the aggravation? But she was my case manager, after all, and there were things I had to see her about—my visitors' list, disputes about discipline, et cetera. One day I went into her office, and it was a rainy day. I was getting close to going home. There were some forms I had to fill out. I walked into her office. Her hair was a little wet from the rain. The damp hair stuck to her neck a little. And she was sitting there at her desk sucking on a red lollipop. She looked up when I came in. "Hello, John," she says. And she is really going at that lollipop.

I'm sayin' to myself, That lollipop looks awful good in her fuckin' mouth. And I haven't had a woman in many, many years, whether she's black, white, or whatever at this point, you know.

"John, before we get going, can you help me out with something?"

Miss Monroe gets up. "This damn fax machine," she says, and she turns to go to the back of the office, and I see that ass. I can see the crack down the middle and a small sliver of her back. But I'm cool. I'm staying very cool. I'm near the end of my time, I'll be home soon, and I'll get all the pussy I want.

So we get back to the fax machine. I don't know where to begin. I figure I'll check the plug first, why not? I reach down to see where the cord goes, and I see something that makes me freeze: her bare feet.

A woman's bare feet there on the carpet. Naked feet. Not that I'm into feet or anything, but she might as well have had nothing on. She caught me staring. I didn't move.

"Oh. Oh, don't mind my shoes being off," she said. "My shoes got all wet, and I had to take them off."

"Yeah, yeah. No problem. No. None at all," I said. "You know, I really don't know anything about fax machines, I'm sorry. I never used one."

And I went back to the front of her office and sat down. "But take your time," I said. It took me a while to cool down.

Miss Monroe was with me through some things that let her know something about me. When a reporter from WBZ in Boston called and wanted to interview me, I talked to him in her office. I wasn't interested in talking to this guy about Whitey, or Whitey's whereabouts, or what I thought about Whitey being an FBI informant. He talked about my reputation as a stand-up guy, and Miss Monroe heard all that. He thought I was afraid to be seen on camera and offered to let me appear behind a screen.

"Are you kidding me? Why would I need a screen? I got nothing to say to you about anything. Good luck with your career, and don't call me again. Got that? End of story."

32

BETRAYAL

Whitey's undoing began with a couple of Jewish bookies—Chico Krantz and Jimmy Katz—and ended with what the press has called his "surrogate son," Kevin Weeks.

Krantz and Katz got busted by a bug at a place called Heller's Café, through which a lot of bookie action was being laundered. And they were paying Whitey big tribute for many years, and they got nabbed and then flipped. The feds knew they had some gold on Whitey and Stevie Flemmi, and they piled it on. They began to throw in other findings they had from other buggings and indictments that were in the works. Then Paul Moore and his cousin Jackie Cherry, who had been indicted with me back in 1990, who'd gotten sentenced to nine years and eight years respectively, got hauled up to a grand jury and were asked tough questions about Whitey. Paul couldn't say no without adding to his sentence. If he refused to answer, he would have been held in contempt and given another eighteen months or more. So he said yes and yes and yes. Pole Cat the skunk became Paul Moore the rat.

Paul and Jackie were taken from Plymouth to federal district court in Boston. They were put in lockup. Paul was taken from lockup and brought upstairs in front of the grand jury. He never came back down. An agent came to Jackie's cell and whispered to him, "Jackie, Paul's on our team now." Jackie replied, "Fuck him, and fuck you, too." Jackie Cherry told them nothing and did his eighteen months like the man he is.

Whitey took off, smart as always. Flemmi waited a little too long, and he got arrested. Whitey drove cross-country with one of his ladies, Catherine Grieg, after he dropped off his longtime paramour Theresa Stanley and has eluded the authorities ever since.

It was no shock to me that Whitey went on the lam. He had been planning it his entire life. Fake passports, money everywhere, safety-deposit boxes around the world. A master of disguises, dressed up like a little old lady. He could slip in and out of town without anyone batting an eyelash. But I was surprised that he had been left with only that choice. He had always been one step ahead of the government. Maybe his slip was showing.

It was.

About three years later, Tony Cardinale was hard at work representing Frank Salemme, while Ken Fishman, who Cardinale worked with at F. Lee Bailey's office many years ago, represented Stevie Flemmi. Whitey was somewhere—Ireland, the Caribbean, England, all kinds of rumors. Early on, Flemmi had reached out to me for some advice on what lawyer he should hire. I immediately had my man, Fran Hurley, see him and advise him who would be the best lawyer to hire given the circumstances. Fran had worked with Fishman on some cases and told Stevie that he was the man for the job. Also, I had some information on some of the rats on Stevie's case, and Fran and I were providing this information and any assistance we could to Stevie's lawyer to discredit the testimony of these rats. Stevie was so happy with this assistance that he sent back a message to me that he would be indebted to me forever.

Cardinale felt that the racketeering case against Salemme involved unacknowledged informants, and he petitioned the judge to require the government to reveal if that was so. The judge agreed and asked for a specific list of names to check. Among the fives names Cardinale turned over to the judge was one Whitey Bulger.

The climax came when a guy from the Justice Department by the name of Paul Coffey came forth and stated officially that James J. Bulger was an informant for the FBI. In the course of things, Flemmi was revealed as a rat as well.

Rumors had been swirling around Boston for years that Whitey and Stevie might be rats. But I never believed it. When a guy came into my cell to tell me, I was not really bothered. Bullshit, I figured. I'd heard it ever since my first day in Danbury. But I decided to call Deirdre and check it out. She wasn't in, and I waited on the phone while her sister reluctantly got up the courage to tell me it was true.

In fact, she had videotaped coverage on the local news and cued it up for me. There I heard local news reporter Ron Gollobin detail the revelations. He even mentioned my case.

I felt like someone had reached down the wire, right through me, grabbed my heart, and tore it out. My knees buckled from the shock. I hung up the phone and realized I was physically sick.

I walked it off in the compound. I must've walked ten miles, 'round and 'round. I couldn't sleep at all that night. I went over in my head everything I had ever thought or felt, seen or heard, that could have predicted this. And there was plenty, when you look at it—but what I couldn't figure was how Whitey could speak with such ferocious conviction about honor and the code and self-discipline and still be a fuckin' rat bastard. The next day I called Kevin Weeks.

I'd always considered Kevin Weeks a friend. I'd known him since I was a kid. I can remember him railing about someone in Southie being a rat. *He's no fuckin' good. Fuck that fuckin' rat motherfucker,* he'd say.

I can hear him saying those words, and I of course agreed that there was only one way to deal with rats. Exterminate them.

But when I called Kevin, what I wanted to hear was that it was all bullshit, someone setting up Whitey. If not that, I wanted to hear fuckin' outrage that this guy had done this to himself, to us, to what we thought was sacred: the trust we had among ourselves.

But I didn't hear any of that from Kevin. He said, "John, I can live with it."

I said, "What? You can live with that? You can fucking live with that? I can never live with that! They're fuckin' rats!"

I hung up the phone. And those were the last words I'd ever speak to him.

Now I only refer to him as "Two Weeks," to reflect the length of time he was in jail before he decided to become a rat.

Among the things that Two Weeks did to save his ass was to lead the authorities to corpses—bodies of people killed by his bosses, Whitey and Stevie. Two Weeks brought the feds to the grave sites of Bucky Barrett, John McIntyre, Deborah Hussey, Tommy King, and Paulie McGonagle. Some of these bodies Weeks had helped move from one site to another.

Tommy King and Paulie were Southie guys who grew up with Whitey. They were all part of the Mullin Gang. In Whitey's rise to power, these two ended up on the wrong side and paid the ultimate price. Some would say that they were killed because they were considered a threat and never would have bowed to King Whitey.

If what I hear is true about those guys, then they are rolling over in their graves dying at the hands of a fuckin' rat, dishonored even in their deaths.

King and McGonagle were unearthed at the edge of Tenean Beach in Dorchester, which borders Southie. They were buried at low tide and would have laid below the gray waters of Boston Harbor forever if not for Two Weeks.

I heard Kevin said that every time Whitey drove by that spot, he would say, "Say hello to Tommy King."

Bucky Barrett, John McIntyre, and Deborah Hussey were buried in a grassy area adjacent to the Southeast Expressway, which runs right through Boston north to south. This was an area that would never have been disturbed, buried underneath a massive highway.

Two Weeks revealed that Barrett was killed because Whitey wanted his money from the Guaranty Trust robbery, and Bucky wasn't giving it up. McIntyre was suspected of being an informant and revealing secrets of the gang's relationship with the IRA.

Deborah Hussey, the daughter of one of Stevie Flemmi's longtime girlfriends, was strangled to death by Whitey's own hands because of her sexual relationship with Stevie. She was going to tell her mother about their relationship but never got the chance. When they found the body, she had no fingers, no toes, no teeth.

At Two Weeks's plea hearing, faced with a litany of charges in the indictment, Kevin told the court, "I did it all."

I beg to differ. He did what he was told, and then he told it all. Nothing more than a fuckin' rat.

33

LOVE AND HONOR

These guys let me down—Whitey, Weeks, Paul Moore. I looked up to these guys, and they went and violated everything I lived by, everything I thought they lived by. I have only the vaguest memories of my own father—that and the words of my mother and sister are the only connection I have to his existence. In some way or manner, it's pretty clear that I've been searching for a father, someone to give me a father's love and acceptance, all of my life. Whitey, Kevin, Paul, they showed me that love. Paul would take me everywhere with him. Walk his dogs down in Plymouth near his house, run together, box together. He took me in when my mother threw me out. Kevin was like an older brother. Someone I could talk to, confide in. And Whitey taught me about life and about *the* life. What to do and how to do it right. Most of all he preached to me about honor. He passed on to me what had been passed on to him from the generation of Irish goodfellas that came before him. It was a code of honor and silence. When I got indicted, he told me, "John, it takes a strong person to reach inside himself and say, 'I'm here because of me.' "

Whitey was strong, powerful, larger than life, intelligent, and supremely confident. A real man. He was everything I wanted to be.

I remember one time I came into the Variety Store. Whitey's there

with his reading glasses on reading the paper. Kevin's there, too. I turn to
Kevin, "How ya doin'?" Whitey looks up from his paper and sees I'm
sporting a little tail from the back of my scalp, a little braid of hair.

"What's that, John?" he says calmly. "On your head there . . . ?"

"Oh," I say, "it's just a little tail. It's the style. What?"

He folds his paper up, still looking at me over his reading glasses.
"That doesn't look so good on you, John. You're a clean-cut kid. You
don't need that. Kevin'll cut it off for you."

"Yeah," says Kevin. "C'mere."

"Really?" I say. I reach around behind me and touch it. "It doesn't
look good?"

"It's not you," says Whitey. Fatherly. He says it more like advice.

"Okay," I say.

Kevin comes over with the scissors.

"You'll cut it even?" I ask.

"Don't worry, John. Trust me. Turn around."

I hear Whitey get up to look. I figure he wants to make sure Kevin
cuts it right. I can hear both of them right behind me.

I hear Whitey say, "That's it." Then I hear the clip of the shears.

"There you go," says Kevin. He shows me the little braid of hair in
his palm.

"See?" says Whitey. "You look better."

"Yeah," I say, looking at my reflection in the store window. "Thanks."

They both seem pleased.

It's a small thing, but Whitey was looking out for me. It was something personal. Something a father would do for his son.

34

THE CUBAN

As the end of my sentence drew near, I grew more and more excited. Maybe "agitated" is the word. I couldn't get over the fact—the FACT!—that Whitey was a rat. It flew in the face of everything I had believed in. Part of what had gotten me through this mess was living up to the lessons I'd been taught, the way I'd been schooled as to what a man was. And it wasn't being a rat. But here it is, in black and white: Whitey Bulger, Informant. That cartoon in the *Boston Globe* all those years ago, when I first got to Danbury—with Whitey as a pigeon—was true. That thing that I denied to everyone who brought it up—to the point that people didn't bring it up—was true. Did I feel stupid? Suckered? No. Did I feel betrayed? Yeah. But I felt most of all right. It was right what I was taught, and it was still right and always would be right. That will never change, not in my book.

So I could hardly wait to get out. But you can't hurry anything, not in the joint. Time is time. And just like I explained to Dominic Scabetta and Vinny Black and countless others, you can't let your fear of doing the time make you rat or take your self-respect away. Toward the end of my time, I got to prove that, unlike Whitey Bulger, I could not only talk the talk but walk the walk.

I was in the TV room one Sunday night, and the place was packed. The Red Sox were on, against the Yankees, a nationally televised game. I knew a lot of guys in the room; it was going to be a good night. A little ball breaking about the Red Sox and the Yankees between me and some of the New York guys. We were having some fun going back and forth. It was a tie game. Some Yankee hit a ball deep to right center in Fenway, and Trot Nixon went for the ball, and it hit his glove and then bounced into the bullpen—a Yankee home run. I cursed.

"Fucking Trot Nixon," I said.

"What's your problem?" I hear from the back of the room. It's some fuckin' Cuban I don't know.

I said, "Watch the replay. The ball hit Nixon's glove and bounced into the bullpen. Fuckin' Trot Nixon just blew the play. If he doesn't touch it, it hits off the bullpen fence."

"No, man," he says, "that was a home run all the way."

So we watch the replay. "Watch, do you see. Do you see?" I say. "The ball hit off Nixon's glove and into the bullpen. The replay shows it."

"I didn't see nothing hit his glove. It was a home run. He never touch it," says the Cuban, wise like.

I said, "That figures. You're a fuckin' Yankee fan."

I'm sitting with my back to him and still watching the game.

He yells out from behind me, "Fuck you, you fuckin' punk!" And he jumps out of his chair and walks over and stands right in front of me.

"Fuck you, you fuckin' punk, you fuckin' piece of shit, you fuckin' pussy!" he continues. "I'll fuckin' machine-gun you!" and he starts jumping around like Tony Montana in *Scarface* with an Uzi. He even has the sound effects.

I put my index finger to my lips and tell him to be quiet and sit down. He doesn't listen to me. He keeps it up.

Some of the other guys in the room chime in. They tell him in Spanish. "Listen to him. He's no joke."

He keeps it up.

"You're a pussy and a coward! You won't even get out of your chair."

I ignore him now because I know count time is coming. He doesn't realize it, but his time is also coming.

Count time comes, and we all have to go back to our cells to be counted. The Sox are losing. When I got back to my cell, I knew what I had to do. I tell my roommate, Mike Sallonen, "I might not be back here tonight."

Mike said, "What's the problem?"

"I got some business to take care of."

When count is over, I go right back to the TV room. When I get there, who do I see outside the room but the Cuban. I step up so I am right on top of him.

"What's up, tough guy? You want me?"

Now I could see he wasn't so sure of himself.

He hesitates a little but says, "Yeah."

"Are you sure?"

He says, "Yeah." And I hit him with a left hook, a sharp left hook. His eyes roll back in his head. I hit him again with another one. He melted like an ice cube right down the wall of the corridor outside the TV room. As he was sliding down the wall, I had my right hand cocked and was ready to drive it through the back of his skull. If necessary. He fell to the floor unconscious. I bent down and whispered in his ear.

"A real pussy, huh?" I'm talkin' to him as he is stretched out on the floor, his jaw ballooning.

A couple of guys pick him up and get him out of there before the guards come.

I watch myself for a couple of days. I figure some kind of retaliation is coming. I carry around a homemade shiv, because the Cuban knows he can't do it with his hands. If he's going to come, it's going to be with a weapon.

Next thing you know, they send a cop up to my room. It's just before count time. He says, "Hey, man, how ya doing? Everything all right?"

"Yeah," I say, but he can see my hand is still pretty swollen.

"What happened?" he asks.

"I was hitting the heavy bag," I say.

He left, but he'd done his little investigation.

I was standing for count next to the window and just happened to look out my window, and they're taking the Cuban to the infirmary. A guard named Duffy is taking him and making sure I see him. The Cuban is walking in front of him. The Cuban gives me a shake of the head and a look like, *Shea, you're done.*

I tell my bunkmate, "Mike, I'm a goner. I most likely won't see you again. I'll be leaving for home from the hole."

"Ah, man, that's fucking terrible," he says. "You're just about home."

"Fuck it," I say. "It's worth it. That cocksucker had it coming."

Sure enough, thirty days in the hole: narrow bunk, twenty-three hours a day lockdown, meals shoved at you through the door, no company, nothing. But I did what I had to do. If I didn't stand up to this Cuban, I'd be like Vinny Black and Dominic. No matter when it happens, even if it's two minutes before I'm supposed to be released, no one is going to fuckin' treat me like a punk. If it means staying in jail, picking up a new case, or another ten years, so be it. I walked into prison a man, I am going to leave a man, no matter what. Can't let it happen, as I told these guys and as I proved. Practice what you preach.

Miss Monroe came down to the hole to visit. She was still my case manager and felt bad that I got solitary. But she brought a little sunshine with her, and my last day in there she put her hand up to the window, and I did the same on the other side. A good-bye.

In a week I was walking out of there, to a waiting car, to Fran Hurley and Michael and George Hogan and the rest of my life.

35

HOME

It was hot when I got home, August. I saw my mother, who cried when she saw me. I talked to my sisters—two of them—on the phone. I called Penelope. Oh, sweet Penelope.

She had sent me, literally, a Dear John letter in prison about halfway through my time. I had received many letters from her over the years, painful letters, full of tears, anger, sorrow. Less and less was there any hope. I had given her permission to see other people, to get on with her life. She was too young and beautiful to be wasting away waiting for me. At first she declined. "I'll wait for you, John. I'm saving for our house. I want your children. I will see no other man."

I told her that was her choice but that she could not lie to me. I said to her, "Penelope, you know I will find out, and I won't accept that if you tell me you're going to be true. If you're going to be with me, keep me and us in your heart, and don't betray me. I'm telling you, you don't have to do that."

With the Dear John, she released herself. I gave her, of course, my blessing, though I was crushed inside.

Still, I had hope that this one person that I ever truly loved would still be there when I got out.

But when I called her after I got back, I couldn't get to her.

"John, it's too painful. There are too many bad memories."

She didn't want to even see me. Still, I insisted. I knew that her mother wanted to see me, so we agreed that I'd come by her mother's house.

Fran dropped me off at the house in Quincy. Her mother met me at the door and was very welcoming. I could smell dinner cooking. Penelope was still upstairs. "Oh, she's dressing, John. You know girls."

It took her forever to come down. Her mother and I made small talk. She said I looked great. But I couldn't wait to see Penelope.

When she came down, she was wearing jeans. She could hardly look at me. We went to the kitchen and had dinner—my favorite, beef braciole. It was a little uncomfortable. I mostly asked them about their lives, trying to catch up. Penelope was vague about what she was doing. She was working in a construction-company office, and she was studying for some test. The meal was delicious, but the mood was very sad, of course. We had vanilla ice cream with butterscotch for dessert, and then it was time for me to leave.

Penelope said she'd drive me home. When she turned her head around to back the car out, I saw in her face and her neck all the years of pain. I could see that she had been crying. I wanted to hold her so much. And I stopped her, and she cried hard. I thought maybe she was melting back to a possibility for us. She wasn't really seeing anybody, she told me, but she said it in a way I knew was the truth: that it was over for us. And then she told me, "John, I'm too old for you now. You need someone young, someone who can give you kids."

I could see that somehow she hated herself for what had happened, for falling in love with me. I realized she saw me as a punishment for her own bad judgment. I realized, too, that we were no more.

The next day I took a walk around downtown Boston. I bought a sandwich and ate in one of the parks, in the shade of the trees, feeling a little breeze, euphoric being free, but sad as can be for Penelope.

I took a walk down memory lane and went over toward the federal courthouse where so much of my fate had been decided, and I spotted the assistant federal prosecutor, George Vien, about half a block away, talking to someone. It was lunchtime, and there were a lot of courthouse people walking here and there.

I turned around when I spotted him, just to make sure it was him. It had been almost ten years since I'd seen him in the courtroom, this guy who was part of the prosecution in all the bail hearings and the eventual sentencing.

I had already talked to Tony Cardinale, who told me he'd run into Vien and told him I was about to get out. Word travels fast.

So I waited for George Vien to finish his conversation. I was just waiting a block away till he was done. I approached him from the back, so he couldn't see me coming unless he could sense it. And after he finished his conversation, he stood there waiting for the cross light to change, and I moved up and stood right next to him, shoulder to shoulder, on a corner across from the courthouse. And I waited for him to turn. I mean I literally stood next to him. I waited for him to turn, but he looked straight ahead. The sweat was beading on his forehead. He wouldn't look at me. He was just looking and waiting for the light to change. He wanted to walk. It was a hot, hot day.

Finally I said, "How are you, George?"

And he looked surprised—"Oh, John!"—as if he didn't know I was there all along.

"How are you, John?" he asked.

"I'm good, George. Are you walking this way?"

"Yeah," he said.

"I'll walk with you."

The light changed, and we walked together across the street to the opposite corner.

"Everything going well, John?" he asked.

"As well as can be," I said.

He asked if I was working.

"Yeah, I'm about to get in the union."

He was a little nervous, still sweating, his eyes darting around looking for familiar faces.

I spoke to him real deliberately, like maybe I'm all business, like I have business with him, unfinished business, like maybe I've been waiting for him.

But then I put my hand on his shoulder. "George, I got something to say to you."

"Yes?" he said, his voice a little weak.

"I want you to know that you're a fair man. You had a job to do, I had a job to do, but you were fair about it."

He looked very relieved and said to me, "If I can ever, ever do anything for you, ever, just let me know. You were young, John."

"Thanks, George."

But both our jobs were done.

As I walked around Boston in those early days, I thought a lot about my story. I thought about the questions I might be asked. If someone was going to tell my story—if I was going to tell my story—there are certain questions I'd have to ask, and answer.

Do I believe in an afterlife? Of course. Do I believe in forgiveness? Of course. Do I believe I will be forgiven? Somehow I don't really think so. I know it's not up to me, it's up to the big guy upstairs. But right now I figure I'm going to hell.

We all have choices, and I made mine. I could have made others. My mother always told me what was right, what was wrong. Everyone did. It was all around me. I didn't listen. I chose the life that I was good at. I hurt a lot of people, and some of those people didn't deserve to be hurt— Penelope of course, my family. But some innocent people I didn't even know got fucked up by me for no good reason. Strangers I beat up for the fuck of it, kids who didn't know any better wandering onto the wrong turf and paying for it big-time. All the other fucks, though, the guys in the life, in the life of crime, I have no regrets whatsoever. It's the innocents that will come back to haunt me, as they should.

But within what I was, I lived right. Within the gangster life, I was as honest as a man can be, and that was a very hard trial. Look at the guys who couldn't do it, guys I respected, including Whitey, of course, and the Kevins and Paul Moore and Stevie Flemmi. But they didn't have the stuff. In the end, they were lowly rats. There's no forgiving that, not from me, nor should anyone forgive that.

When I think about Judgment Day, I get emotional. It's a heavy thing. But I did what I did, and there's no erasing it. Nothing I do from here on out is going to change it. I can write an honest book, be an honest man, help little old ladies across the street. But what's done is done. There's no escaping that.

Whatever it is, I'll do my time, even if it's for an eternity.

36

TODAY

These days I'm working construction. We're at 80 Broad Street in downtown Boston, putting up condominiums. I'm doing demolition, chipping concrete. A laborer. I put in a good day's work; I give the company a good day.

Yesterday morning I'm waiting for the elevator that goes up the side of the site—we call it a frackle. We are starting to dismantle the thing, from the top down. I'm standing there with my hard hat on and a T-shirt that says HELL'S KITCHEN on it, waiting to go up. Another laborer is there. Looking at my shirt, he says to me, "Irish, eh?"

"Yeah," I say.

"From New York?"

"Nope," I say.

He says, "I saw a documentary on Hell's Kitchen. That Jimmy Coonan was a sick fuck."

"Yeah?" I say.

"Yeah. Like Killeen up here. Back in the day. You from here, then?"

"Yeah, Southie."

"Then you know Killeen, he was a bad guy. Whitey killed 'em, he killed them all."

"I don't know about that," I say.

"Yeah, he killed 'em all. But it turns out Whitey and his guys were all rats."

The elevator arrives finally, and we step on.

"Not all of them," I say.

"What?" he says.

"Not all of them were rats."

"You know," he says, "that's right, that's right. There was one guy . . . just got out of prison not long ago. I can't remember his name. One guy stood up and took it. The rest of them—you couldn't shut 'em up."

I let it pass. I got off at the top. I could see all of Boston below me. I could see the sea.

EPILOGUE

Whitey Bulger has been on the run for eleven years now. He remains on the FBI's Ten Most Wanted list, with a reward for his capture second only to that offered for Osama bin Laden. Though he lives as a fugitive, Whitey never did his time. Not like me. As we know, Whitey was protected. As we know, Whitey was a rat. Still, I don't wish that he gets caught, I don't wish jail for him. That would be a violation of the philosophy I learned from him, the philosophy that is right, the philosophy that Whitey himself couldn't live up to.

I don't like wishes anyway. What is a wish? A hope that someone or something makes something happen for you? Like wishing the law on someone, like hoping that the law takes care of some problem for you? That's not how a man handles things, that's not how I was taught. That's how a rat thinks.

But I do have a problem. At times I feel like I'm being pulled both ways emotionally. On the one hand, Whitey Bulger was a hero to me, someone who taught me the streets, the code, someone who was respected and feared by everyone, with a few notable exceptions. He was a man's man, and what I learned from him made me what I am today. I wanted to be like Whitey Bulger. I wanted to emulate him. I wanted to be respected and feared. On the other hand, Whitey was a total fraud.

He took care of himself and gave the rest of us up. He couldn't face the music. He didn't practice what he preached. It is still incomprehensible to me that a guy of his character, who presented himself as he did, who schooled me so well, could be a rat. Yet it's a fact.

As I said, I'm not running to the law. I never did and never will. I don't root for any man to be sent to jail, and I would never, ever have the law do my work for me. That's not to say that if I saw Whitey Bulger somewhere, I wouldn't want to settle the score. But if I did want that, it would be for me to do. It's no one else's job.

I do keep having this dream of seeing Whitey on the streets of New York, with him stepping out from behind a pillar. Maybe there, in that dream, is the final justice for me.